Sacred Rice

ISSUES OF GLOBALIZATION

Case Studies in Contemporary Anthropology

Series Editors: Carla Freeman and Li Zhang

Labor and Legality:
An Ethnography of a Mexican Immigrant Network
Ruth Gomberg-Muñoz

Listen, Here Is a Story:
Ethnographic Life Narratives from Aka and
Ngandu Women of the Congo Basin
Bonnie L. Hewlett

Cuban Color in Tourism and La Lucha:
An Ethnography of Racial Meanings
L. Kaifa Roland

Gangsters Without Borders:
An Ethnography of a Salvadoran Street Gang
T. W. Ward

Sacred Rice

An Ethnography of Identity, Environment, and Development in Rural West Africa

JOANNA DAVIDSON
Boston University

New York   Oxford
OXFORD UNIVERSITY PRESS

Oxford University Press is a department of the University of Oxford.
It furthers the University's objective of excellence in research,
scholarship, and education by publishing worldwide.

Oxford   New York
Auckland   Cape Town   Dar es Salaam   Hong Kong   Karachi
Kuala Lumpur   Madrid   Melbourne   Mexico City   Nairobi
New Delhi   Shanghai   Taipei   Toronto

With offices in
Argentina   Austria   Brazil   Chile   Czech Republic   France   Greece
Guatemala   Hungary   Italy   Japan   Poland   Portugal   Singapore
South Korea   Switzerland   Thailand   Turkey   Ukraine   Vietnam

For titles covered by Section 112 of the US Higher Education
Opportunity Act, please visit www.oup.com/us/he for the
latest information about pricing and alternate formats.

Published by Oxford University Press
198 Madison Avenue, New York, NY 10016
http://www.oup.com

Oxford is a registered trademark of Oxford University Press

Library of Congress Cataloging-in-Publication Data
Davidson, Joanna, 1969- author.
Sacred rice : an ethnography of identity, environment, and development in rural
West Africa / Joanna Davidson, Boston University.
    pages cm. -- (Issues of globalization)
    Includes bibliographical references.
    ISBN 978-0-19-935868-7 (pbk. : alk. paper)
    1. Diola (African people)--Guinea-Bissau--Social life and customs. 2. Diola
(African people)--Agriculture. 3. Rice farmers--Guinea-Bissau. 4. Rice--Social
aspects--Guinea-Bissau. 5. Climatic changes--Economic aspects--Guinea-Bissau.
I. Title. II. Series: Issues of globalization.
    DT613.45.D56 D38   2015
    305.896'32--dc23
                                                                    2015004269

Printing number: 9 8 7 6 5 4 3

Printed in the United States of America
on acid-free paper

For Jasper & Zoly,
Di eyer lernen di hiner

CONTENTS

....

List of Illustrations   viii
Acknowledgments   x

Introduction: Sacred Rice   1

CHAPTER 1   A Rice Complex   18

CHAPTER 2   Ampa Badji and Nho Keboral   48

CHAPTER 3   "We Work Hard"   85

CHAPTER 4   Cultivating Knowledge   101

CHAPTER 5   Of Rice and Men   135

CHAPTER 6   Transgressive Segregation Revisited   155

CHAPTER 7   *Jopai,* and the Limits of Legibility   176

CHAPTER 8   Conclusions: Structural Uncertainty   190

Glossary   197
Notes   200
Bibliography   217
Index   236

LIST OF ILLUSTRATIONS

Figures

Figure 1. Evolution of rainfall over the years   7
Figure 2. Evolution of rainfall from the beginning and the end of the rainy season, 1950–1995, Pirada   8
Figure 3. Rice imports into sub-Saharan Africa during the period 2008–2012   29
Figure 4. Guinea-Bissau milled rice imports by year   29
Figure 5. Jola agricultural calendar wheel   38
Figure 6. Kinship chart for all named characters   61

Maps

Map 1. Evolution and spread of the geographical races of *Oryza sativa*   20
Map 2. Map of Guinea-Bissau and neighboring countries   40
Map 3. Map of several Jola villages from São Domingos to Varela   41
Map 4. Sketch map of Esana   59

Photographs

Transporting rice seedlings from forest nursery to inundated rice paddies, Esana 2003   22
Transplanting rice seedlings [*borokabu*], Esana 2003   22
Unloading sacks of imported rice at the Dakar port, 2010   28
Children gather around a bowl of rice at a wedding celebration, Esana 2003   34
Bundles of rice decorate a woman's headdress at an inter-village wrestling tournament, Karuay 2002   35

A funeral platform is piled high with rice from the deceased's granary, Esana
   2002   35

A young girl wears a skirt made from unhusked rice at a carnival performance,
   Esana 2010   36

Tilling a paddy with a *bujandabu*, Esana 2002   37

Padre Spartaco Marmugi in Esana, 1950s   68

Construction of the PIME Mission facilities in Esana   69

Walls and fence surrounding PIME Mission, Esana 2002   70

A Jola Christian working in the *oficina*, Esana 2003   71

Jola *ai-i* at an inter-village wrestling tournament, Karuay 2002   144

Jola wrestlers, Karuay 2002   145

Second grade classroom, Cassolol 2003   167

Nursery school classroom, Esana 2010   168

ACKNOWLEDGMENTS

There is no single word for "thank you" in the Jola language. Jola often express gratitude with gestures (a nod of the head, a quick dance) or a blessing invoking their supreme diety, *Emitaï*. More recently Jola villagers in Guinea-Bissau have adopted various "thank yous" from other languages in their midst, and people now pepper their conversations with "merci," "obrigadu," or "jerrijef." It is in the spirit of this multiplicity of ways to express gratitude that I would like to recognize the many individuals, institutions, families, and foundations that have helped this book come into being.

Although this is my first book, it is not a revision of my PhD dissertation. It certainly relies heavily upon and builds from the foundational research I conducted in Guinea-Bissau as part of my doctoral studies from 2001 to 2003. But the framework, central insights, and narrative structure of the book emerged during my second stint of long-term fieldwork, in 2010, as a postdoctoral fellow in the Carnegie Corporation–funded States at Regional Risk (SARR) project. I thank Bruce Knauft, the Director of the SARR program at Emory University, for providing the support—financial, advisorial, and collegial—that enabled continued research in West Africa, as well as the time and space to begin the writing process.

I owe an enormous debt to Ivan Karp, who has been my best source of intellectual inspiration and my most critical reader. Ivan passed away in 2011, but he remains, in my mind, a generative and wise mentor, and he is very much present in this book. Eric Gable has discussed, read, and provided wonderful insights into this material over many years, and he continues to be my most treasured interlocutor and favorite ethnographer.

My conversations and collaborations with Ellen Foley—whether in Dakar or Middle Earth—have significantly enriched my work. Carla Freeman saw something worthwhile in this project before I did; I am so lucky to have her as a role model, champion, and friend.

I have been fortunate to have had two congenial academic homes that have nurtured this project at different phases. At Emory University, as a graduate student and then a postdoctoral fellow, I had many teachers, colleagues, and fellow students who added immeasurable value to my work. In particular, I thank Bruce Knauft, Don Donham, Cory Kratz, David Nugent, and Benjamin Junge. At Boston University, I am grateful for the warm welcome and unparalleled collegiality of my fellow faculty members in the Department of Anthropology and the African Studies Center. I would like to recognize, especially, Parker Shipton, Rob Weller, Corky White, Jim McCann, and Kimberly Arkin.

Many people—friends, colleagues, teachers, and students—have read various earlier and drafty versions of this book. Whether commenting on just a chapter or on the full manuscript, they have been generous readers and critics. I would like to thank Robert Baum, Marina Temudo, Fallou Ngom, and the reviewers for Oxford University Press, a few of whom were able to explain to me, finally, what this book is really about: Allison Alexy, University of Virginia; Laurence Becker, Oregon State University; Crystal Biruk, Oberlin College; Eric Gable, University of Mary Washington; David Hicks, Stony Brook University; Jayne Howell, California State University, Long Beach; Mark Moritz, Ohio State University; Mark Allen Peterson, Miami University; and Cassandra White, Georgia State University. I am eternally grateful to Arianna Huhn, who not only foisted an earlier version of the manuscript on her students and sent me their candid assessments, but also helped in countless vital ways by organizing and managing the unwieldy bibliography and creating maps and charts that were beyond my graphic design skills.

The various phases of research and writing that have culminated in this book have been supported by a wide range of institutions and grants. My field research benefitted from the financial support of the Social Science Research Council's Global Security and Cooperation Program, the National Science Foundation, the Wenner-Gren Foundation for Anthropological Research, and the Carnegie Corporation's States at Regional Risk project. Fellowships from the Woodrow Wilson Foundation (the Charlotte W. Newcombe Doctoral Dissertation Fellowship) and, most recently, the Boston University Center for the Humanities (BUCH) gave me time and space to complete significant amounts of writing and re-writing.

I also thank the Wellfleet Public Library for simply existing, and for being the very best place to indulge in binge writing.

A few of the chapters in this book are significant revisions of articles that have been published in the following journals: *American Ethnologist*, *African Studies Review*, *Culture, Agriculture, Food & Environment*, and the *Journal of the Study of Nature, Religion, and Culture*. I thank these journals for permission to reprint some of this material.

It has been a delight to work with the team at Oxford University Press. I especially want to thank Sherith Pankratz, Meredith Keffer, and Lori Bradshaw for their expertise at all levels of the production process.

Many people in Guinea-Bissau and its neighboring countries facilitated my research through their hospitality, friendship, and collegiality. In Bissau, I want to acknowledge Rui Ribeiro and other colleagues at the Instituto Nacional de Estudos e Pesquisa (INEP) for stimulating discussions and access to archives and other documentary resources. In Dakar, Gary Engelberg always provided a welcome refuge, abundant food, and a never-ending cast of vibrant characters with whom to share stories and ideas. Gary and his colleagues at Africa Consultants International (ACI) also helped enormously in 2010 by hosting me in the ACI offices as I transcribed the interviews and jotted down the notes that eventually turned into this book.

I am most indebted, of course, to the residents of northwestern Guinea-Bissau. Many, many villagers invited me into their homes, fed me rice and palm wine, included me in their celebrations and mourning ceremonies, taught me how to "work hard," and shared their stories, worries, and hopes with me. I cannot possibly list them all here, nor adequately express the depth of my gratitude to all of them, but I hope this book is, in some small way, an offering of thanks to them. I do want to express particular thanks to Zacarias Sipalunto, Marie Buinem Manga, Bernardo Djibugei, Nene Ulandjebe, Manel Massima Neves Trindade, Mida Sipalunto, and all of the women in my work association for their extraordinary warmth, insights, and patience. Since my first visit to the village of Esana in 2000, I have seen children grow up, friends and neighbors die, and new babies fill their parents' homes with laughter. My host father's hair has turned grey (much to his own amusement), and my younger siblings have become parents. And they have seen me become a mother and have welcomed my daughter into their homes. After almost fifteen years, my attachment to this field site is primarily affective and social, and I hope the strength and increasing density of these relationships continues to grow for many years to come.

Finally, I thank my family. My parents, Frances and Jonathan Davidson, inititiated me from infancy into an itinerant life, instilled in me an appreciation for all things cultural, and helped me cultivate the subtle (and profoundly ethnographic) craft of eavesdropping. My niece, Lyna, has enriched all of our lives simply by being herself. My husband, Bobby Milstein, has been a steadfast partner and my best friend throughout. I dedicate this book to my children, Jasper and Zoly, who make each day better.

Sacred Rice

How can we make any progress in the understanding of
cultures, ancient or modern, if we persist in dividing what
the people join and in joining what they keep apart?

—A. M. Hocart,
The Life-giving Myth

All sorrows can be borne if you put them into a story or tell
a story about them.

—Isak Dinesen

....

In 2009 a Portuguese nongovernmental organization (NGO) working
on basic healthcare in northwestern Guinea-Bissau decided to tackle
one of the most urgent problems in the region: the rapidly decreasing
supply of potable water. In order to drum up European support for their
plan to dig pump wells in rural Guinea-Bissau, they came up with an effective if gimmicky fundraising ploy that involved showcasing a Jola woman
from one of the villages in this area at the Lisbon marathon. The tagline
went: Guinean women have to run a marathon every day in order to secure
enough safe drinking water for their families.

The woman they chose was Nho Keboral, a mother of six, grand-
mother of five, and generally recognized by her friends and neighbors as a
hard worker and straight talker.[1] Nho Keboral had lived her entire life in
the central Jola village of Esana. She was born there, she grew up there, she
married a Jola man from within the village, she raised her children and
worked within the daily rhythms of a rice-cultivating society, season after
season, harvest after harvest.[2] Notwithstanding her occasional visits to the
capital city, Bissau, to seek medical treatment or to the Senegalese border

1

to sell palm oil, she had stayed put in her village. So when representatives from the Portuguese NGO asked if she would come with them to Lisbon, she balked. But after talking it over with her husband—who had spent most of his life dreaming of such an opportunity for himself—she agreed to go. The NGO staff person based in Bissau arranged for a passport, bought her some warm clothing, and secured a pair of sneakers for the marathon. Once in Lisbon, Nho Keboral was paraded around the stadium and interviewed for several days on various talk shows and morning news programs, her Crioulo words being interpreted into Portuguese by a Guinean employee of the NGO. By all accounts she was a huge hit. She straightforwardly explained the hardships of rural Guinean life, and she graciously responded to questions about polygamy and paganism. Much money was raised, and the project for digging seven pump wells in the increasingly parched region was soon underway.

I knew Nho Keboral well from my time residing in her village from 2001–2003. When I went back for a visit in February 2010, this is how Nho Keboral related her experience in Portugal to me:

> I was so hungry, Joanna. I just couldn't eat their food, I just couldn't. They kept asking me, 'What do you want? What can we get you?' And I told them, 'Just rice. All I want is rice.' Oh! They tried so hard. They took me to all their restaurants and offered me all kinds of food. . . . They invited me to try, oh, I don't know what any of it is called. All I wanted was rice. I was so hungry. Then they started to feel bad—I made them feel bad—because how could they eat when I wasn't eating? No one had any will to eat because I wasn't eating their food. I don't understand— why didn't they just have a bowl of rice? They even tried taking me to a Chinese restaurant, because they said maybe there I would be happy, but that didn't work. All they had was a small amount of rice, and it didn't taste right. I was so hungry I cried.

I had imagined that Nho Keboral would be struck by the cold weather, or by the concrete landscape, or by the hurried rhythms of urban life. But she was principally focused on the rice. Everything else about this un- imaginably rare opportunity faded into the background as she ached for lack of sufficient rice.[3]

When she first told me this story I laughed—as she did—at the ridicu- lous aspects of her experience. Other listeners, especially her own family, also laughed, but followed up with understanding nods and agreed that Nho Keboral had suffered. In some ways, her repeated recitation of this story could be seen as part of her ongoing strategic effort to convince her friends and neighbors that she did indeed suffer on their behalf—to get wells for the village—and that she was not the recipient of special gifts and money, as everyone assumed she would be. Given social dynamics in this region, Nho Keboral's return to the village after her brief stint in Portugal was met with much whispering and gossip about what she had benefitted and how she was now "above them all." This is dangerous talk in the social world of Jola villagers, and Nho Keboral spent an enormous amount of time and energy visiting people door to door to give a firsthand account of her trip, its community-oriented motives, and its empirical hardships. Even months later when I arrived for a visit she was still engaged in her counter-gossip campaign, and I spent several days walking around the village with her and hearing the same story over and over again. So, at first, I thought the focus on the lack of rice and the ensuing hunger were just part of the same rhetorical strategy. But I eventually began to understand other reasons for why Nho Keboral was focused on this aspect of her experience in Portugal, not necessarily instead of but in addition to her reputation-rescuing efforts.

And here I will make a bold statement: rice has been a central feature— perhaps *the* central feature—that has textured land and livelihoods, persons and population flows, desires and dreams and disappointments, spiritual and moral life, and interactions and transactions across and beyond this region of West Africa. The area we now call the Upper Guinea Coast was known as the Grain or Rice Coast for several centuries, signaling European recognition of the importance, abundance, and defining aspect of rice in this region (or, more selfishly, highlighting their own interest in securing this rice in their trade along the coast). But both before and after European presence in this area, rice has played a defining role in the interactions among residents with each other and with the various outsiders who have traded, raided, and invaded in their midst. Rice in this region has been linked to the rise of the great precolonial West African states of Ghana, Mali, and Songhai (Grist 1959; Osseo-Asare 2005). The rice-growing landscape—especially the mangrove swamps—that evokes the topographical imaginary of this region has often served as a refuge from various external forces and foes: from centuries-old Islamic incursions (Linares 1981) to more recent iconoclasts (Sarró 2009), from Atlantic slavers (Hawthorne 2003) to more recent civil strife (Richards 2006).

A seemingly trivial and partially self-preserving account of a contemporary Guinean villager's experience in urban Europe might reveal more than I first assumed about the ways in which people in this region see themselves in relation to others, even when these selves and others change over time. And Nho Keboral's experience becomes even more poignant given current conditions in the rice-growing regions of Guinea-Bissau. Her complaint now extends far beyond one Jola villager's hunger for rice in an unfamiliar landscape. Most Jola in contemporary Guinea-Bissau will tell you that they no longer have enough rice. Nho Keboral's story opens up questions about the connections among food, identity, place, and development. It also opens up the possibility for understanding the notion of hunger more broadly: as nostalgia for an imagined past and desire for the development-driven promises of a different future. Although Nho Keboral's hunger was personal, and perhaps even performative, it still speaks to a more collective contemporary Jola dilemma: who are we without our rice?

Sacred Rice

Scholars of the Jola have consistently offered rich portrayals of this rice-oriented (some would say rice-obsessed) society. Even when rice is not their intended subject, its presence still pervades their pages.[4] As Olga Linares, a long-time ethnographer of the Senegalese Jola, sums up, "Rice is the symbol of ethnicity, of continuity, of all that is traditionally Jola. . . . Rice keeps men tied to the land, village-bound, and wholeheartedly peasant" (Linares 1970:223). I, myself, did not go to the Jola region of northwest Guinea-Bissau to study rice. And yet I still find myself, more than a decade after my first Jola rice harvest, returning again and again to rice, not only as a central organizing feature of Jola social life but as the "thing" that mediates their encounters and exchanges with others, as well as their reflections and reassessments of themselves.

Jola regularly convey the central and multivalent character of rice in their lives. "The Jola was created in order that he farm [rice]"—a proverb collected by Francis Snyder (1973:170; see also Baum 1999)—still reverberates among contemporary Jola when they say, "Rice is our life." As Robert Baum explains, "Rice was seen as part of a covenant between *Emitaï* [the Jola supreme deity] and a people, a covenant based on the Diola's hard work in cultivating the crop and *Emitaï*'s responsibility to send them rain to nourish it" (Baum 1999:28). I saw this covenant in action throughout my fieldwork in 2001–2003 and during my return visits over the past decade through Jola farmers' arduous efforts in the rice paddies, their commitment to well-organized work groups at crucial moments in the agricultural cycle, their regular libations and occasional costly sacrifices at spirit shrines to propitiate their gods and bargain for rain, and their careful child-rearing practices that socialized young people into an ethical life of hard work and no theft (Davidson 2007, 2009). And I heard these sentiments regularly expressed in anthropomorphic and deistic references to rice.[5] "The rice is pregnant," my work associates would note as we walked through a paddy. "Rice," my neighbors would tell me, "is sacred."[6]

Sacred rice is, above all, the idiom Jola use to talk about their central crop. Translated to anthropological terms, rice for Jola is a total social phenomenon in the classic Maussian sense. Marcel Mauss's famous phrase "total social phenomenon" (or, as it is often translated, "total social fact") has been parsed, evoked, deployed, and debated by anthropologists and other social scientists since it was first offered by Mauss in his classic essay on the gift (Mauss 1967), and yet it remains what Gofman calls "a vague but suggestive concept" (Gofman 1998). What I take it to mean, and why I think it is particularly apt for understanding the role of rice in Jola society, has to do with both its epistemological and ontological facets. By "total," Mauss was signaling the need for a relational approach to the study of social phenomena; that is, a methodological orientation that refuses dissection or extraction of particular practices and institutions along traditional disciplinary lines, and instead seeks out the links among seemingly distinct material and social forms, in the same spirit advocated by Hocart in this chapter's epigraph. "We are dealing then with something more than a set of themes," Mauss said,

> More than institutional elements, more than institutions, more even than systems of institutions divisible into legal, economic, religious, and other parts. We are concerned with "wholes," with systems in their entirety. We have not described them as if they were fixed, in a static or skeletal condition, and still less have we dissected them into rules and myths and values, and so on of which they are composed. It is only by considering them as wholes that we have been able to see their essence, their operation and their living aspect, and to catch the fleeting moment when the society and its members take emotional stock of themselves and their situation as regards others" (Mauss 1967:77–78).

It is this very orientation that secured Mauss's place in the canon of anthropological theory, and it continues to be a guidepost for anthropological inquiry regardless of topic or world area, perhaps even more important (and challenging) in a world increasingly dominated by partitioned specialization. But it is the last sentence that provides a particularly powerful entrée into a specific analysis of what Jola mean when they talk about "sacred rice." "Total," in this sense, refers to "phenomena which penetrate every aspect of the concrete social system; they concentrate it and constitute its focus . . . they are the generators and the motors of the system" (Gofman 1998:67). Rice, for Jola, has worked in this way. It has mediated all social spheres and held together the contradictions across them. It has been the means through which people present themselves to themselves and to others.[7]

In some senses, rice as a total social phenomenon reflects one of the hallmarks of African agriculture more generally: the "intense dependence of a people on a single crop" even when that crop differs (Harlan, De Wet, and Stemler 1976). That is, whether with yams, sorghum, millet, or rice, people cultivating these crops tend to be singularly and intensely focused on them.

> African agriculture is characterized by a rather unusual number of dominant crops. In Arabic *'aish* means "life," and in the Sudanic savanna the word is applied to sorghum—the staff of life, the source of sustenance. Life without sorghum is unthinkable. To the north in the Sahel, *'aish* means "pearl millet." Life itself depends on pearl millet, and pearl millet alone, in that ecological zone. To the west around the Bend of the Niger, the word may be applied to rice by some Arabic speakers. Certainly in West Africa, from Senegambia to central Ivory Coast, a meal without rice is considered no meal at all. The same intense dependence of a people on a single crop is found in the yam zone. Existence itself depends on yams. In different parts of the continent other dominant crops are ensete, tef, and fonio. . . . The current dependence of some people on maize and others on cassava indicates that dependence on single crops does not take long to establish (Harlan et al. 1976:14).[8]

The concept of sacred rice is the centerpiece of Senegalese filmmaker Ousmane Sembène's (Sembène 1971) portrayal of French colonial brutality in southern Senegal in his film *Emitaï*. After conscripting young Jola men to fight in the French army in World War II, colonial officials demanded locally produced rice as a tax from the Casamance Jola villagers so adept at producing a surplus. In this otherwise caricatured portrayal of Jola religious life—elders sit among human skulls and sacrifice animal after animal in order to appease their gods, while their wives are held at gunpoint under a scorching sun until they hand over their rice—Sembène did, I think, capture a central dilemma in Jola (and probably other rice-cultivating people's) social and spiritual life. In addition to rendering a quite accurate portrayal of the physical rhythms of rice cultivation, Sembène shows Jola struggling (and divided) over a thorny conundrum: How can they give away their rice, which is sacred to them? But how could their gods abandon them—the humans that propitiate them—for the sake of rice? This is encapsulated in perhaps the most problematic scene, when the dying "chief" argues with the gods about what is more valuable: Rice? The people? The gods themselves?

These questions never get answered, and they might still be asked today although under very different circumstances. At that moment, Jola were pressured to give their surplus rice to the French colonial authorities, which they insisted was a violation of their principle of sacred rice. In contemporary Jola-land in Guinea-Bissau, the main problem is this: Jola can no longer grow *enough* rice, not only to meet their ceremonial needs or to have surplus for a potential tax, but even to feed their families. Jola villagers are on the frontlines of global climate change. Within the past fifty years declining rainfall, desertification, and widespread erosion in northern Guinea-Bissau have increasingly challenged Jola villagers' ability to provision themselves through the wet rice cultivation practices that have long defined them as a people. These environmental factors have combined with neglectful and disadvantageous government policies and programs with regard to rural development, difficult marketing conditions, and diminished labor capacity due to out-migration of youth, all of which have worsened conditions in rural rice-growing regions of the country (Abreu 2010; Bigman 1993; Galli 1987a, 1987b; Temudo 2011; Temudo and Abrantes 2015; Vogel 2005).

The notion of sacred rice is often offered (by outsiders and Jola themselves) as the period at the end of every sentence regarding Jola beliefs and practices. This book attempts to turn it, instead, into a question, or a set of questions: What does it actually *mean* for a crop to be sacred? How does it play itself out in Jola social life? How did this come into being? And, perhaps most importantly given the current context of declining rice

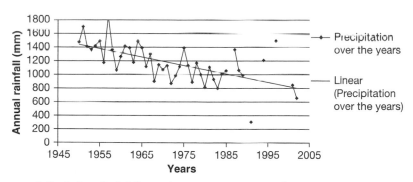

FIGURE 1 **Evolution of rainfall over the years** *(Embaló 2008:16).*[9]

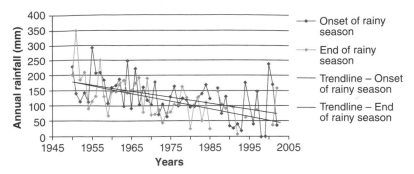

FIGURE 2 Evolution of rainfall from the beginning and the end of the rainy season, 1950–1995, Pirada *(Embaló 2008:15)*.

production, how do ideas and practices around rice change? How are various people in Jola villages re-negotiating their relationships with the production, consumption, and sacralization of rice?

The concept of sacrality when applied to rice in the Jola context thus invites us to consider the historicity of the sacred: how did it emerge and what is happening to it now? Following Sheridan and Nyamweru's (2008) challenge to the assumptions attached to sacred groves in Africa as based on a rather old-fashioned set of assumptions about tropical ecology, religious belief systems, and African societies, I want to push the concept of "sacred rice" from multiple angles—historical, ethnographic, political ecological—and redefine sacred rice through a dynamic lens by exploring the processes that led to its emergence, the dimensions that explain its continuity, and the challenges that may lead to its undoing. Rather than accept the notion of sacred rice as the final word, the answer to all enigmas about Jola behavior, the code to Jola cultural logic—or worse, from a development perspective, to write off this "fact" as so much traditional cultural baggage, a kind of relic ill-suited to the demands of development and progress—I explore the notion of sacred rice as a field where "ecological, social, political, and symbolic dynamics intersect (and perhaps disconnect) over time," (Sheridan and Nyamweru 2008:10) and try to tease out the dynamics of an increasingly contested core cultural ideal.

The central question that animates this book is: Once rice is understood as a Maussian total social phenomenon for Jola villagers, what happens when this changes? How does something so totalizing unravel and disentangle itself from spheres of social, cosmological, moral, economic, political, and familial life? Mauss understood that total social phenomena change, and he was quite clear on the dynamism of social life.[10] But his was a largely theoretical formulation; he did not take us into the "how" of such processes. This study tries to tackle this very question: How are Jola farmers responding to changes in their environmental and economic conditions given the centrality of rice?

Decline in Rain and Rice

Much scholarship on the transformation of agrarian work regimes throughout Africa has explored how shifts in agricultural production during the late colonial and early postcolonial era—through the introduction of new crops and technologies, the intensifying pressures on land, and the need to respond to increased commercialization—have significantly altered social relations, especially gender roles, within cultural groups.[11] In West Africa, in particular, the long history of food insecurity due to shifting and unpredictable environmental conditions—most famously the droughts of the 1970s and 1980s—as well as social and political upheaval is well-covered academic ground.[12]

Another important contribution to the scholarship on environmental change in Africa has criticized the reductive, crisis-oriented, and exaggerated claims of dominant depictions of African environmental change—especially in terms of soil erosion, desertification, and deforestation—and has instead offered a corrective to the singular narrative of African environmental decline by introducing evidence that suggests longer-term historical shifts in land use that might indicate a more complicated picture than a downward trajectory would lead us to believe. Most important in this line of research is James Fairhead and Melissa Leach's (1996) work on the forest savannah complex in Guinea, through which they challenge conventional climate change analyses on the assumptions they make about past conditions. Environmental scientists and policymakers had judged forest areas in Guinea to be degraded and forest inhabitants as culpable in abusing the land. Fairhead and Leach demonstrated that it was these very inhabitants who actually enriched these forests, and that experts had been "misreading the African landscape." Their work, and others that have followed in its wake, provides an important corrective to the received wisdom of African environmental history.[13]

This literature helps contextualize contemporary problems in Jola-land within a longer history of shifting structures and demands on agrarian populations across the continent. Nonetheless, there is a growing consensus (among scientists and rural Africans alike) that the impact, intensity, and confluence of the particular changes of the past few decades present especially dramatic challenges to agrarian populations. The legacy of colonially imposed cash-cropping schemes; the postcolonial World Bank and IMF-imposed structural adjustment policies that shifted national attention away from food security and toward efficiency, and mandated a dramatic reduction in government support of agriculture; other economic liberalization regulatory mechanisms that put African farmers in a disadvantageous position vis-à-vis global tariffs, import and export policies, and subsidy practices; the increasing environmental pressures that place agrarian populations across Africa on the frontlines of global climate change; and many other factors have generated chronic food insecurity and poverty, cyclical famine, and dependence on food aid among millions of Africa's rural residents.[14] In the past several years, food prices have soared, food riots have proliferated, and the "global food crisis" alarm is being rung around the world.[15]

Guineans certainly recognize these changes. Even the lush southern "rice-bowl region" of the country suffered food shortages in 2006 because of lack of rain (IRIN 2006). Scholars have begun to explore the impact of these pressures on agrarian societies in the region. Temudo and Schiefer, for example, note that

> While mangrove cultivation still allows the production of a marketable surplus, today rain-fed production is in crisis. The Cubucaré [southern] region still produces surplus rice. But while many producers sell their surplus outside the region, more and more families inside the region fail to meet their yearly requirements in rice from their own production. . . . Contrary to the ritual invocations of success by development ideologists, the agrarian societies have been sliding downwards on a negative spiral since the beginning of the 1960s (2003:401).

Likewise, in the country's northwest, environmental changes were already being felt by villagers who depended upon abundant rain to desalinate and irrigate their rice paddies. Every day villagers complained that they were suffering because of the decline in rain and rice.

Jola villagers regularly invoked a recent past during which their mode of production yielded an abundance of surplus paddy rice, often stored for decades and used in great quantities for ceremonial purposes. The decrease in rice stores had significant consequences for Jola ritual activities. Most shrine ceremonies require copious paddy rice expenditures—"sack rice," what Jola call imported rice, even if it could be purchased in sufficient quantities, would not be acceptable in most ritual contexts.[16]

Such ceremonies—including inter-village wrestling matches—were more often than not canceled. The previously elaborate rites during which adepts at various spirit-shrines were inducted as priests had also taken on a compromised quality. For instance, in May 2003, as I sat chatting with some men in a rice shop, a small procession of adepts from the spirit-shrine *Amumau* danced through the village's main street. "It used to be a big deal, this business, when it rained more," one of the men commented. "A big affair, lots of rice. But now, it's like nothing. No one has rice anymore."

Beyond its impact on ritual life, diminishing crop yields have led to changes in what might be called the Jola social security system, particularly with regard to vulnerable segments of Jola society like widows. Given the already strained situation of monogamous households providing for their members, the levirate (*botunabu*) practice in which a widow and her children were customarily absorbed into her late husband's brother's household has all but disappeared, leaving an increasing number of widows to fend for themselves on the margins of society.[17] And, at the most basic level, decreased rice in Jola-land has contributed to increased anxiety around sustenance, and many Jola villagers lead a worrisome quotidian experience and a more intense working life in what was already a taxing labor regime. According to a household survey I conducted in 2002, for the previous decade paddy rice harvested for any particular year could feed a household for an average of three months. Some households with more paddy or fewer mouths to feed could subsist on paddy rice for up to eight months. But not a single household was able to say that paddy rice carried them through the full year.

For the past decade I have seen Jola villagers respond to the decrease in rain and rice in varied, and mostly highly individualized, ways. When you ask most Jola how they get by they respond by saying, "*kuji-kuji, son*," referring to what chickens do to find insects and grubs on a day-to-day survival basis. They scrape together what they can in order to buy a kilo of sack rice. Another common strategy among adult Jola—those with families to care for—is to work *harder* and to scold (and often punish) those shifting their primary allegiance away from rice cultivation and toward other livelihood strategies. Some Jola have invested in spirit shrine ceremonies to contract for more rain. Others have sought new religious identities and institutions—Catholic and Protestant are the two options available in this area—that enable both access to new resources and a religiously sanctioned opt-out from traditional strictures that require exclusive devotion to rice. Increasingly, Jola families are investing in schooling for their children and pinning their hopes for the future on their children's academic success. In Guinea-Bissau, school is a fragile thing to pin one's hopes to, and there have been some unexpected hurdles in the process of sending adolescent girls to schools outside the village: most have come back as pregnant drop-outs. Boys often have their studies interrupted because of political turmoil or lack of economic wherewithal, and as they wait around the capital they are not only unable to contribute their much-needed labor back home but are far more likely to lead precarious lives, particularly in a nation where drug trafficking is ever-more entrenched and offers one of the only viable economic alternatives to a laborious (and food-insecure) rural life and a paralyzed (and unfulfilled) postsecondary school urban life.

All of these strategies reflect efforts among Jola villagers to confront their collective dilemma: who are we without our rice? For now, Jola are hungry—some of them literally so as they struggle to feed themselves and their families, others more metaphorically as they search for new paths to social security through schooling, new religious institutions, and escape. Understanding the many dimensions of this hunger contributes to a deeper appreciation for the complex dynamics of agrarian life. This has implications for development policies and practices for Jola and other agrarian populations in this region and beyond. The interpenetration of rice across all social domains requires that any development response— particularly in increasingly food-insecure regions—take into account the totalizing quality of rice agriculture. And the concomitant challenge for scholars is not only to articulate such complexity, but to do so while pragmatically engaging both the anxieties of present-day rice farmers and an agricultural development discourse that disproportionately focuses on efficiency and quantity.

Structure of the Book

Sacred Rice explores the cultural intricacies and the reinforcement of difficulties through which Jola farmers are responding to changes in their environmental and economic conditions given the centrality of a crop that is the lynchpin for their economic, social, religious, and political worlds. Based on over ten years of ethnographic and historical research on rural Guinea-Bissau, this book is about the relationship among people, plants, and identity, as it explores how a society comes to define itself through the production, consumption, and reverence of rice. In that sense, it is a story profoundly tied to a particular place: the tangled mangrove landscape that surrounds the people who have ingeniously turned it into rice paddies. But it is also a story of various encounters with outsiders of all kinds— colonial officials, missionaries, development practitioners, merchants, and schoolteachers—often mediated through rice. Finally, even though the focal point is a remote area of West Africa, it is a story that illuminates the nexus of identity, environment, and development more generally, especially in an era when many people—rural and urban—are confronting environmental and economic changes that challenge their livelihoods and lifestyles. Rural Jola farmers in Guinea-Bissau may be an extreme and out-of-the-way case, but their stories resonate with a larger story about acknowledging a disappearing resource base, whether in a rice economy, an oil-based economy, a postindustrial town, or a megalopolis reaching its limits. Anchored in an environmental dilemma that profoundly effects social relations, moral economy, and cosmological understandings, the story of contemporary Jola rice farmers has much to teach us about the implications of climate change beyond its environmental dimensions.

Sacred Rice thus engages enduring anthropological concerns with sustenance, cosmology, and social structure to explore contemporary problems. It builds on classic and contemporary scholarship in anthropology that places an appreciation of people's cosmologies and cultural understandings at the center of studies on the environment and development (Croll and Parkin 1992). Through detailed life histories and social dramas, it explores how Jola villagers in Guinea-Bissau bring their cultural imaginations to bear on the current circumstances of environmental change that challenge not only their longstanding livelihood practices, but the ways in which these practices are linked to their identity, their values, and their ideas about the past, present, and future.

In the following chapters you will read about the lives and memories of three main characters. Two of them—Ampa Badji and Nho Keboral (whom you already met on the first page)—have lived through the most significant milestones of the past half-century: the waning era of Portuguese colonialism, the eleven-year independence war, the arrival of many missionaries, the still-shaky transition to independence, the ongoing turbulence of an economically weak and often violent state, the introduction of formal schooling, and a fluctuating set of environmental conditions and unpredictable patterns of rainfall throughout. Their life stories tell a compact history of the last century in Guinea-Bissau as they reflect upon their parents and grandparents, provide candid accounts of their own biographies, and hazard predictions about what is to come for their children and grandchildren. Ampa Badji and Nho Keboral are also husband and wife, and the way they experience and narrate many of the same events highlights differences in gender, family position, and perspective, as well as vibrantly demonstrates how such challenges and changes are negotiated under one roof.

The third character is one of their daughters, Marina, who was fourteen years old when I met her and is now twenty-six with a daughter of her own. Her story gives us yet more insight into the best-laid plans of her parents, and how these were implemented and experienced by the third eldest of their six children. Like Marina, the vast majority of teenagers who left village life to continue their studies and seek out new livelihoods have come back unmarried with infants in tow, a new phenomenon in Jola family dynamics given the strict sexual mores that previously regulated reproduction. Their families—already stretched thin in their ability to provide for their own children—take on the additional needs of their grandchildren. Marina and the peers who populate her anecdotes are members of a new social group—and, arguably, a new social order—in this part of rural Africa. They have grown up within the constraints of a diminished economy, pursued the modernist dream of education as an escape from poverty, and found themselves back in the doldrums of village life, unable and unwilling to take their parent's place as subsistence farmers.

This book thus provides portraits of particular Jola lives, but in the context of global shifts in climate, agricultural regimes, and the nature of work in its broadest sense. These personal stories and family histories chronicle changing political economies and life possibilities, and each individual's account illuminates processes of cultural reproduction and improvisation. This is a moment of transition, a time when Jola and other agrarian groups are struggling to re-define their relationships to the land, to each other, to the supernatural, and to the future. Grappling with the decline of rain and rice and the implausibility of continuing to eke out an existence in the paddies provides one set of challenges. But, as we see through the shift of household resources and a new emphasis on schooling, leaving one set of troubles behind leads Jola families into a new set of unexpected challenges. The individuals portrayed in this ethnography personify predicaments facing many rural populations in other parts of the world as they strive to farm and live in ways that are meaningful and dignified to them, and as they struggle keep their families together, but under conditions that make those efforts ever more uncertain.

These character studies are not, however, merely an entrée into a story of typicality. Rather, it is by seeing how they bump into each other—and perhaps even rub up against readers—and by drawing out the uncertainty, contradiction, contingency, paradox, and constrained agency of their lives, that we get a more accurate narrative of the conflicts that construct society, not the typicality that keeps it out of focus. It is also through these paradoxes and conflicts that we gain further understanding of the basic but ever-varied anthropological insight that culture at once opens up and constrains possibility.

Even more, these in-depth portrayals of particular individuals provide a theoretical antidote to two dominant but inadequate approaches to the study of marginalized peoples. The first trope emphasizes death, doom, and disaster through depictions of demise, disappearing cultures, and decline. The second broad approach focuses on the resilience and resistance of impoverished populations, revealing how they subvert oppression and cleverly cope with myriad forces against them through their cultural creativity. Although aspects of these analyses might resonate in the case of Jola rice farmers, neither of them suffices for this story. I address the analytic problem of how Jola are coping with the contemporary challenges of production and reproduction through character-driven narratives that are at once more tragic and more hopeful than either of these over-determined tropes and ideological traps. The intimacy of these stories situated within the wider world of regional politics and global development practices will, I hope, enable readers to move from what is often imagined as either the tangled pathology or the romanticized resilience of the African rural poor toward a feeling of resonance with the challenges of coping with a changing environment.

It for these reasons that I rely heavily on the rhetorical strategy of storytelling, not merely as a means to an expository end but as an analytic method in its own right. As the Australian cultural historian Tom Griffiths suggests,

> Story is sometimes underestimated as something that is easy and instinctive. But story is actually a piece of disciplined magic, of highly refined science. . . . It is also a privileged carrier of truth, a way of allowing for multiplicity and complexity at the same time as guaranteeing memorability. Story creates an atmosphere in which truth becomes discernible as a pattern. And so I would argue that narrative is not just a means, it is a method, and a rigorous and demanding one. The conventional scientific method separates causes from one another, it isolates each one and tests them individually in turn. Narrative, by contrast, carries multiple causes along together, it enacts connectivity (2007:5).

Enacting connectivity is precisely how storytelling links to Mauss's assertion of the "total" as the distinct (and necessary) framework for meaningful sociological analysis. Stories—in their refusal to artificially partition reality, in their insistent preserving of multiple possibilities, and in their roundness—enable a kind of knowledge that enriches our understanding (and compassion) for particular people, moves us away from flattened renderings of problems and populations, and potentially breaks the hold of a tenacious orientation to knowledge and practice (at play both inside and outside the academy) that is committed to certainty at the cost of complexity, and to knowability over and above intimacy and ambiguity. Story is a potent strategy, for Jola villagers and their ethnographers alike, to counter what the Greeks recognized as *hubris*, and what currently holds sway as expertise.

The narrative architecture of this book thus mirrors its theoretical scope by interspersing sections devoted to the life histories of specific Jola villagers with sections on the structural and historical conditions in which these lives unfold. As the story shifts over multiple generations, we observe how Jola villagers have conformed to or subverted those very conditions, and we witness the range of dilemmas Jola have confronted over the past century. Particularly through Ampa Badji's accounts, we gain insight into a people that has surmounted forces and events—the slave trade, colonialism, missionization, state violence—that have annihilated others. Part of my argument, however, hinges on the fundamental difference of the challenges that Jola face in this generation. As we will see, there were quintessentially Jola responses and solutions—such as evasion or compromise—to these past problems that are no longer possible. Whereas, in the past, Jola have met with (and dealt with) dramatic transformations and led lives (as we all do) thick with uncertainty, the current challenges that undermine the work of rice as a total social phenomenon cut to the core of Jola personhood, and this has led to a kind of structural uncertainty that demands a different set of responses.

All of this is happening in the context of worldwide concern over climate change, increasing anxiety over decreasing arable land, and escalating fears about declining agricultural output. Although the topic of climate change is receiving intensified attention from scholars, policymakers, and journalists, relatively little is known about its impact on the cultures and consciousnesses of the agrarian populations most vulnerable to its effects.[18] This book explores one such group's responses to the changes—environmental and other—that challenge its longstanding beliefs and practices. It is through these characters that we see how pressures on Jola livelihoods ripple across all social and cosmological spheres.

Dominant development approaches, however, continue to address these concerns largely through a focus on food productivity and the technological improvement of agricultural methods. Each chapter thus also considers how the current development apparatus is ill equipped to grapple seriously with connections among material, social, and spiritual needs. Even more, we see how the Jola desire for development—manifest most obviously in their hunger for formal schooling—creates new dilemmas that Jola are ill equipped to deal with themselves.

The next chapter introduces yet one more central character in this story: rice itself. It charts the epic global history of rice, focusing on its spread across West Africa, its importance for Jola and other agrarian groups in this region, and the varied efforts to produce ever more of it.

CHAPTER 1

A Rice Complex

[S]ocial issues . . . are sometimes described, and dismissed, as 'micro-issues,' irrelevant to the broad sweep of African farming history and to the monumental plans now deemed necessary to rescue Africa's agriculture. Yet such 'small issues' have always been the downfall of grandiose schemes, something which should not be a surprise to those familiar with African literature, whether in its modern guise, or its ancient epics.

—James Fairhead and Melissa Leach,
The Centrality of the Social in African Farming

....

A Very Condensed World History of Rice

The history of rice is often told with a focus on its abundance and adaptation across various ecological and political landscapes. Most general publications about rice tend to start with bold statements about the global importance of its production and consumption, the antiquity and ubiquity of its cultivation, and the urgent need for more of it. "Rice," much of the rice literature repeats, "is one of the world's most important cereals, providing nourishment for a greater number of people than any other grain" (Irvine 1974:130). "Rice has been cultivated for such countless ages that its origin must always be a matter of conjecture" (Grist 1959:3). And "The hope for improved nourishment of the world's population depends on the development of better rice varieties and improved methods for rice production and utilization" (Luh 1991:v). What emerges from the wealth of rice scholarship over the last 50 years is a chorus singing rice's praises based largely on quantity and adaptability, a logic which leads inexorably to clarion calls for more.

Rice is cultivated on all the continents of the world except Antarctica (Sharma 2010). But rice, both in the popular imagination and—until recently—in the scholarly literature, is also decidedly Asian. Authors who take a global and historical view have tended to give short shrift to the role of rice in Africa, partly because rice is, indeed, produced in much greater quantities in Asia, and partly because, until the 1970s, it was assumed that all rice was of Asian origin. In a 1969 publication on West African crops, for instance, the entry on rice focused exclusively on Asian rice and never mentioned African indigenous rice (Irvine 1974:130–135). Even the 1977 proceedings of a conference on rice in Africa, held in Ibadan, Nigeria, began with the question: "Rice in Africa? Rice connotes, to most of us, Asian civilization and its base in the permanent rice agriculture in the alluvial deltas of the great Asian rivers" (Buddenhagen 1978:ix).

The epic history of Asian rice is indeed a grand tale. Although the precise time and place of the emergence of *Oryza sativa*—the Asian rice cultigen—are still debated, most scholars chart the grain's early journey from the Indus Valley to Southeast Asia, through southern China, on to Ceylon and the East Indies, across to the Philippines, New Guinea, and tropical Australia, and eventually to Japan, where rice, as the anthropologist Emiko Ohnuki-Tierney (1993) has argued, is now synonymous with the Japanese self. More recent accounts locate *Oryza sativa*'s first site of domestication in China along the Zhu Jiang (Pearl River) and Yangtze River areas (Huang et al. 2012; Molina et al. 2011). Migration of people across the Asian continent went hand in hand with the spread of rice; prehistoric people, it seems, traveled with their plants (Chang 1976a). Greeks and Romans used Asian rice as a trade commodity rather than a crop they farmed themselves, but after 700 CE rice appeared in Islamic agriculture, especially in Mesopotamia, Egypt, and the Nile valley. Asian rice then made its way through Mediterranean Europe, as well as across the Indian Ocean to Madagascar. Eventually, around the 1600s, Spanish explorers brought rice to the Americas, where it was planted in the Caribbean and mainland South America, and then traveled northward (possibly from the Madagascar strain) to the British colonies along the Carolina coast, where it was cultivated as a slave plantation crop (Sauer 1993; Chang 1976b; Carney 2001, 2004). Even with this wide geographic diffusion, *Oryza sativa* is "exceptional among major grain crops ... in having its present production so heavily concentrated within its ancient geographic range. Asia still produces and consumes over 90% of the world's rice crop" (Sauer 1993:209). In other words, Asian rice, despite its presence on all inhabited continents of the world, is still decidedly Asian.

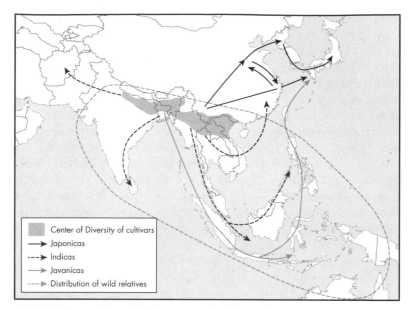

MAP 1 Evolution and spread of the geographical races of *Oryza sativa* (*Chang 1976b:101*).

Until quite recently the conventional understanding was that *Oryza sativa* made its way to West Africa, perhaps with Portuguese explorers along the Upper Guinea Coast in the mid-fifteenth century, or even earlier via Malayo-Indonesian voyagers across the Indian Ocean, where they introduced the plant to Madagascar and it eventually spread to mainland east Africa and then across the continent to West Africa (Purseglove 1976; Clark 1970). But, starting in the 1950s, collecting expeditions and botanical analyses of rice varieties in Africa opened up the question of an independent site of rice domestication. This was a time of great interest among agricultural scientists and historians regarding the Vavilovian paradigm shift in understanding the Neolithic Revolution. Researchers and scholars were pushing against the conventional theory (based on V. Gordon Childe's work) that the birthplace of agriculture was in a single center—the lush valleys of Mesopotamia—and proposing multiple cradles of plant domestication and agricultural innovation. While the Russian geneticist Nikolai Vavilov went far in locating multiple centers, he limited such sites in Africa to Ethiopia. It took another generation of scientists to show that Africa was home to several centers of independent domestication. Roland Portères, writing very much in the Vavilovian tradition of identifying primary centers of domestication and cultivation of certain crops, extended Vavilov's focus on Ethiopia to two other "cradles of agriculture": West Africa and East Africa.[1] It is West Africa that was home to an indigenous species of cultivated rice—*Oryza glaberrima*—that was first named and described by Ernst Gottlieb von Steudel, a German physician and authority on grasses, in 1855. According to Portères, and confirmed by subsequent studies, *Oryza glaberrima* was first cultivated in the Inner Delta of the Niger River (in what is now the country of Mali) around 3,500 years ago (Portères 1970, 1976; Carpenter 1978; Chang 1976a, 1976b; Grist 1959; Sanni et al. 2013). Two secondary centers of varietal diversification can be found on either side of the coastal Gambia River (Portères 1970, 1976). As Portères unequivocally concludes, "West Africa thus possesses a rice-growing cradle of agriculture peculiar to itself and anterior to the arrival of Asiatic rice. . . . Rice cultivation in West Africa was therefore not promoted by the Portuguese; they did no more than introduce varieties of a different species" (Portères 1970:47–48).

Rice cultivation in West Africa developed under quite different climatic conditions than the present day. The Upper Guinea Coast was a wetter place, with the rainy season lasting for five months, typically from June to October (Irvine 1969; Buddenhagen 1978; Portères 1976). Rice is unusual among grain crops in terms of its semi-aquatic nature; most of its growth cycle occurs underwater (Grist 1959; Moormann and Veldkamp 1978:29). Water is thus the most essential ingredient—and constraining factor—in rice cultivation, more so than soil conditions or other environmental factors (Latham 1998; de Datta 1975).[2] Since rice cultivation is so deeply dependent on rainfall, and rainfall is and never was predictable in this region, yields have always fluctuated from year to year (Will 1978:216). These particular conditions—the intrinsic characteristics of a semi-aquatic plant, the topography of a coastal mangrove landscape, and the challenges of variable rainfall—led to the development of agricultural innovations and strategies that are now trademark features of the Upper Guinea Coast, particularly the *crue* and *décrue* techniques, which take advantage of flooding and subsequently receding waters, matching seed varieties in accordance with these patterns, and transplanting rice seedlings from an inland nursery to an inundated paddy at appropriate moments in the agricultural and climatological cycle. All of these now well-known features of West African rice farming corroborate what some have seen as another hallmark feature of African agriculture more generally: that techniques conform to the opportunities and challenges of a

Transporting rice seedlings from forest nursery to inundated rice paddies, Esana 2003 *(photo by Joanna Davidson).*

Transplanting rice seedlings [*borokabu*], Esana 2003 *(photo by Joanna Davidson, 2003).*

particular environmental context, rather than radically transforming those conditions (Harlan, De Wet, and Stemler 1976; McCann 2005).

Even with the irrefutable evidence that rice was independently domesticated and cultivated in West Africa prior to the arrival of non-Africans, rice scholarship still tends to quickly dismiss the importance of African rice as of "only local importance and ... antiquarian interest" (Sauer 1993). Part of the focus on Asian rice, even after the "discovery" of the African *O. glaberrima* variety, stems from the fact that, since the introduction of *O. sativa* to Africa, it has been steadily replacing African rice even in the "cradles" of indigenous African rice domestication (Sauer 1993; Chang 1976a, 1976b; Peel and Richards 1981).[3] Also, most authors are quick to point out the inferiority of *Oryza glaberrima* as compared with its more robust Asian cousin. "Compared with *O. sativa*, the African rice (*O. glaberrima*) has many shortcomings: its grains often shatter on the ground even before reaching the threshing floor, the rice is red-skinned and, when cooked, tastes gritty. Its per acre yield is low and it has not become a trade commodity" (Sharma 2010:18). Many rice experts point to the relative lack of diversity and complexity of both the African grain itself and the methods for cultivating it (Chang 1976a; Purseglove 1976; Badawi et al. 2010). Others are more measured in their assessment of the differences between the two cultigens, pointing out *O. glaberrima*'s adaptive responses to the soil, climate, and pest conditions of West Africa, as well as its higher protein content. But, until recently, the overall consensus seemed to hold that African rice was less hardy, less diverse, and confined to a relatively small area, whereas Asian rice was dominant in terms of yield, resistance, and span of the globe. Comparing the narratives of the two rice species, the language of diffusion, migration, and domination rings out for the Asian species, and the tone of confinement, primitivity, and subordination resounds for the African species (Purseglove 1976; Luh 1991; Chang 1976a, 1976b; Chandler 1979; Sharma 2010; Carpenter 1978). *Oryza sativa* is said to have botanically colonized its African counterpart (Buddenhagen 1978), and one source contends that African rice "lingers on only as a weed of Asian rice fields" (Harlan, De Wet, and Stemler 1976:10).[4] As Chandler sums up the reigning view of the time: "Most rice specialists consider *O. glaberrima* to be inferior to *O. sativa* in yielding ability and disease resistance" (Chandler 1979:14).[5]

Perhaps because of these assessments, agricultural development efforts focused on rice-growing regions in West Africa have, until recently, channeled their energy into improving *Oryza sativa* through breeding programs, as Buddenhagen explains: "Indigenous rice culture in these areas [of West Africa] was primitive and stagnant, and modern efforts to expand rice production in Africa have focused on the recently introduced *O. sativa* and on Asian techniques of rice growing and rice improvement, largely ignoring the African heritage" (Buddenhagen 1978:11). Thus, rice improvement schemes along the Upper Guinea Coast have involved the introduction—and often imposition—of not only a new species of rice but of Asian techniques of growing it, based on the assumption that Africans did not have the best—or even adequate—cultivation methods. Although the editors of the 1978 conference proceedings on "Rice in Africa" quickly dispelled the reigning myth that rice came only from Asia, the contributors went on to largely focus on *Oryza sativa* as the right rice to develop for Africa (Buddenhagen 1978; Moormann and Veldkamp 1978).

Such attitudes reflect the kind of hubris that was characteristic of colonial science and that led to so many mistakes in the implementation of Green Revolution approaches to agricultural development in Latin America and Asia.[6] Paul Richards (1985, 1986, 2006) has consistently argued against such approaches to agricultural development in Africa, calling instead for development practitioners to enlist themselves in the service of an African-led indigenous agricultural revolution.[7] Although some of these sentiments have entered the rhetoric of policymakers and development practitioners in the past few years, they have not been put into practice in the transformative ways Richards seeks (see Davidson 2012a).

Before returning to the current conditions of rice-growing regions in West Africa, I want to devote some attention to this long "ignored African heritage" of rice.

Rice on the Upper Guinea Coast

The last several decades have actually seen a flourishing of influential studies of rice in Africa, and in Atlantic studies more broadly, rectifying many of the biased assumptions in previous understandings—both scholarly and popular—regarding rice's origins and importance being located exclusively in Asia. A considerable literature now attests to the important role of rice in shaping societies on both sides of the Atlantic. The weight of evidence—historical (Pélissier 1966; Lauer 1969; Alpern 2008), botanical (Portères 1970, 1976; Harlan, De Wet, and Stemler 1976), climatological (Brooks 1985), geographical (Cormier-Salem 1999), archaeological (Linares 1970, 2002), linguistic (Fields-Black 2008), political ecological (Paul Richards 1985, 1996a), and genealogical (Carney 2001, 2004)—restores rice history to its proper place in West Africa, even if the extension of such accounts across the Atlantic into New World systems continues to be debated (Eltis, Morgan, and Richardson 2007). That rice was grown 3,500 years ago in the Inner Delta of the Niger River; that it diffused to two secondary centers; that both the plant and the people adapted to the particular conditions—saline, insalubrious, unpredictable—to thrive in a challenging landscape and develop a range of rice planting methods; that rice production even increased, in some cases, in spite of the ravages of the Atlantic slave trade (Hawthorne 2003)— all of this is now, unlike the semi-aquatic rice pant itself, on terra firma.

Carney's (2001) watershed study consolidates such evidence to demonstrate Africans' roles in developing both the domesticated rice plant, *Oryza glaberrima*, and the highly sophisticated water management systems, cultivation techniques, and trademark tools involved in successfully growing the crop in a tricky and unpredictable environment, long before European influence in the area. Building on Wood (1974) and Littlefield (1981), Carney breaks the narrative of African rice out of its relegated confinement to West Africa, of "local importance and antiquarian interest" (Sauer 1993), and provides as compelling a travel narrative for African rice as the more familiar accounts charted for the Asian cultigen. Just as for Asia, as African people and plants moved across the oceans to different ecosystems—whether of their own volition or not—they brought with them both the seeds and the skills that would transform the environments, economies, and societies wherever they went (and wherever they left behind). It is a transnational story of the West African "rice knowledge system" that builds upon classics of this kind for other crops (Crosby 1972; Mintz 1985).

Putting aside her more controversial extension of this argument, which focuses on the influence of this indigenous African rice knowledge system in the Americas via the Atlantic slave trade,[8] I want to take up a point Carney and others writing in her wake emphasize regarding the development of rice agriculture in West Africa and ask about its implications today. Carney (2001), Hawthorne (2003), and Fields-Black (2008) each emphasize the *innovative* qualities of rice cultivation on the Upper Guinea Coast as a technologically ingenious approach to a challenging mangrove ecosystem, particularly in terms of its sophisticated *crue/décrue* method of water management (Carney 2001:40–46; Fields-Black 2008) and its socially innovative responses to the pressures of the Atlantic slave trade (Hawthorne 2003). Whereas the aims of these authors were to establish a solid historical basis for rice-oriented cultures and their continual adaptation to myriad challenges—Mandinka expansion, European slave raiding, colonially enforced cash cropping, shaky transitions to independence, and throughout all a fluctuating set of environmental conditions and unpredictable pattern of rainfall—my experience as an ethnographer among Jola rice cultivators in postcolonial Guinea-Bissau leads me to ask: What now?

Rice Metrics: The Institutional History of Rice Science and Agricultural Development

In order to approach this question I first take a brief look at the history of efforts to improve rice growing—and agricultural production more broadly—in West Africa, focusing particularly on the frame of reference through which such approaches have been developed and implemented. Rice is a quintessentially developing world staple crop. As such, it is evaluated most often in terms of quantity, and its use is considered to be primarily belly filling. This is perhaps why rice researchers—agronomists and policymakers alike—tend to have a Malthusian tone. Most rice scholarship focuses on quantity, and a consistent thread that runs through the literature calls for the need—often urgently—to increase yield. As one source states, "The importance of rice as the number one staple in the developing countries will grow as the human population increases at a higher rate in such countries as compared to the developed world. By the year 2000 rice will be the chief source of energy for about 40% of the world's people, thereby passing wheat" (Luh 1991:10). Particularly in Africa, the upward trend in rice consumption (largely driven by urbanization) coupled with significant dependence on imports has led to consistent rhetorical and practical efforts aimed at rapidly and dramatically boosting rice production (see Seck et al. 2013). Authors such as these are concerned about population increase in the developing world and the ability to meet increased consumption needs for rice. This makes for simultaneously urgent and banal statements that feeding the growing world population means finding ways to increase rice production.[9] And it is why assessments of rice production—in both Asia and Africa—have tended to emphasize the inefficiency of rice production and the limited value of rice as a trade commodity (Pearson, Stryker, and Humphreys 1981; Latham 1998; Sayamwala and Haykin 1983).[10] For instance, a Stanford University study on rice in West Africa in the early 1980s provided a set of country-based case studies that focused largely on economic analyses of production and regulation schemes. The authors concluded that rice growing was simply "not economic"—meaning it was inefficient—in many West African countries (Pearson et al. 1981). Such emphases are not just relics of Green Revolution programs of the 1970s. They are very much present in key agricultural development policies and programs today, as exemplified by a recent resurgence in promoting a "new" Green Revolution for Africa (see Davidson 2012a).

Considering the future of rice in West Africa must, of course, go hand in hand with an historical view of the decreasing self-sufficiency of what was once called the Rice Coast, which takes into account the shift from staple to cash crops during the colonial era in Africa, as well as a continued de-emphasis on agricultural development in the postcolonial period (see, e.g., Bigman 1993; Galli 1987a; Lofchie 1975). Once defined by its abundant rice production, the Upper Guinea Coast has seen a dramatic increase in rice imports over the past half-century. Colonial policies shifted African agricultural efforts away from food crops for local sustenance toward cash crops for European consumption.

Newly independent African nations in the 1960s and 1970s declared their intention to attain self-sufficiency in food production, framing such a goal both as a pragmatic approach to meet the demands of population growth and address Africa's marginal position in the international market, and as a political and symbolic reversal of the colonial project.[11] But since independence the increased influence of the cash economy combined with rapid demographic shifts and a concomitant focus on urban development have conspired to keep rural development efforts in a marginalized position vis-à-vis large-scale improvement schemes, and food imports have only increased. Such trends in importing basic staples, especially rice, rapidly accelerated during the early 1970s given the twin impact of the Sahelian drought and the availability of cheaper rice on the international market, due to surplus yields in Asia as a result of new intensive approaches and high-yield seed varieties of the Green Revolution. Thus, in the independence era, "The amount of rice imported into West Africa increased from 276,000 tons/year in 1960–1964 to 496,000 tons/year in 1970–1974, an increase of 80%, at a time when total world rice exports were unchanged" (Aw 1978:71). In Senegal, for example, such import trends continued from the colonial to the postcolonial era:

> During the colonial period, rice was imported in large quantities in order to keep food prices under control and at the same time promote groundnut production as an important cash crop. . . . A further factor encouraging rice imports was that in the French colonies in Indo-China, rice production and export were under French control. That region exported the bulk of rice coming to the West African colonies. During the first two decades after independence, this import policy remained unchanged, and there was a continued interest in exporting groundnuts and importing rice. . . . Senegal currently imports more than three-quarters of its rice for domestic consumption. . . . In

Unloading sacks of imported rice at the Dakar port, 2010 *(photo by Bobby Milstein)*.

addition, many rice farmers have difficulty selling their crop, because the markets are inundated with cheaper imported rice from Asia (Badawi et al. 2010:396, 399).

Neighboring Guinea-Bissau followed a similar trajectory, even if under quite different circumstances. Despite its stated post-independence commitment to boost rice self-sufficiency (Bigman 1993; da Silva 1978; Galli 1987a), Guinea-Bissau's rice imports have steadily increased since independence (Temudo 2011). As Temudo notes, "In recent years rice imports in the sub-region have been increasing from an annual growth rate of 5.54% in 1991–2000 up to 10.51% in 2001–2005 (WARDA 2008:30). Despite research and development efforts focused on the selection and diffusion of modern varieties, rice consumption has been increasing faster than production, and the self-sufficiency ratio decreased from 0.78 in the nineties to 0.58 during 2001–2005 (WARDA 2008:8–12)." (Temudo 2011:309).

To answer post-independence Africa's call for self-sufficiency in rice production, the West African Rice Development Association (WARDA) was established in 1971, based in Monrovia, Liberia, and later joined the Consultative Group on International Agricultural Research (CGIAR). WARDA was one of several agricultural research and development centers dedicated to improving the yields of African farmers, and it was the only

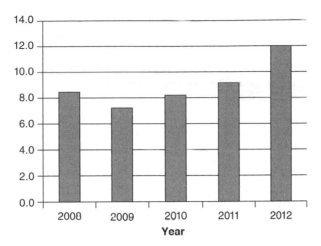

FIGURE 3   Rice imports into sub-Saharan Africa during the period 2008–2012 (Seck 2013:30).

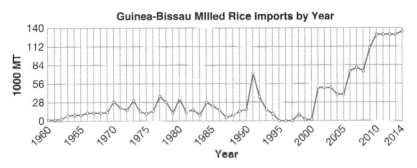

FIGURE 4   Guinea-Bissau milled rice imports by year (United States Department of Agriculture 2014).

one focused exclusively on rice.[12] Since its establishment in 1971, WARDA has been a moveable feast, relocating from Liberia to Cote d'Ivoire to Mali and then finally to Benin in response to the eruption of violent conflicts across this swath of West Africa; in 2009, it officially changed its name to Africa Rice Center (AfricaRice). Although conscious of the particularities of environmental, political, and cultural factors that condition rural development work in West Africa, WARDA largely followed the model of other agricultural research and development entities in terms of its focus on the technical aspects of growing rice.[13] The characteristic approach of agricultural development since the Green Revolution, and even before, has been to apply the latest innovations in agricultural science—especially plant breeding, fertilizers, and irrigation—to impoverished rural communities across the world, and to move agricultural production from sustenance to surplus to sale. Generally couched in the development discourse of poverty eradication and food security, the goals are primarily quantitative— higher yields, more crop per drop—and even though the latest iteration of the Green Revolution for Africa has incorporated the language of sustainability, holism, and gender into its rhetoric (Tollens et al. 2013; Agboh-Noameshie, Kabore, and Misiko 2013), the creation of high-yield seeds continues to be the Holy Grail for rural development.

WARDA's chief contribution in this vein has been the development of New Rice for Africa (NERICA) varieties—the first successful hybrid between *Oryza sativa* and *Oryza glaberrima*—that are being distributed to rice-cultivating populations across the continent. NERICA was first named "wide crossing" to highlight the achievement of bringing together two rice species from widely divergent sources (Walsh 2001). It also reflected a shift in attitudes toward African indigenous rice, long considered inferior and marginal to rice breeding programs. As Walsh explains, looking back on several decades of rice breeding efforts, WARDA scientists realized that they had made limited gains because of the concentration on imported grains, so they began to "reclaim *glaberrima*"—analyzing the long-ignored indigenous rice species to see what could be learned from its long history and adaptation to West African conditions (Walsh 2001). A recent publication from AfricaRice went so far as to assert that "*Oryza glaberrima* constitutes a rich reservoir of adaptive traits essential for new rice varieties for Africa" (Sanni et al. 2013:90). A senior plant geneticist at AfricaRice (then WARDA) described the process as "time consuming, but it's worth doing because eventually we are going to get an interspecific hybrid that will combine important traits between *glaberrima* and *sativa*" (Walsh 2001:65). And it did indeed pay off, at least in terms of scientific recognition, when WARDA won the prestigious King Baudouin International Agriculture Research Award for NERICA in 2000, its leading rice breeder Monty Jones won the World Food Prize in 2004, and hopes began to soar regarding the possibility of revitalizing rice production across the continent.

In some senses NERICA brings the epic journey of rice full circle. It is now generally accepted that *Oryza sativa* and *Oryza glaberrima* shared a common progenitor and that the genus *Oryza* originated in the Gondwanaland supercontinent before being widely distributed across the tropics. From a common origin in a geologically conjoined world, followed by a long history of independent domestication and cultivation to the extent that attempted crosses between the two species—*O. sativa* and *O. glaberrima*—were sterile, and a subsequent "colonization" of African rice by the Asian variety in *glaberrima's* homeland, we have finally come back to a different kind of conjoining, one conjured in the laboratory, where Asia and Africa are brought back together in the microcosm of a single grain, rhetorically touted as the "best of Africa mixed with the best of Asia" and having hopes pinned on it to feed a hungry world. "The NERICA rice varieties," states a recent comprehensive publication on rice, "offer great hope to the next generation in Africa" (Badawi et al. 2010:404).

But what do rice farmers across West Africa hope for the next generation? So far, early evidence suggests that adoption of new seed varieties, including NERICA, among rice-growing populations, at least in Guinea-Bissau, has not been successful (Temudo 2011).[14]

A 1978 publication declared: "The challenge for research and development on rice in tropical Africa is enormous, and the problems are many. The opportunity to answer this challenge mainly lies with the scientists and development officers of Africa" (Buddenhagen and Persley 1978:x). So, in 1978 the answer was to be found in science and development. This became bound up with structural adjustment policies in the 1980s, which were based on the belief that "the market would take care of seeds, fertilizer and everything else" (African Rice Center [WARDA] 2009). But this belief—manifested in economic development practices—has not borne itself out in Africa. Reliance on the global market and dependence on rice imports for an accelerating urban population has actually intensified the impact of international market shocks on both rural and urban populations.

Much can be said about the failed economic policies across Africa throughout the last several decades, and in particular how they have impacted rural agrarian populations. In Guinea-Bissau's case, after winning independence in 1974 through an eleven-year liberation war, the government established a centralized economy in which, as Temudo describes,

> Agriculture was relegated in practice to function as a supplier of food for the urban population, of raw materials for industry, and of export commodities. Assuming that farmers would not respond to price incentives, the government maintained artificially low prices for agricultural commodities, forcing producers into direct exchanges of crops for other essential goods supplied (in a tremendously inefficient manner) by state enterprises. The aggregate effects of these measures were the stagnation

of agriculture, the impoverishment of farmers, and the increase of informal trade networks (Temudo 2011:311).

Shortly after independence the state froze the price of rice and required farmers to sell their harvests only to state stores, thereby establishing a monopoly over the rice trade (Ribeiro 1989). This lasted until the mid-1980s, which brought in the era of economic liberalization, but with it new market policies and development priorities that further disadvantaged Guinea-Bissau's already vulnerable farmers (Bigman 1993; Galli 1990; Handem 1987).

It has been almost forty years, which happens to be close to the life span of an average Guinean man (CIA 2015), since scientists and development officers were charged with the task of improving rice production, but they have made little headway in Guinea-Bissau. It has been thirty years since neoliberal market policies, especially through structural adjustment schemes, were meant to eradicate entrenched poverty, but instead they have continued to worsen agricultural production and the conditions of the rural poor. There have been plenty of anthropological and other analyses to help explain such failures—the most compelling of which follow Ferguson's (1994) anti-politics approach and Scott's (1998) critique of legibility and high modernism. I am not going to rehearse those arguments here, although it will become evident that my own thinking has been deeply influenced by them. Unfortunately, although such arguments have had a major impact on social science scholarship, they have not had a similar impact on large-scale international development efforts themselves. The main international agricultural development initiative currently underway across most of Africa—under the auspices of the Alliance for a Green Revolution for Africa (AGRA)—is a continuation of these same approaches outlined earlier: policies and projects firmly rooted in the belief that high-modernist science and the market hold the answers to agricultural transformation. Elsewhere, I have challenged the premises and programs behind this supposedly "new" effort (Davidson 2012a). My main concern is that such approaches to agricultural transformation and rural development tend to extract agriculture outside of its social, political, and cosmological contexts and, by doing so, miss the multidimensionality of how farmers see, understand, and perform their work. Ultimately, even the most well-intentioned interventions miss the mark and tend to flounder or even worsen the conditions of their would-be beneficiaries.

Plant breeders do their best to achieve what they call "transgressive segregation," in which the offspring of a particular seed variety does better than the best of its parents. Such a notion of progress is in direct contra-distinction to the current experiences of rice farmers themselves. Most of the villagers whom I came to know during the course of my fieldwork insisted that their parents and grandparents were much better off than they were, and they worried constantly about what would become of their children.

So far, I have chronicled the global history of rice, its spread across West Africa, and shifts in the portrayals of the West African cultigen—*Oryza glaberrima*—and those who cultivated it. I have briefly charted the deleterious impact of colonial, postcolonial, and neoliberal policies on rice production, and the mostly failed efforts of rice scientists and development officials to bolster production and self-sufficiency. I now turn to the farmers themselves, re-embedding this study of rice into a particular historical, social, cultural, religious, and moral context. I begin by highlighting the centrality of rice, not as a staple crop that is meant to feed the developing world's growing population, but as a multivalent complex that ties together and defines a particular agrarian population.

The Jola Rice Complex

Soon after I arrived in a Jola village in northwestern Guinea-Bissau, I became deeply immersed into a life in which rice dominates one's actions, preoccupations, and even dreams. I harvested ripe rice at the height of the dry season, carried heavy baskets laden with freshly cut rice from the paddies to the village, helped pound and winnow rice at my adopted family's home, and cooked rice over wood fires in large pots of heavily salted water. I ate rice every day, at least three times a day, sometimes adorned with small fish or a sauce of boiled hibiscus leaves, but mostly plain rice—*kutangu*, as it is called in Crioulo—morning, afternoon, and night. I ate such rice in my daily meals and also in ceremonial contexts, when it is prepared in enormous pots and distributed among participants who gather in small groups around a shared tin bowl. I saw un-husked rice used to decorate funeral grounds, strung on cords connecting gigantic cottonwood trees, and hung in bouquets around the central platform where the corpse had been seated. Small sachets of rice often encircled a young girl's waist at a neighborhood dance, and delicately balanced bundles were worn as headdresses by the celebrants at inter-village wrestling matches. I discussed rice with my neighbors and friends, or rather, listened as they spoke endlessly of rice, sometimes in technical terms (seed variations, irrigation methods, transplantation practices), sometimes in worried tones ("there's not enough rice to go around anymore," "our granaries are empty"), and sometimes in metaphorical tropes ("our money is rice," "rice is our life").

Rice is omnipresent in Jola economic, social, and symbolic life. It is the center of social gossip, and people regularly discuss whose supply is abundant and whose is depleted. Rice is the medium of exchange during life-cycle redistributive processes, such as weddings, funerals, and initiations. And rice is the ticket to ritual power, as spirit shine ceremonies require abundant expenditures of one's crop. Jola lives, like those of most rice-growing people in this region, are permeated by rice. Growing, eating, displaying, wearing, discussing, and revering rice. It was ubiquitous. I closed my eyes at night and panicles of rice swayed behind my eyelids.

Jola villagers along the Upper Guinea Coast have long been recognized for their capacity to grow rice in their landscape of tangled mangroves and thick oil palm forests. Archaeological evidence suggests that Jola have been practicing their trademark wet rice cultivation techniques in this region for at least a thousand years (Linares 1981).[15] Jola survival and success—despite periodic droughts and other environmental hazards,

Children gather around a bowl of rice at a wedding celebration, Esana 2003 *(photo by Joanna Davidson)*.

Bundles of rice decorate a woman's headdress at an inter-village wrestling tournament, Karuay 2002 *(photo by Joanna Davidson)*.

A funeral platform (on which the corpse is seated) is piled high with rice from the deceased's granary, Esana 2002 *(photo by Joanna Davidson)*.

A young girl wears a skirt made from unhusked rice at a carnival performance, Esana 2010 *(photo by Joanna Davidson)*.

as well as myriad social and political upheavals—are a testament to both their complex and intricate system of agricultural knowledge (Carney 2001) and their commitment to hard work.

Rice cultivation is a major feature of most cultural groups in Guinea-Bissau, not just the Jola. Aquatic rice occupies 80 percent of the total rice area, and of this, 75 percent is in mangrove swamps (Da Silva 1978:324–325). This makes Guinea-Bissau the country with the greatest proportion of total land under mangrove rice cultivation (Écoutin 1999; Temudo 2011). A smaller amount of upland rice is grown as well, but the popular imaginary of rice cultivation in the country is very much tied to the inundated mangrove paddies. As Temudo notes, "The mangrove swamp ecology is highly productive even without the use of chemical fertilizers and modern varieties, but is work-intensive throughout the whole year and needs constant monitoring and repair of the dikes and canals to remain productive" (2011:312).

It takes an enormous amount of physical work to grow rice, and it requires a sophisticated approach to coordinating collective labor at certain crucial moments in the agricultural cycle. Jola have accomplished this through a household-based gendered division of labor in which men till the paddies and women transplant rice seedlings from their forest nurseries to the inundated paddies at the height of the rainy season, and then harvest ripe rice at the height of the dry season. All of this labor is manual. Men use the *bujandabu*, an iron-tipped fulcrum shovel employed by Jola and other cultural groups in the area, to till the heavy soil, and every Jola household has at least one, and sometimes several, of these long-handled shovels tucked into the rafters of the veranda.[16]

Most rice cultivation tasks are fulfilled at a household level, with children joining their parents in the forests and paddies when they become old enough to participate. At crucial moments in the cultivation cycle, though, there is a need for more collective labor, some of which is addressed through kin-based reciprocal labor, but most of which (and increasingly so) is managed through collective work groups. These are also gender-based; each neighborhood in a village has a group of married men, another of in-married women, a group of unmarried male youth, and a final group of unmarried young women. Any of these groups can be contracted by a household to perform particular tasks: usually tilling (either to prepare a forest nursery or till the mounds of an inundated paddy), transplanting

Tilling a paddy with a *bujandabu*, Esana 2002 *(photo by Joanna Davidson)*.

seedlings, or harvesting ripe rice. Increasingly, collective groups have been used to clear-cut sections of a forested area for upland rice cultivation. I discuss these work groups in more detail in Chapters Three and Six.

Jola consume rice every day for every meal. Typically, in October, they harvest the upland rice from their forest groves, which ideally lasts them through late December or early January. Any surplus rice would be stored in the household granary. In late December, during the dry season, they harvest the paddy rice. In the past, paddy rice would last them through the year with plenty left over. But, as I discuss below, yields have decreased significantly during the past few decades.

Before getting into these details, however, let me pause here to provide some background on just who these Jola villagers are. In Guinea-Bissau,

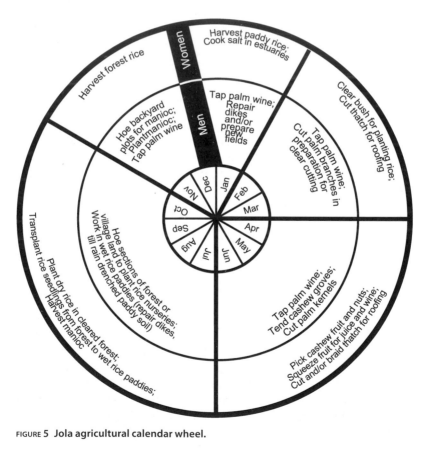

FIGURE 5 Jola agricultural calendar wheel.

Jola[17] are a minority group and occupy just a small strip of mangrove and forested land in the northwest of the country, along the Senegalese border. They number 15,000 to 20,000, under 2 percent of Guinea-Bissau's overall population of 1.5 million (Lobban and Mendy 2013), but across the border they are far more numerous. Jola populations stretch from their southernmost villages in Guinea-Bissau, across the Casamance region of southern Senegal, and into the Gambia, with a total population estimated at 500,000 (the vast majority in the Casamance).[18] Although they share some fundamental social and cultural principles, there is significant variation among and within these communities. Jola tend to share a diffuse political structure; a lineage-based religio-political official—an *ai* (plural: *ai-i*)—maintains a certain amount of ritual authority at a village level, and there is one paramount *ai* for all Jola who resides in the Guinean village of Karuay. The village-based *ai-i* are supported by a cadre of *amangen-i*—sometimes glossed loosely as "elders"—who are generally spirit-shrine priests with authority over one or more particular shrines. Although both *ai-i* and *amangen-i* can exert their authority over certain domains—especially in the ritual arena—most Jola decision-making happens at the household level.

There are three major dialects among the Jola: Fonyi in the north, Kasa in the middle, and Edjamat in south, including Guinea-Bissau.[19] Even within these dialects there is a great deal of linguistic variation, sometimes from village to village. Furthermore, Jola in the Gambia, Senegal, and Guinea-Bissau were subject to different colonial regimes—British, French, and Portuguese, respectively—each of which, to varying degrees, left its particular legacy on Jola populations. Religious conversion has also affected Jola across these countries in distinct and uneven ways. The northernmost population of Jola, north of the Casamance River and along the Gambian border, were Islamicized by the 1930s (Lambert 2002; Mark 1978, 1992). South of the Casamance River, but still within Senegal, several Catholic missions have had—and continue to have—significant influence (Baum 1990). The southernmost subgroup of Jola, in Guinea-Bissau, has remained most impervious to religious missionization on both Islamic and Christian fronts, maintaining their adherence to traditional Jola (*awasena*) beliefs and practices, although this is beginning to change with the presence of foreign Catholic and Protestant evangelical missionaries.[20] Religious conversion among Guinean villagers across the Upper Guinea Coast is a dynamic and varied phenomenon, and the ways in which Jola have incorporated new elements from Islam and/or Christianity while maintaining (and sometimes strengthening) traditional Jola religious practices have been the subject of several scholarly works on Senegalese Jola (Baum 1990;

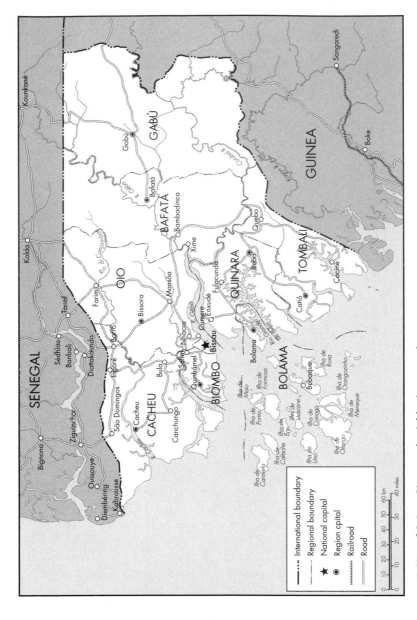

MAP 2 **Map of Guinea-Bissau and neighboring countries.**

40

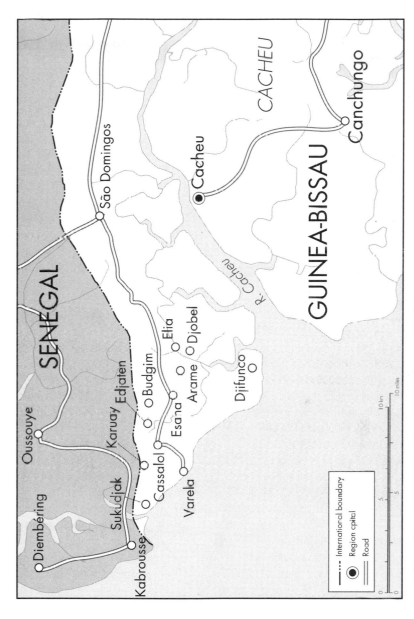

MAP 3 Map of several Jola villages from São Domingos to Varela.

41

Lambert 2002; Linares 1981, 1992; Mark 1978, 1992; Palmeri 2009). Differences in external pressures—whether from the colonial and postcolonial state or from religious missionaries—have had implications for diversity in Jola social organization, gender roles, and agricultural practices, and it is difficult to generalize very much regarding Jola populations across this swath of West Africa. One of the unifying characteristics across Jola populations in these three countries, however, is their relationship to rice, although even this has a great deal of variation in its historic and contemporary manifestations (Linares 1981). My research focused on the Jola residents populating the cluster of twenty villages in northwestern Guinea-Bissau, and in this book I use the term "Jola" to refer to them (except when otherwise noted), even though I acknowledge that conditions and practices among Jola villagers just across the border might be quite different.

Guinea-Bissau's "Orbit"

Part of the reason for this difference lies in the history and current conditions of each country. Jola villagers often lamented to me the unfortunate fact that they resided in the poorest and least capacitated of these three nation-states, especially when we watched planes just across the border spraying Senegalese rice fields with insecticide while Guinean Jola paddy rice was being devoured by insects. Guinea-Bissau occupies a negligible piece of international attention; it is one of the most obscure nation-states in the world, and even neighboring Africans are hard-pressed to locate it on a map of their continent. Most publications on the country—regardless of discipline or audience—often begin by doing just that, and I have found myself repeating the same stock sentence in this regard ("Guinea-Bissau is a small country on the west coast of Africa sandwiched between Senegal and the Republic of Guinea") since I began working there. Its peripherality in geopolitical affairs is certainly felt by Guinean residents themselves. For instance, when I was living there in 2002 many Guineans were tuned into the news of a possible U.S. invasion of Iraq. I was visiting the national research center (INEP) in the capital city one day as various staff members held their radios to their ears and listened as then-President George W. Bush listed his growing "coalition of the willing"—countries that had aligned with the U.S. in their mounting campaign against Saddam Hussein. As several countries were listed—the Marshall Islands, Estonia, Palau—one of my INEP colleagues quipped, "They never even asked us. Perhaps we would have been willing. But Guinea-Bissau—we're not even in their orbit."

Guinea-Bissau has entered the international media and political "orbit" more frequently in the past several years, however, largely due to dramatic political upheavals and its position, since 2004, as a trans-shipment point for funneling Colombian cocaine into Europe. This latter development has garnered more international attention—from the media and various UN agencies—than anything else in Guinea-Bissau's history, including the eleven-year independence war in the 1960s–1970s and eleven-month civil war in 1998–1999. It has finally put Guinea-Bissau on the map, so to speak, on the radar of international interest, both because of the salaciousness of the subject and because of the illicit and destabilizing nature of the drug trade itself. Since longstanding drug trafficking routes through the Caribbean—especially Jamaica and Panama—have become more intensively policed, cocaine cartels have been forced to evade international law enforcement agencies by switching channels across the Atlantic Ocean to meet increasing demand from European consumers. From a narco-trafficker's perspective, West Africa—and Guinea-Bissau in particular—is an appealing transit hub for geographic, political, and economic reasons. Guinea-Bissau is a straight shot across the Atlantic Ocean from the coca fields of Latin America. Planes from Colombia and Brazil, and ships from Brazil and Venezuela, have been carrying billions of dollars' worth of cocaine across the Atlantic to Guinea-Bissau's largely unmonitored islands and ports. From there, the drugs are sent by ship to Spain and Portugal (as gateways to other European countries), travel overland to Morocco, or arrive in various European capitals using mules on commercial airline flights.

Between 1998 and 2003, the total quantity of cocaine seized each year in Africa was approximately 600kg. By 2006, the figure had risen five-fold and during the first nine months of 2007 had already reached 5.6 tons. In 2010, the most recent year with United Nations Office of Drugs and Crime (UNODC) statistics for the region, an estimated 33 tons of cocaine were smuggled from South America to West Africa, and 18 tons transited through West Africa destined for European consumers, representing US$1.25 billion.[21] Although precise statistics disaggregating Guinea-Bissau's piece of this trade are, of course, difficult to obtain, one recent source estimates that 40 metric tons of cocaine leave Guinea-Bissau each year (Smoltczyk 2013). UN officials have labeled Guinea-Bissau Africa's first de facto narco-state.

Traffickers have been able to exploit Guinea-Bissau's political and economic fragility to rapidly expand their presence in the region. Experienced and sophisticated drug cartels have capitalized on the incapacity of governmental institutions, police, and the judiciary to control trafficking. There are widespread allegations of high-ranking military complicity and government collusion, although sufficient evidence remains elusive. The Guinean government's general lack of resources—the police force has few vehicles, limited gasoline, no radios, and very few handcuffs—is no match for the wealthy, well-armed, technologically advanced narco-traffickers.

The money brought into the country by funneling drugs dwarfs all other economic sectors combined. The business in Guinea-Bissau alone is worth an estimated $1.6 billion per year, more than five times the national gross domestic product. Although it has been impossible to verify how much of that money stays in Guinea-Bissau for bribes and logistical support, a Dakar-based representative of the UNODC calculated that "even if only 1% of this cash stays in the country, it is enough to co-opt security forces and other state authorities, and to disrupt what is largely a poor, agrarian economy significantly. . . . The flow of money can't be compared to any other sector; it's money falling from the sky."[22]

Concerns expressed by external observers—such as UN officials, journalists, and European and United States representatives—have largely been framed in terms of national and regional instability. Some have emphasized the deep penetration of drug money into national political institutions. Others have noted that the money generated through drug trafficking can become an "explosive tool . . . it can affect democratic rule. It can finance rebellions. [It can] be a reason for taking up arms and perpetuate corruption, bad governance and instability."[23] Because of the assumed enticement of easy money, youth involvement could lead to violent competition between drug lords, increasing national instability, and a return to civil war. Similarly, other observers have expressed anxiety about cocaine catalyzing resource-driven civil and regional wars, akin to those in oil- and diamond-rich countries like Nigeria, Liberia, and Sierra Leone. International concern (especially as expressed in Europe and the United States) has also focused on the link between drug barons, arms trafficking from neighboring post-conflict countries, and ultimately financing for terrorism. Finally, although Guinea-Bissau is being used primarily as a storage warehouse and transit hub, there is widespread apprehension about an increase in local addiction. Given its ranking as one of the world's poorest countries, the vast majority of Guineans cannot afford to buy the drugs they are helping to ship to Europe. But local traffickers are sometimes paid for their services in kind, leading some observers to suggest that addiction among Guineans will proliferate.

Long neglected by these same media outlets and international agencies, Guinea-Bissau is suddenly finding itself at the center of global concern. Since 2006, the UN and other multilateral and bilateral agencies have been trying to quickly catch up in their efforts to establish a presence and programs focused on what they perceive as an emergency situation in Guinea-Bissau.

The UN Security Council, for example, asked its Peacebuilding Commission to explore the possibility of establishing a strategy for Guinea-Bissau, and I was invited in October 2007 (along with two other "Guinea-Bissau experts") to brief a range of UN agencies on emerging conflicts and potential sites of engagement toward this end. The discussion at these meetings was dominated throughout by the drug trafficking situation, and it became clear that any form of UN involvement in Guinea-Bissau, no matter the rhetorical commitment to deeper structural issues such as weak state institutions and long-standing environmental and economic pressures on rural livelihoods, would necessarily focus on eradicating Colombian drug cartels from the country.

As one of a handful of international scholars who works on Guinea-Bissau, I have since participated in three similar UN roundtables and briefings, each one preceded by another "crisis" in the country. Although the expertise among officials involved in international agencies with links to Guinea-Bissau has certainly increased over the years since 2007, and my own role in these sessions has moved from one where I provided the most basic background information to engaging in much more advanced analyses that can, legitimately, presuppose a high level of familiarity with the country and its history, these discussions, nevertheless, are still dominated by a focus on drug trafficking and coups, and more structural issues and pressing problems of the majority of the country's residents get sidelined by the urgency and eagerness of international agencies to respond to a perceived emergency.

The drug trade is undeniably a feature of the landscape in contemporary Guinea-Bissau. But the rural residents of northwestern Guinea-Bissau are (so far) largely untouched by it. They are aware of it, of course, because they listen to the news on their battery-powered radios, and some of them are stung by the fact that Guinea-Bissau is now mostly perceived—on the global stage—as a narco-state. But they are not nearly as concerned with their country's ever-deepening involvement with the international drug trade as are the participants at UN briefings. Although cocaine has put Guinea-Bissau on the international agenda, it has also blinded international actors and agencies—not to mention journalists—to other important dimensions of the country. So, while solving the drug trafficking problem is necessary, it is not sufficient in terms of a sustained and meaningful program of international involvement in Guinea-Bissau.

Likewise for the periodic political dramas in Bissau that briefly catch international attention. The independence period, in general, has been characterized by ongoing partisan political upheaval, government irregularities, and a civil war (1998–1999), which wrecked the already fragile economy and has been followed by several years of political instability and economic decline. No president has ever served his full term in Guinea-Bissau. There have been several coups d'état since independence in 1974, the most media-captivating of which happened in March 2009, with the double assassination of the army chief (General Batista Tagme na Waie) and president (João Bernardo "Nino" Vieira) within hours of each other. In April 2012, just a few weeks before the second round of presidential elections, the Guinean military took power again, detaining the leading candidate and several other prominent political figures. Two years and one day later, on April 13, 2014, Guinea-Bissau gave way to international pressure and held legislative and presidential elections (see International Crisis Group 2014), and the African Party for the Independence of Guinea and Cape Verde (PAIGC) was restored to power with José Mário Vaz as president.

Much of the chronic national political instability is linked to the out-sized role of the military in Guinea-Bissau. As one UN official commented, "Most countries have an army. Guinea-Bissau is an army that has a country."[24] The Guinean military has commanded enormous respect and legitimacy across a broad swath of the civilian population, primarily because of the legacy of the eleven-year War of Independence during which the weakening Portuguese colonial foothold in the country was ultimately militarily defeated, in 1974, through prolonged armed conflict with the PAIGC. In this sense, many Guineans still feel indebted to their military for the very existence of their independent state, and Guinea-Bissau can be more accurately characterized as a post-liberation society than as a post-conflict society along the lines of other neighboring countries in West Africa. But since independence the military has continued to grow and play an increasingly problematic role vis-à-vis the state. Militarization across the country is extensive and largely normalized. There are barracks in even the most outlying areas, including the village in which I resided, and often the only connection rural Guineans have to the state is through particular military personnel.

But other than these rather loose connections, the urban-rural divide that has long characterized Guinea-Bissau continues to be a defining feature of the country. Sometimes this divide has been Guinea-Bissau's saving grace in the face of persistent Bissau-based political upheavals; rural people have continued to get by in spite of chronic coups, national political instability, and state bankruptcy. There are many patterns that provide insight into this rural capacity and relative autonomy, and to the unusual model of urban-rural relations in the country. For instance, urban-rural remittances tend to flow in an atypical direction in Guinea-Bissau, with rural households more often than not supporting urban family members with rice and money, rather than vice-versa. Furthermore, rural communities often provide funding and other means of support for even the most basic supposed state services, like education and health care. For the many years when the bankrupt state could not pay its teachers and health care workers, schools and hospitals closed in the capital, but they continued to function in the interior as salaries were collected through community contributions.[25] That rural populations have generally gotten on with business despite the continued instability in the capital speaks not only to the strength and resilience of rural communities in much of the country, but also to the irrelevance of political dramas in Bissau—what captivates most international attention—for the majority of Guineans (Bordonaro 2009).

Although the latest coup, in April 2012, captured more media attention and international response than many previous ones, this state of affairs is nothing new for Guinea-Bissau, nor should it be the focal point (along with drug trafficking) of international concern and involvement in the country. The impact of these national-level political dynamics is felt unevenly throughout the country. In general, though, these are events that have a major bearing on political workings in the capital city and on the continued exasperation of international agencies eager to establish stability in the country, but outside of Bissau the postcolonial state, with the exception of a few military personnel stationed throughout the country, has played a limited role in its citizens' lives (see Forrest 1992, 2003). In rural Jola-land, for instance, no taxes are collected, most conflicts are resolved through local channels and adjudication at spirit shrines, and state services—such as building roads, providing water, etc.—simply do not exist. Most residents in contemporary northwestern Guinea-Bissau do not factor the state into much of their thinking, planning, decision-making, or even anxieties.

What *does* contribute to the anxieties of Guinea-Bissau's rural population is their experience of dwindling harvests, which most of them link to declining precipitation. By the time I arrived in Guinea-Bissau in 2001, most Jola villagers' granaries were empty. Many people regularly told me "We used to be able to do this," referring to the complex technical, social, and ritual system through which Jola produce, consume, and revere rice. "Now we cannot."

The following chapter begins to elaborate on some of these anxieties as we see them played out in the lives of particular rural Jola individuals. It also provides a more local and personal set of perspectives on the broad historical outline chronicled through this chapter, as Ampa Badji, Nho Keboral, and their kin and neighbors narrate how they experienced colonialism, independence, missionization, schooling, changing environmental conditions, and other regional and institutional shifts that confronted them.

....

CHAPTER 2

Ampa Badji and Nho Keboral

What, then, can be accomplished through storytelling?
And can our stories be equated with our theories about
the world—symbolic techniques of control and comprehension, born of our need to believe that we can grasp reality and determine the course of our lives? The answer to
this question cannot be provided by philosophy alone,
though a first step is to suspend our conventional notions
about the essential differences between fact and fiction,
science and myth, the real and the illusory, in order to explore, on a case by case basis, what consequences follow
from any behavior, and what effects our actions have upon
our lives and the lives of others. . . . Storytelling gives us a
sense that though we do not exactly determine the course
of our lives we at least have a hand in defining their
meaning.

—MICHAEL JACKSON,
The Politics of Storytelling

....

"I am a rice farmer," Ampa Badji told me, again and again. Once, when
he had just returned home on his bicycle from teaching primary
school in the neighboring village of Arame, I asked him—somewhat
provocatively—what his job was. His answer was, again, unequivocal:
"I am a farmer. I cultivate rice." A few minutes later he got back on his bicycle
and pedaled off to his forest grove to tap palm wine. Many of his peers—
some teachers, some soldiers, some mechanics at the Catholic Mission's
workshop—answered the same way.

The more I came to know Ampa Badji, and the more I learned about his life growing up in Esana, the more extraordinary and compelling this seemingly simple assertion came to be. Ampa Badji grew up during a time of unprecedented change in rural Jola-land, particularly in the institutional landscape of Esana and surrounding villages. Born in 1960, Ampa Badji's childhood coincided with the waning era—although increasing military character—of Portuguese colonialism, the expansion and solidification of an Italian-sponsored Catholic Mission in Jola-land, the introduction of formal schooling, the violence of the eleven-year liberation struggle, and the emergence of Guinea-Bissau's one-party state. Although each of these new external actors and institutional arrangements both enlarged and constrained Ampa Badji's opportunities and choices, his own recounting of his life history—as well as his perspectives on his immediate forebears and his own children—were refracted through rice. Being a rice farmer was not, for Ampa Badji, an occupation, nor even a vocation, but was ontologically bound up with what it meant to be a Jola person, even when new religions and governments and other institutions entered the rural landscape and sometimes seemed to take center stage. His consistent statement exposed one of the most fundamental aspects of Jola understandings of themselves and their environment, not as separate entities, or as dominant and subordinate agents, but each as constituting the other. "I am a rice farmer," Ampa Badji insisted, even (or perhaps especially) when I tried to challenge him on this assertion. "*Inje miwañ*," he would say in Jola. Or, more often in Crioulo, "*Ami labradur di aruz.*"

This chapter takes Ampa Badji's insistent self-ascription as a point of departure to narrate elements of both his and Nho Keboral's biographies. In doing so, it chronicles a century of this region's history from their perspectives and positions as repositories of their parents' and grandparents' memories, as witnesses of major institutional shifts, and as participants in some of the new possibilities and challenges that emerged during their lifetimes. There are other scholarly accounts of this time period in Guinea-Bissau and across the Upper Guinea Coast, and readers may want to refer to them to get a more conventional sense of these same events.[1] My intention here is to acquaint readers with Ampa Badji, Nho Keboral, and their families, to provide a broad overview of this place and its people through their stories, and to convey enough background information and context to make the subsequent chapters intelligible.

*   *   *

A Note on Method: Cultivating Central Characters

Ampa Badji was one of the very first residents in Esana I came to know, a circumstance that does not often lead to sustained collaboration in field-work, as an ethnographer's judgment and capacity to connect to truly valuable informants (let alone friends) is something that develops over time. Many anthropologists have false starts in establishing long-term and meaningful relationships with their most prized interlocutors in the field. I certainly had my share of false starts in this and other areas, but Ampa Badji proved to be the first, the deepest, and the most sustained of my friendships in the field, and it is still his house where I stay on my ongoing visits to the village. Ampa Badji hosted me in his home when I first arrived in Esana, before I was able to set up a house of my own. Even after I was no longer living in his house (although I was just around the corner) I continued to eat with his family every evening, and after our shared bowl of rice Ampa Badji would extract a liter of palm wine he had carried home from his forest grove, pour it into a large plastic *kaneka*, and pass it around, everyone taking a few sips. And then we would talk. I never got tired of these talks, and without my consciously realizing it they started to form the backbone of my understanding of Ampa Badji, his family, Esana, and Jola society. In particular, my knowledge of his life and his character (in the non-novelistic sense) came from this kind of rhythmic building up of story upon story, conversation after conversation, whether in his home or in his forest grove, where I often visited after a day's work with Nho Keboral or my women's work association in the paddies or the forest. I regularly sought his input on questions or confusions I was experiencing, and he was patient in his explanations, especially given how very busy he was. But our conversations were by no means one-sided inquiries on my part; they were more often than not genuine exchanges on topics ranging from differences among various religions, the political situation in various parts of the globe, the nature of violence, and the mechanics of homosexuality. Ampa Badji was intrigued by my Jewishness, and we had many illuminating conversations about the intersection among—and sometimes the boundary between—identity, culture, religion, and history. He was (and continues to be) a wonderful partner in conversation: thoughtful, intelligent, inquisitive, and calm.

Ampa Badji was also a consummate storyteller. Jola have no established class of people who specialize in this skill and it is largely considered a personal propensity. Ampa Badji had both exquisite observational sensibilities and an extraordinary memory, and he could recount in staggering detail episodes from his own life as well as stories he had heard from his parents and even plots of books he had read or films he had seen many years ago. He once showed me a sack he kept stashed away filled with Portuguese novels—romances and westerns, mostly—that he had acquired as colonial leftovers during his stint as a teacher elsewhere in the country. The books were moldy and termite ridden, but he read them all ages ago and he often related the narratives to me chapter by chapter. Another time we were sitting on his veranda and he gave me a frame-by-frame rendition of a film he had seen in one of the makeshift video salons that cropped up in Bissau in the 1990s. He was in the capital for a required teacher's training and stumbled upon the salon. It was a Chuck Norris movie, and Ampa Badji gave me a theatrical and impeccably detailed blow-by-blow account of Norris's adventures throughout the film, which he had seen fifteen years previously.

And yet it did not occur to me to make him one of the central characters in this book until I returned to Esana in 2010 and discussed the idea with him. Just like rice was so obviously central to Jola social, moral, and religious life that I had become temporarily blind—or perhaps desensitized—to its importance, so too had I somehow taken for granted the importance and illuminating quality of Ampa Badji's life history for making intelligible the very questions (and perhaps even providing some tentative answers) I wanted to pursue. So it was only in 2010 that I began more proactively to seek out what I felt to be the missing pieces in his story and to push further with particular questions about his life choices. But there was never enough time, nor the appropriate conditions (given the lack of privacy and constant interruptions that characterize village life) to do the sort of interviews I knew I needed for this kind of deeply biographical approach. That had always been a challenge of fieldwork among Jola: lack of time (they work so hard!), lack of space (one on one time is basically impossible in Jola households), and a lack of fit between the kind of directness an interview requires and Jola modes of communication (cf. Chapter Four). During my years in the field I had addressed these challenges in various ways. I worked alongside my Jola hosts in the paddies and the forests, not only in order to engage in the requisite participant observation by experiencing for myself their primary tasks, but if I had not done agricultural work with them I would have almost never seen them. I established my own residence, centrally located enough so that people could casually stop by and discuss whatever they wished out of earshot of the neighbors and kin whose surveillance everyone was constantly aware of. And, with some exceptions, I gave up on formal and tape-recorded interviews, instead engaging in conversations on their own terms, and writing down lengthy fieldnotes late into the night in an attempt to record as best I could whatever I had heard and seen that day.

As for Nho Keboral, I spent my very first full day in Esana with her, harvesting rice. We left her house after a quick breakfast of the previous night's leftover rice, and we walked a few kilometers down the main dirt road, then turned onto a bush path passing cashew orchards and palm trees and eventually arriving onto the flat terrain of furrowed rice paddies. We were joined by various women along the way, all of whom I later recognized as members of the same neighborhood work association I eventually joined. Once we arrived at our destination all of the women got straight to work. Nho Keboral had told me to bring a knife and she showed me brusquely how to cut ripe rice. She insisted that I use only my right hand to cut the stalks and my left hand to hold them. After gathering a handful and holding the chaff apart with my left thumb, I learned—by a quick demonstration—how to pull and discard the chaff. After several rounds of cutting and pulling, an older woman observed my poor technique and showed me—more slowly this time—a better method.

This was not only my introduction to Jola agricultural work, but also, as I came to realize, an initial glimpse into Nho Keboral's personality and what came to be the texture of our interactions over the following years. Even several months later, when we went to transplant rice seedlings from the forest to the inundated paddies at the height of the rainy season, Nho Keboral's manner was consistent with that very first day. She gruffly showed me how to pull up the seedlings, with no verbal explanation, and I was on my own. Later that day, as we moved into the paddies to punch the delicate seedlings underwater into the tilled muddy earth, I felt that my learning curve had been quite rapid, and that I had even figured out the spacing of the seedlings by following Nho Keboral and her daughters' examples. After transplanting in what I thought was exactly the same way as I had been for a few rows, Nho Keboral criticized my work: "You started off good, but now you're doing badly." It was not clear to me what was different about the way I was planting compared with the good job I had been doing before, nor was it explained to me when I asked.

Despite these interactions, Nho Keboral became one of my closest companions and a very good friend. As we spent more time together and became more comfortable around each other, we developed an easy teasing rapport and shared many personal confidences. But Nho Keboral was not only an impatient teacher, she was a terrible informant in the conventional anthropological sense. I quickly learned that her answers to my questions yielded little, if any, real information, and that I was better off going elsewhere to learn most things, from the basic techniques of agricultural tasks to the ins and outs of Jola kinship, ceremonies, and other ethnographic fundamentals. Although I often tagged along with Nho Keboral wherever she went—whether to the forest or paddies to work, to neighbors and relatives to visit, or to funerals and spirit shrine ceremonies—she was my guide only in the most rudimentary way. Explanations about any of these activities came later, through other interlocutors.

For instance, I once asked her what happened at the *harimanahu*, where women related to a deceased person gather at his or her house and, I later learned, compose short eulogistic songs about their dead relative. Nho Keboral's answer was "we just sit." End of story. Other times I asked for basic explanations of songs or particular articles of clothing, and the answer, accompanied by a shrug and usually delivered while we hurriedly walked somewhere, was always "just for fun." Even when our conversations did venture beyond these terse remarks, Nho Keboral was often quick to express what felt to me like awkward clichés about the difference between white people and Africans. One evening, after we had finished eating from our collective rice bowl, Ampa Badji, Nho Keboral, and I were talking about witches, whom Jola often refer to as those who "have head." Nho Keboral repeated a line she had often used during such conservations: "'That's why Africans are no good and white people are good. Because God gave white people a head and they use it for work; to make things like computers. But God gave Black people a head and they use it only for bad things, like curses and eating others' souls." I had long since learned that it was pointless to push back, challenge, or offer counterexamples to this kind of explanation. It was Nho Keboral's way of articulating her annoyance with the world, as well as her often-successful way of shutting down a conversation.

But Nho Keboral was an eager participant when it came to telling her own life story. Unlike Ampa Badji, who told his life story and answered my endless questions through reflective, methodical, and highly sophisticated narratives, Nho Keboral's stories about her life were scattered, repetitive, and full of complaints. "Work is killing us," she would often lament. "We're being punished; our life is punishment." Although this was, indeed, true, especially from Nho Keboral's perspective, it was repeated so frequently that I found myself getting annoyed at this constant refrain. It was partly for this reason—perhaps guilt over my annoyance—that I wanted to probe further and dig for the substance behind the complaint by stitching together the details of Nho Keboral's life. She was a willing collaborator in this process, partly because she loved to talk about her own life and partly because it gave her even more opportunities to complain.

When I came back to Esana in February 2010, knowing that my time would be too brief to fill in all the gaps in Ampa Badji and Nho Keboral's life stories, I gave them each a small tape recorder and long list of questions and topics and asked them to record their thoughts and stories when they were able to. Since Nho Keboral did not read, I discussed with her the general outline of what I was looking for, and asked Ampa Badji to review the questions with her as needed. I had no idea if this would really work, and I could only have done this with the two of them given our long history together and an already well-established mutual understanding—although still often challenged and treated as bizarre—of why on earth I kept bothering them. But it turned out that, especially in Ampa Badji's case, this yielded a treasure trove of material. Even though at first they both found it a bit awkward to talk by themselves into a tape recorder, they soon got used to it and the method circumvented many of the interviewing challenges mentioned earlier. Ampa Badji recorded many entries in his forest grove after tapping his palm trees and waiting for his liter bottle to fill up with sap. I can hear the familiar sounds of the forest in the background of his recordings, and can often tell what time of day it is based on these sounds and the tone of his voice. Nho Keboral, who rarely sat still, managed to hide herself away from her constant domestic and agricultural work and provide snatches of her memories of childhood and motherhood, and long soliloquies on her current anxieties. The background noise that accompanies her recordings are the sounds of domestic animals—chickens clucking, pigs shuffling and snorting, an occasional rooster crowing and drowning out her already hushed words—and the muffled voices of people passing outside her window, sometimes calling out a greeting to her. When I came back to collect the recordings, I was thrilled to see how much they had been able to do, and then filled with dread at the thought of the thousands of hours of transcription that awaited me. It was worth it. Their self-recordings combined with my daily interaction with them over two years and my long-term and maturing relationship with them over more than a decade all contribute to what I hope are rich, interesting—although never complete—accounts of their lives.

One final word on this matter: as we worked on their self-recordings together, I asked them if they wanted to choose their own code names. I explained why ethnographers often change the names of their interlocutors, and they each nodded in comprehension and said they would consider it. Knowing that such consideration could take a very long time, I reminded them regularly over the next several weeks and offered some options of possible code names, which they politely declined. Finally, the day before I once again left Esana indefinitely, they separately announced to me their chosen names. I was immediately taken aback by the care with which they had chosen them, and by how much their chosen names reflected their very different positions and personalities. In both cases, they opted for the most common prefix of male and female Jola names— "Ampa" and "Nho," respectively—although neither of them had these prefixes in their actual names. Such prefixes are archetypal of Jola names but are considered rather old-fashioned by current standards. In choosing them, it seemed to me that they were positioning themselves (or at least their characters in my book) as irrefutably Jola and solidly in the past. Ampa Badji's chosen name took this even further, as Badji is the name of his patriclan. This name located him squarely as a member of a particular lineage and carried with it all of the rights and obligations of that lineage, even though, in his actual life, he had distanced himself both spatially and symbolically from those very things, especially those that involved spirit shrine practices. Ampa Badji did, however, continue to farm in his ancestors' paddy and forest land, and continued to redistribute both land and labor among his agnatic kin. By naming himself a male member of Badji, he was signaling his deep connection to his family's history, and to the agricultural landholdings in the same space where his ancestors had settled long ago. Nho Keboral's name did not evoke any such sense of history or belonging, but instead highlighted, in a rather cryptic way, a specific aspect of her personality and perspectives. "Keboral" is an encoded reference to defeating an opponent; it might roughly be translated as "whacking someone on the head with a stick." It was most often used in the context of wrestling matches—the dominant sport among Jola, which has both athletic and religious dimensions—although actually *doing* this during wrestling matches was no longer allowed. Although she was not a violent person, Nho Keboral was certainly known for her brusque manner (something that I came to tease her about), and perhaps she was presenting this aspect of herself through her chosen name. Or maybe she was hinting at something deeper; a desire to defeat her various opponents (futile and backbreaking work; chronic sickness and poverty; anxiety and uncertainty about her children's future) with an efficacious and satisfying whack on the head. Although I tried to probe her thinking behind her chosen name, she simply shrugged and said, "You know, Joanna. Just for fun."

Ampa Badji

When Ampa Badji was born, the women in the powerful *kenyalen* society (see Journet 1987; Journet and Girard 1976; van Tilburg 1998) made some very soft rice and gently coaxed the newborn baby to eat some of it. Rice is what makes a newly born baby into a Jola person, so babies are fed a light rice mush from the moment of their birth.

For his parents, Ampa Badji's birth was perhaps one of the few moments of relief and joy—even if short-lived—in their otherwise difficult lives. Since their marriage, his mother, Nha Buhel, had struggled with miscarriages and infant deaths, and the couple had been locked in a cycle of births and burials—what Jola now refer to in Crioulo as *padi/ntera*—for far too long. Ampa Badji's father, Akabau, had been plagued by a lack of reproductive success since before his marriage to Nha Buhel. Akabau was born in Esana's Katama neighborhood, which had been home base for his lineage since they had left the forest hamlet of Lhikeu during the internecine wars among Jola in the mid-nineteenth century. He was orphaned by the age of two and subsequently raised in his father's brothers' households.[2] But, given their wives' disinterest in him, he was not well cared for. He had to sleep outside on a woodpile at the side of the house, and he often spent his days searching for his own food by gathering oysters or crabs in the mangroves. Akabau managed to endure the hardships of his childhood quite simply because there was nothing else to do and nowhere else to go. "They were people who didn't go anywhere," Ampa Badji said of his father's generation. "When they went out, they went to prepare a palm tree and waited until that palm tree was dry and then they tapped it and drank palm wine."[3] Migration in search of a better life (except in the extreme case of seeking refuge from colonial brutality and war) was not pursued as an option as it was among the Manjaco just a little further south (see Crowley 1990; Gable 1990, 2000; van Binsbergen 1988) or Jola across the Senegalese border (see Baum 1999; Foucher 2002; Lambert 2002, 2007; Mark 1978).

Ampa Badji remembered his father as deeply dark-skinned with almond-shaped eyes and pitch-black hair before it turned white with age. Despite his childhood struggles he grew up to be respected as a strong worker with abundant rice. But he was also known—as many were in his time—for his troubles with producing children. "My father had a big problem," Ampa Badji recalled. "The problem that he suffered was *padi/ntera*, birth and burial. When a child was born he would bury it, when another was born he would bury it, just like that."

Jola funerals for adults and children include an inquisition into the spiritual and social causes of death, called a *kasaabaku*. The cloth-covered corpse is carried on a makeshift wooden frame, like a stretcher, by *kasaabaku* specialists who are led by the corpse in particular directions that are interpreted as responses to questions regarding the cause of death. At each of Akabau's children's funerals, the *kasaabaku* process provided a clear indication that Akabau's classificatory brothers were killing his children (both born and unborn) in order to eliminate his progeny who were in line to inherit the important initiation spirit shrine—*Karenghaku*—that was maintained in Akabau's lineage.

Some background on spirit shrines and their relation to land and lineage is required here. As a great deal of Africanist ethnography and history has attested, land tenure is not only about the procedures for inheriting and distributing land but also about a particular group's relationship to that land. One of the ways Jola conceive of land has to do with the relationship between land, lineage, and spirit shrines. Each lineage has, as its "possessions," plots of forestland (*butat*), rice paddy (*butondu*), and, in many cases, a *bakinabu* (spirit shrine; pl. *ukinau*) associated with them. When new Jola settlers arrived on the coast in the sweeping cycles of migration that characterized Upper Guinea Coast precolonial demographic patterns, in most cases they were integrated into existing kinship and land tenure processes. But they were never given rights to inherit the *bakinabu* originally associated with firstcomers to that land. In many cases this has caused conflicts within extended families who have integrated their land holdings and households, and for all intents and purposes are considered to be kin, but whose fault line between original and latecomer factions is keenly felt in the denial of *bakinabu* inheritance to the latecomer branch.

In Ampa Badji's family, for instance, this is the case between Ampa Badji and his classificatory brothers. Many generations ago, the forebears of the two men Ampa Badji considers as his brothers came to settle amongst Ampa Badji's people in Lhikeu, a small forest hamlet on the outskirts of present-day Esana, and the forest base where Ampa Badji and his agnatic kin continue to tap palm trees and plant rice nurseries.[4] Ampa Badji's ancestors gave land to these settlers and integrated them into the family, and they are now considered to be of the same lineage and continue to divide land amongst themselves. But the fact that his classificatory brothers' ancestors were settlers amongst Ampa Badji's forebears is never forgotten, and they can never have rights to the *bakinabu*—which happens to be a particularly important one, *Karenghaku*, associated with male initiation—that Ampa Badji is meant to inherit.

In terms of the Jola relationship to land, such associations attach a sense of sacrality to an otherwise utilitarian approach to land ownership and use, and land—through its attachment to spirit shrines—is seen not just as a cultivable tract, but an historical text. Jola history and settlement patterns are indelibly recorded in the land, and even though the functional aspects of land distribution might erase apparent differences between firstcomers and latecomers, rights to land-based spirit shrines encode and maintain them. In this way, lineage-based *ukinau* serve as a permanent record of lineage history, and as an intractable boundary between firstcomers and latecomers.

As far as Ampa Badji was concerned, this distinction should end, especially as he does not want to inherit *Karenghaku* since it has, from his perspective, only caused friction—most often in the form of witchcraft—amongst the branches of his family. Like Ampa Badji, many people in contemporary Esana who were in a position to inherit ritual authority of a particular *bakinabu* refused to do so. But even when those designated to inherit *ukinau* eschew this responsibility the position is not opened up to other (even closely related) lineages.

In the case of Ampa Badji's father, the cause of his problems in producing progeny was diagnosed within this framework of land, lineage, spirit shrines, and jealousy. The successive *kasaabaku* all pointed to Akabau's classificatory kin residing in his midst in Katama, the same patrilineal neighborhood they had settled together after leaving Lhikeu during Esana's consolidation campaign many generations ago. So Akabau left Katama to reside with his mother's brothers in Nhakun, where his wife entered the *kenyalen* birth society and stayed under its protection until she gave birth to Ampa Badji.[5]

Ampa Badji's mother, Nha Buhel, also had her share of childhood troubles. Her father was originally from Nhakun, but because of his constant health problems he left his natal neighborhood and moved to Esana's other ward. During that time, traveling from one ward of the village through the dense forest that separated it from the other ward was not a regular event. Although now the distance seems so short and the village has a constant flow of foot-traffic moving from one end to the other in the course of any day, just a generation ago a child would rarely leave his or her own lineage-based neighborhood. But adults could re-locate to a different neighborhood in the same ward, or to the other ward across the forest, often using their links with maternal kin to establish residence outside of their natal compound. Jola virilocal marriages tended to be endogamous at a village level but exogamous at a neighborhood level, so one's mother's

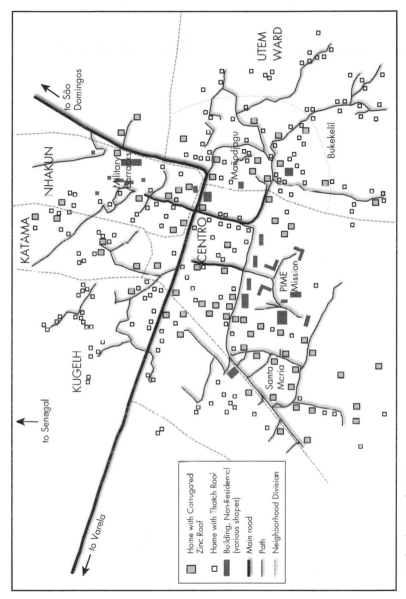

MAP 4 **Sketch map of Esana.**

Home with Corrugated
Zinc Roof

Home with Thatch Roof

Building, Non-Residencial
(various shapes)

Main road

Path

Neighborhood Division

UTEM WARD

Bukekelil

Mañodipgu

CENTRO

PIME Mission

Santa Maria

NHAKUN

Military Barracks

KATAMA

KUGELH

to São Domingos

to Senegal

to Varela

kin were often called upon to provide refuge outside one's own neighborhood. As in Akabau's case, reasons for seeking such refuge were generally
linked to suspicions of witchcraft within one's own neighborhood that
were seen to be the cause of poor health, reproductive problems, and high
infant mortality (the *padi/ntera* dynamic). Like Akabau, and like Nha
Buhel's father, many Jola escaped what they saw as the predations of their
own patrilineal kin in the hopes of better health and better luck just a few
hundred meters away. Nha Buhel's father moved across to Utem when he
was still a boy, and he remained there throughout his childhood and ado-
lescence. When it was time to find a wife, he chose one in the same ward
and completed all of the life-cycle ceremonies and marriage preparation
rituals as a resident of Utem. But shortly after Nha Buhel was born, her
mother and father died in quick succession, and she—like her future
husband—was orphaned at a young age.

Nha Buhel's father, Tegilosso, was a very large man and hard worker
despite a lifetime's struggle with illness. He was so beleaguered by sickness
that he sought help across the Senegalese border with a traditional healer.
This was—and is—quite common; specific healers known for their curative
capacities are sought out by far-flung villagers with a range of physical and
mental ailments, and often serve as hosts for their patients for extended
periods of time. Such was the case with Tegilosso, who was sent by his kin
in Esana to Senegal to seek out a well-known healer. He stayed there for
more than a year, receiving treatment and recuperating, and he began to
feel healthy again. As he was preparing to return to Esana, the healer
stopped him and insisted he stay put. "Don't go now," he said. "I know you
Jola; if you go now you'll start working hard and you'll get sick again. I
want you to stay with me. Stay for two years and then you can return to
Esana." Tegilosso, however, did not want to stay. He was eager to return to
his home and tend to his paddies. But he did not say anything to the healer;
he simply acquiesced and stayed put. Most Jola are generally loathe to
engage in direct confrontation in any interaction, and are more likely to
agree in words and make their intentions clear in deeds, which is precisely
what Tegilosso did. He stayed in the healer's household for another three
months waiting for his opportunity. Eventually, the healer left on a short
trip and Tegilosso snuck away to Esana the following day. He headed
straight for Esana and started tapping his palm trees and engaging in the
arduous labor of rice cultivation, and after just a few months he started to
become ill again. His head ached and he felt chills all over his body—the
same symptoms as his previous sickness. His body became so weak that he
was unable to work at all. Despite the urgings of his kin, he was too ashamed

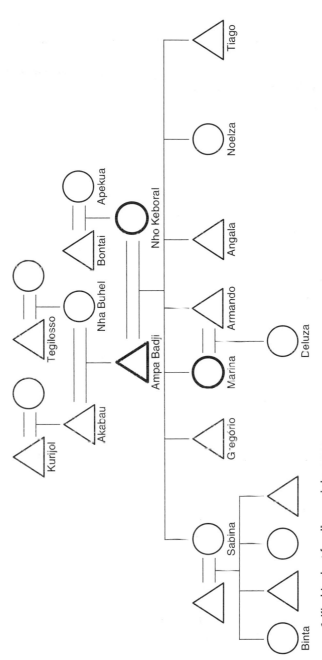

FIGURE 6 Kinship chart for all named characters.

61

to return to the Senegalese healer given his abrupt departure in the face of the healer's warnings. Tegilosso stayed put in Esana. His body weakened, and although he sought additional treatments through local medicines, he soon died, leaving his daughter, Ampa Badji's mother, an orphan.

Nha Buhel was raised by her father's sister, and although she suffered from a great deal of health problems, she was not treated as badly as Akabau was in his adopted home. She stayed in her aunt's home until she married Akabau, began her own *padi/ntera* cycle, and eventually gave birth to Ampa Badji through the *kenyalen* society.[6] A few years later, Nha Buhel gave birth to a girl, and then to another boy. But both children died in 1968, the year Ampa Badji participated in the once-in-every-thirty-years male initiation ceremonies. At that time, measles was spreading around the village and many people died. After his siblings died, the *kenyalen* members came to warn his mother that perhaps Ampa Badji, too, would die, and this was more than she could bear. "Her body just gave up. You wouldn't even recognize her as my mother. I, myself, I wondered why my mother's body dried up like that, what kind of thoughts did she have that made her body give up on her like that, and so since her body was wasting away like that, wasting away, wasting away . . . it was that very body she had until the day that she died."

Ampa Badji's mother died in 1998, thirty years after her two young children had died from measles, and in the same year as Esana's most recent male initiation. She died just a month before the men entered the initiation forest, but she got to see her only son grow up, get married, and have six children of his own, three of whom he took into the initiation forest just after she died. She had buried five babies and had miscarried many times. She continued to try to bear children, and every time she was pregnant she would say, "Wait, maybe I can give birth to this one, maybe this one will be saved."

*   *   *

Reaching Further Back: Portuguese Colonialism

Not long after Esana had been consolidated into a federated village, a new and often violent presence came to the area in the form of Portuguese colonial troops. Guinea-Bissau's colonial history is inextricably intertwined with the Cape Verde Islands. Portuguese activities in this region were headquartered in Cape Verde, which was an important slave depot and port for ships involved in the Atlantic trade (Crowley 1990). The

Portuguese established their administrative base on Cape Verde, and "although the Portuguese experimented with a number of different ways to administer the Guinea-Bissau region, for most of the time from its discovery [sic] in 1446 until it acquired an autonomous government in 1879, the area that is now Guinea-Bissau was a dependency of the Cape Verde Islands and seemed to be more of a colony of Cape Verde than of Portugal" (Crowley 1990:97). Such an infrastructure helps explain the limited control and influence the Portuguese exerted in Guinea-Bissau during this period, especially since "communications between Cape Verde and its dependency were infrequent. During the entire period of colonial rule only six governors posted in Cape Verde ever visited Guinea" (Crowley 1990:103–104). It was only with the decline of the slave trade that, in 1879, Portuguese Guinea became an autonomous overseas colony and was administered separately from Cape Verde for the first time, after almost four hundred years of Portuguese presence.

Even so, the turning point in the Portuguese colonial administration of Guinea-Bissau did not come until 1912–1915, which marked the beginning of effective Portuguese domination and occupation through a series of "pacification" campaigns. This period of colonial occupation ran roughly from 1915 to 1960. Portuguese Guinea was never a settler colony. The Portuguese effort to subdue the population through its "pacification" campaigns was unevenly felt, focusing primarily on the Bijagós Islands and the coastal regions. There was no massive re-organization of land familiar from neighboring countries, and there were relatively few attempts to shift agricultural practices. In many parts of the country, the presence of colonial authority was negligible.

To be sure, Portuguese colonialism was a violent endeavor (Bigman 1993; Birmingham 1995, 1999, 2006; Cabral 1969, 1970, 1980, Chilcote 1967, 1977; Davidson 1969, 1981; Dhada 1993; Forrest 1987, 1992, 1998, 2003; Galli and Jones 1987; Hawthorne 2003; Lobban and Forrest 1988; Lobban and Mendy 1996, 2013; Lopes 1987; MacQueen 1997). But compared with neighboring colonial policies and practices of the French and English, and even Portugal's flagship African colonies of Angola and Mozambique, the tentacles of colonial power did not reach as deeply and extensively into Guinean social life as they did in these other regions. The typical constellation of colonial presence through its impact on land, labor, and taxation was certainly felt by the local population, but not to the extent that such policies and practices impacted other areas in Africa. Colonial power was limited, and although it was still a major feature during a significant period of Guinean history, it probably has less to do with what happened in this area than it did in other places.

In Jola-land, Esana was the site of a Portuguese colonial outpost in the 1940s, although the Portuguese were at first rebuffed by Esana residents, and set up in three other villages before forcibly situating themselves in Esana.[7] The Portuguese established themselves in the center of Esana and erected a military post to house newly arrived soldiers that would disembark a few kilometers away on the riverbank at Buatche. The Portuguese base in Esana primarily served to train these new soldiers before they were sent to other parts of the colony.

Jola relations with these Portuguese soldiers shifted over time, as will be explored over three generations of Ampa Badji's family. In some ways, their arrival marked the beginning of what is still an ongoing external military presence in Esana. The barracks they built were taken over by the Guinean national army after independence and have been occupied by Guinean troops—sometime just a few, sometimes swelling with a surge of new arrivals—to address a range of conflict and security issues in this region over the last thirty-five years, especially given Esana's proximity to the Senegalese border and the Casamance separatist movement that has affected border relations since 1982.[8] Esana residents have become quite nonplussed about the chronic military presence in their midst, and each generation has developed its own way of interacting with the soldiers, whether Portuguese or Guinean. Currently, relations between residents and soldiers are amicable, and often amorous, but it was not always so.

Ampa Badji's paternal grandfather, Kurijol, was a young man in Esana when the Portuguese established themselves in the area. There was widespread opposition to Portuguese presence in Jola-land, but because they were not evenly matched—the Portuguese soldiers had guns, and Jola had only bows and arrows—the typical response at that time was to leave Esana and seek temporary refuge in neighboring villages. But villagers would regularly return to Esana to tend their paddies and forest land, and the Portuguese soldiers took advantage of such returns to round up Jola men in the military post for public *palmatorios*—the infamous Portuguese colonial beating in which one's palms and feet were whipped with a stick. As one Esana man recalled, "When you had received these blows you couldn't walk any more, you would stay like that with your bottom on the ground, you see! So . . . people of Esana said, well, there's no other way, we'll all die here in Esana unless we rise up and have a war against these troops who are here."[9]

But rumors of the planned Jola resistance reached the barracks, and reinforcements arrived. One older Esana resident recalled the story he had heard about this episode:

> You would see troops and you would think it was like fields of hay, there were sooo many of them! Some said there were more than two thousand troops who came. And all of them armed, you see! So when they came here in Esana, whenever they saw a man go to the forest to tap palm trees in the morning, they would shoot him on the spot. They would see him, they would shoot him, they would tie him up, you see!

Esana villagers decided to remove the women and children, so they took them to neighboring villages across the Senegalese border. The men returned to Esana, but the Portuguese troops kept shooting them. This was during the rainy season, and there was no shelter in the forest from the constant rain. The men hid in the forest for about a week, sitting together in small clusters under large palm fronds. But it was futile. So they, too, scattered across the border to Jola villages in Senegal. Ampa Badji's grandfather joined his infant son—Akabau—across the border, but he died there a year later. When a Jola person died away from their own land it was imperative to bring the body back to be buried. Esana refugees hiding in nearby villages brought his body back to Esana, but they were unable to hold a funeral for him because of the menace of Portuguese troops in the barracks. They buried him early in the morning that they arrived and went back to their places of refuge. His family remained as refugees for three years before they and their neighbors began to return. In their absence, much of Esana had turned back into bush. Esana residents sent delegates to the Portuguese post to discuss their return before the bush took over the village entirely. They promised cooperation with the Portuguese troops as long as they could come back safely and resume their work in the paddies. The Portuguese commander agreed, and Esana residents poured back from the border and re-occupied their homes. The most important consideration among Jola at that time was to get back to their abandoned forests and paddies, and cooperation with the Portuguese was the price they paid to do so.

As we can see from even a brief recounting of Ampa Badji's parents' and grandparents' lives, health was a precarious state; sickness and death were rampant; orphanhood and fosterage of young children whose parents had succumbed was common; reproductive challenges and infant mortality were widespread and a constant source of anxiety, vulnerability, and volatility; and various forms of military violence—whether from ongoing wars between Jola villages or the brutality of Portuguese colonial soldiers—shaped their lives, their settlement patterns, and their deaths. And yet Ampa Badji and others of his generation insist that theirs was a time of relative ease and abundance because they did not worry about rain and rice. Their contract with *Emitaï*—that if they worked hard in the paddies, *Emitaï* would send them rain—was still intact. No matter that the hard work sometimes made them sick beyond healing; no matter that the commitment to such work required risking Portuguese bullets. Hard work, according to Ampa Badji and his peers, is what enabled them to withstand these challenges and continue to be Jola.

Despite Kurijol's death and his own childhood hardships—or perhaps because of them—Akabau absorbed this ethic and passed it on to his own son. Ampa Badji credits his father with teaching him how to work, and specifically how to work hard like a proper Jola man. Again, there were no other options at that time besides rice farming. Ampa Badji's mother, Nha Buhel, was also a highly competent and tireless worker, and she raised her son to be the same.

Ampa Badji grew up as a rice farmer, learning both the technical aspects and the attitudinal approach that define Jola cultivation practices. But he also grew up at a time when other influences—especially the continued Portuguese military presence, the establishment of a Catholic missionary school, the violence of the independence struggle, and the emergence of the one-party state—significantly shaped his relationship to many things Jola.

*   *   *

The PIME Catholic Mission: A Brief History

On January 22, 1952, the first priest from the *Pontificio Instituto Missioni Estere* (PIME) diocese arrived in Esana and subsequently established a Catholic Mission that has played a vital and often controversial role in the region's recent history.[10] Padre Spartaco Marmugi traveled to Esana after an exploratory trip by one of his colleagues, who described the life there as "very difficult, poor, and full of sacrifice; [one] literally cannot find things to eat, one cannot buy anything if not in Senegal, at [Esana] there is only the exchange of agricultural products and crafts" (Gheddo 1999:53).[11] Marmugi soon obtained land (with Portuguese colonial backing) in the center of the village, in what was then *matu fitchadu*—dense, un-cut forest. After clearing the land, presumably through forced labor campaigns comprised of local residents often used for such purposes during the late colonial era, he built a school and began recruiting Jola participants in Mission activities.

After several unsuccessful attempts to convince local families to attend mass and send their children to his school, Padre Marmugi enlisted Portuguese colonial backing once again. He convinced the chief colonial administrator in Esana to register the names of all school-aged children in the village. The administrator then sent his *sipaios* to physically catch the children and force them into the school. When Jola families realized what was happening many of them took their children into the thick forest surrounding the village to hide from the authorities, a tactic they used repeatedly during the subsequent forced schooling campaigns. But several young boys and girls were successfully captured, and Padre Marmugi began to teach them rudimentary reading and writing skills.

When the Mission school first started Jola adults called it *kajanay-aku,* derived from the Jola words "ear" and "to hear." Their primary concern with the school was that children would learn things that were forbidden to them, especially regarding sexual reproduction. The school thus marked the first intrusion into the carefully separated gendered domains of knowledge and secrecy that organized Jola social and ritual life.[12] But even though Jola families were deeply suspicious of Padre Marmugi's efforts, colonial officials threatened them with corporal punishment if they refused to enroll their children in the Mission's school. As for the children, they enjoyed the novelty of Mission schooling, and most participants in these first cohorts recall with nostalgia the glee they felt in receiving their first clothing from Padre Marmugi, as well as a weekly ration of soap to wash themselves and their new clothes. Many Jola residents, when talking about this era, do not seem indignant or resentful of these coercive tactics. Rather, they laugh at their own innocence and discuss the proceedings as if they were a playful game. "I used to hide in the bush," my neighbor told me, nonchalantly. "My mother would tell me never to accept a gift from a white person. There was a suspicion that white people who seemingly gave you gifts were really fishing for you because they wanted to catch you and make you a stranger. So I would hide in the forest when they came to capture the other kids for school. But really I wanted to go see what my friends were up to there. And they got a t-shirt from the priest. I wanted a t-shirt, too."

In this way, the first cohort of Jola schoolchildren proceeded. But by the time they had completed a couple of grades, the boys reached the age in which they declared their future wives. Betrothal ceremonies took over school-related activities and Padre Marmugi, deciding it was inappropriate to have students who were married or preparing to be so, expelled the entire group and recruited, through the same methods, a fresh cohort.

When the new cohort of boys neared the age of declaring brides Marmugi sent them away to the Bafatá Mission to continue their schooling. Once they were removed from Esana and the control of their families, they had little recourse but to continue in their Mission-led lives.[13] This strategy worked quite well, and several cohorts of Jola boys were sent to Bafatá, where, according to one member of this group, "things accelerated a bit." When they completed fourth grade in Bafatá, they were considered educated enough to be teachers in their own right, and Marmugi either arranged for them to continue schooling elsewhere or he brought them back to Esana to serve as teachers for the younger students. This is how Esana developed a stable of Jola teachers that, to this day, comprise the majority of teachers at schools scattered across Jola territory.

Padre Marmugi spent twenty-one years in Esana. Despite what seem to be coercive, manipulative, and altogether intrusive tactics, Marmugi remained well loved by Jola Christians and non-Christians alike, especially when compared to his successor. Padre Marmugi died in 1973 and was buried in the still mostly empty Catholic cemetery behind the Mission. Most Esana residents, even non-Christians, recall him with overwhelmingly positive regard, and many still mourn his death, as the Esana Mission headed in quite a different direction under his successor, Padre Luigi.

Padre Spartaco Marmugi in Esana, 1950s *(Gheddo 1999, courtesy of PIME)*.

Padre Luigi joined Padre Marmugi in Esana in 1968, when he was nineteen years old. He arrived during the protracted war for Guinean liberation from Portuguese colonial rule. Although PIME priests had benefited from Portuguese colonial administrative and authoritative structures in establishing their presence around the country, and did not hesitate to use colonial backing—sometimes with physical force—when it served their interests, both Padre Marmugi and Padre Luigi were sympathetic with the Guinean independence movement. Relationships with Portuguese colonial authorities had to be managed delicately, though, especially as Esana served as a base for incoming Portuguese troops, and many of Esana's residents were conscripted into the Portuguese army. At the height of the Independence War Esana's Mission facilities were used by the Portuguese army as a prison and torture camp for suspected African Party for the Independence of Guinea-Bissau and Cape Verde (PAIGC) sympathizers, and several of Esana's residents were killed there. The original church, which had only been built several years prior to its use as a torture facility, was never again used for ceremonial purposes, as Padre Marmugi declared it tainted, and it was eventually torn down after independence.

Construction of the PIME Mission facilities in Esana *(Gheddo 1999, courtesy of PIME)*.

Padre Luigi arrived in Esana as a young man and, due to Padre Marmugi's death, unexpectedly became the senior priest in Esana shortly
thereafter. He has remained in Esana since 1968, and his tenure has been
fraught with tensions and conflicts between himself and Jola villagers.
But his perspective on changes in Esana over the last forty-plus years and
his comments on the emergence of a Jola Catholic community are unparalleled in terms of his often-contentious involvement with Jola in the
region.[14]

The PIME Mission facilities in Esana were surrounded by a brick wall,
topped by a barbed wire fence that gave the entire complex an intimidat-
ing, fortress-like feel.[15] The structures themselves were unlike any in the
surrounding area; they were made of concrete and tile roofs, and stood out
in sharp contrast to the mud and thatch houses that comprised the rest of
the village. The entrance to the Mission—two large, creaking iron gates—
generally remained closed unless one of the priests or nuns needed to
drive their car in or out, after which they were promptly shut. Overall, the
Mission had a rather uninviting physical presence and there was very little
traffic between the Mission grounds and the rest of the village. Those that
did enter the Mission gates did so with trepidation. The priests and nuns

Walls and fence surrounding PIME Mission, Esana 2002 *(photo by Joanna Davidson)*.

A Jola Christian working in the *oficina*, Esana 2003 *(photo by Joanna Davidson)*.

were rarely seen outside the Mission walls except in their cars on their way
to another village or Bissau.

Another major facet in the dynamic between village and Mission
was the role of the Mission as an employer. When Padre Marmugi established the Mission facilities he included a small mechanics shop in which
to train his young charges in the basics of bicycle and automobile repair.[16]
The mechanics' shop has since grown, under Padre Luigi's patronage, to
include a well-equipped carpentry workshop and an automobile repair
shop. Jola converts have been awarded positions as workers in these shops,
where they were apprenticed to more senior employees and received an
hourly wage. The carpentry and automotive center, referred to generically
as the *oficina*, conducted its work internally; that is, workers performed
services only for Mission jobs requiring carpentry and vehicle repair and
maintenance, and Padre Luigi frowned upon accepting work for anyone
else in the community or in surrounding villages. Since it is the only facility of its kind in the northern swath of the country, such requests were
frequent, and Padre Luigi and his *oficina* workers regularly rejected them.
This was seen by community members as Mission selfishness and insular-
ity, which, to some degree, it was, although Padre Luigi insisted that as a

not-for-profit institution, the Mission *oficina* was not in a legal position to take on work outside the Mission itself. Because of the *oficina*, with its constant generator hum and power tool whine and busy Jola workers in an otherwise completely non-industrial setting, the Mission often appeared to be more of a well-functioning business enterprise than a religious institution.

Of course, the Mission also conducted a series of religious activities, such as mass and catechism. But most people's interaction with the Mission and its personnel was business-oriented, whether through the various productive activities, or to sheepishly solicit a favor to borrow equipment, get a ride, send a message to another village or Bissau, or borrow money. And most of these requests were rebuffed by Padre Luigi in patronizing tones, which reinforced the general consensus that "the Mission doesn't help anyone." Even the junior priest who arrived in Esana shortly after my own arrival in 2001 admitted that Padre Luigi's manner in denying requests left much to be desired. He once mentioned to me, as we witnessed the usual line of solicitors at Padre Luigi's office door being turned away, that diplomacy was needed when turning down someone's request, especially here where "people are so sensitive." "One must sometimes say 'no'," he said quietly, "but one can soften the blow."

The current relationship between most villagers, Christian and non-Christian alike, and the Mission is fraught with misunderstandings, built-up resentment, and an uncomfortable combination of dependence and disdain. As a member of one of the first cohorts of captured schoolboys, Ampa Badji had much to say about these matters. His own relationship with the Mission is explored further in Chapter Five.

* * *

"Quero Ser Amigo"

In addition to the PIME Mission, another major dimension of Ampa Badji's childhood was the ever-changing relationship between Esana's villagers and the Portuguese colonial soldiers stationed in their midst. Unlike his grandfather, who had been beaten mercilessly by the post's commander, died as a refugee in a village across the Senegalese border, and was hurriedly and secretly buried in Esana before the village was re-settled, Ampa Badji's memories of the Portuguese troops was overwhelmingly positive, and often recounted with a deep sense of fondness for particular soldiers: "We and they, we had a great friendship, really and truly great." The barracks were already established in Esana long before Ampa Badji was born, so there never has been a time in his life that he has not seen some kind of military presence in Esana. Alongside their other childhood pursuits—like nicking papayas and hunting for small game—Ampa Badji and his friends would frequent the military barracks and try to establish links with newly arrived soldiers. Whenever a new company arrived, they would rush over and repeatedly state the one sentence of Portuguese they had learned: "Quero ser amigo [I want to be your friend]." Eventually, the soldiers would shrug and say, "OK, let's be friends." And a relationship was established that, for the boys, meant access to all kinds of novelties. Their new "friend" might start by giving them a plate from the canteen that they could wash straight from a tube with water coming out of it. Sometimes they would be given soup and bread, and if they were lucky and found the soldier in charge of the mess hall, they would be given red or white wine. Ampa Badji encountered for the first time all kinds of foods that he craves to this day: olives, tinned tuna, corned beef, and bread with jam. Whenever I visit Esana a large portion of my luggage is taken up by the items that still rank among Ampa Badji's favorite foods and continue to evoke memories of his childhood friendships with Portuguese soldiers.

Once the Mission started charging them for school supplies, Ampa Badji and his peers would sell their pilfered papayas and bananas to the Portuguese soldiers so they could pay for their materials. And they believed fervently that the soldiers were protecting them from the "enemy," defending them from "bandits in the bush," which is how the soldiers referred to the PAIGC liberation fighters. Often, their commanders would organize forays outside of Esana to look for the "enemy," and the soldiers told Ampa Badji and his friends, "We're going to hunt down those Moors!" But Ampa Badji was not offended; he was flattered to be let into their confidence. And he was thrilled that he and the soldiers were beginning to understand each other's languages, although still with difficulty.[17]

Most Jola villages had been mobilized by the PAIGC's war effort, but Esana and the neighboring village of Elia remained exceptions and sided (or at least complied) with the Portuguese. Many Esana residents were conscripted into participating in raids to ambush PAIGC "bandits in the bush," although others escaped the Portuguese hold on the village and joined the PAIGC fighters in other parts of the country. Regardless of their affiliation, most villagers recall the liberation war as a time of insecurity and fear; they were often obliged to stay inside their houses given gunfire in the forests surrounding the village, and this, of course, impacted their ability to tend to their agricultural tasks.

The war lasted for eleven years and resulted in Guinea-Bissau's independence from Portuguese colonial rule in 1974. A year before, Ampa Badji had completed fourth grade at the Mission school and, barely fourteen years old, had begun his role as a teacher. After independence he continued teaching in the Mission school, but the new one-party state quickly took over all schools and absorbed teachers into their own corps of civil servants within the newly formed ministry of education. One of their first implemented policies was to post teachers to a school not in their own ethnic territory, perhaps an attempt to put into practice some aspects of Amílcar Cabral's vision of a tolerant multi-ethnic state (Cabral 1970, 1973; Chabal 1983; Chilcote 1991; Mendy 2006).[18] In 1976 Ampa Badji and six of his colleagues were sent to Canchungo, only 80 kilometers away but the farthest any of them had traveled outside Jola-land. After two years there, a new administrator—in a decidedly un-Cabral-like move—removed all non-Manjaco employees in order to fill their posts with members of his own ethnic group. Ampa Badji arrived back in Esana, took his place alongside his father in the rice paddies, and joined his peers in the neighborhood work association of unmarried boys.

It was around this time that he was encouraged to start looking for a wife. In those days, one of the most important steps a young Jola man took in preparation for marriage involved building his own house, generally in his lineage's neighborhood near his father's house. Lineage-based neighborhoods pull strongly on a Jola person's identity and loyalty, and one always identified as "from" one's true neighborhood, which in Ampa Badji's case was Katama. But, as we have seen through Ampa Badji's grandparents and parents, where one fetches up is an entirely different matter. Akabau, his father, had left Katama as a young married man in order to escape what he believed to be the predations of his kin that lay at the root of his *padi/ntera* problem. Even though Esana as a whole is quite compact and travel among the various neighborhoods is now frequent, there is a general belief that if a man moves away from his natal neighborhood he gains a measure of safety for himself and his family. Similar strategies were pursued by the first Jola converts to Catholicism, taking the practice a step further by establishing a new neighborhood—dubbed Santa Maria—alongside the Mission walls.[19]

Akabau built a house in Nhakun, among his maternal kin, where Ampa Badji was born in the *kenyalen* society. Ampa Badji decided to stay in Nhakun despite the pressures from his paternal uncles to build his house in Katama. First, since the PIME Mission had cleared away the thick forest that had long separated Esana's two wards, Nhakun was situated much more in the geographical center of the village. It was close to the main dirt road and to the small shops that Fula merchants had set up near the military barracks. Compared to Katama, which was tucked back deep into the village and accessible only along narrow and winding footpaths, Nhakun had a more vibrant and modern feel, and this appealed to Ampa Badji's growing sense of worldliness. But even more importantly Ampa Badji was continuing his ongoing effort to separate himself from the obligations that traditional life in the "deep" village entailed, especially with regard to the ritual office for *Karenghaku*, which he was in line to inherit. Living in Nhakun provided some amount of physical distance—even if only measurable in meters—from what Ampa Badji felt as the downward tug of traditional spirit shrine-based ceremonial life.

Although he did not have patrilineally based access to land in Nhakun, he built his house on land that belonged to his father's mother's family, and he and his family continue to reside in that same spot. In addition to its function as a stable structure in which to live, building a house is, for Jola, a public display of a young man's proximity to marriage. When Ampa Badji built his house he had already declared Nho Keboral as his bride, and he was eager to complete this final step as a full-fledged Jola man. This is one of the biggest contrasts that contemporary Jola—young and old— point out between the current head of household generation and their young adult children. Although much had changed since their parents' time (schooling, missionization, national independence), Ampa Badji and his peers all declared their brides and built their houses according to Jola traditional norms, even when they improvised on their neighborhood affiliation (a longstanding, if not strictly traditional, practice). They look at their own children and shake their heads. "Now, even if you haven't prepared anything, not even your house, and you get a girl pregnant, you don't marry her, you just have a kid with her. . . . In those times, it wasn't like that. Before the wedding itself you will have built your house, you cover it with thatch, and when you've covered it you announce the wedding day." (I elaborate on these changes in subsequent chapters.)

Ampa Badji's own process of declaring a bride and getting married was filled with anticipation. He had first noticed Nho Keboral at a dance and had been watching her closely. She was being fostered by a family in Kugelh, because her mother had become mentally unstable after burying so many of her own children. When Ampa Badji began to receive a sack of rice as part of his civil servant salary as a teacher, he would bring much of it over to her household. As was the custom, he never spoke directly to Nho Keboral or her family about his intentions. Instead, he sent a delegate

to speak on his behalf. Nho Keboral's family conducted the typical inquiries about her potential husband, finding out if he worked hard, if he had
enough paddy and forest land, and, most importantly, if he was a thief.
Many Jola adults stressed to me over my years in the village that in their
time, if people knew you were a thief, you would have a very difficult time
getting married. Sometimes these investigations were quite prolonged, but
in Ampa Badji's case his proxy returned a third time and Nho Keboral's
family accepted the proposal. Nho Keboral went to the Gambia to be a
domestic worker for a Mandinka family in order to earn the necessary
money for basic household goods a Jola wife needs: a cooking pot, aluminum implements, a bucket for drawing water. Ampa Badji built his house
in 1983, and the couple married that same year. Nho Keboral soon gave
birth to a daughter and, a couple of years later, a son.

When his father died in 1987 Ampa Badji was supposed to be inducted
as *Karenghaku's* shrine priest, but he refused, telling the *amangen-i* that he
was now aligned with the Mission and could not assume responsibility for
the spirit shrine. In fact, Ampa Badji had long since broken with the Mission. The real reason, Ampa Badji admitted, that he refused to assume his
destined position as *Karenghaku's* priest was that "If I accept responsibility
for the shrine, the witchcraft will begin again, and my children will be put
at risk." It was too dangerous, in his opinion, to accept the priesthood.
Like others who evaded their induction into religious offices, Ampa Badji
could be forced into ordination, but only during the *esaangai* proceedings
every six years. So, every six years, Ampa Badji goes into hiding (usually in
Bissau) and returns to Esana when the *esaangai* ceremonies are complete
and the *amangen-i* can no longer abduct him and force him to take responsibility for *Karenghaku*. If he continues to do this they might seek
someone else, like his eldest son Gregório. Ampa Badji once told me that,
despite his disagreements with Padre Luigi and his own doubts about
Christianity, he planned to return to the Mission. "I will go back," he
sighed, "because then the elders will see that I cannot have *Karenghaku*.
My heart is not in it, but I'll go back." When I returned to Esana in 2010
Ampa Badji had already explained some of his concerns about his lineage's
relationship to *Karenghaku* to his sons. "I've given them hints," he said.
"But ultimately it depends on each one, on each one's sensibilities. It's up
to them. I've already told them I'll have nothing to do with it. It could have
a lot of consequences, all kinds of consequences."

This was among the reasons he wanted his own children—especially
his sons—to continue with their studies and stay far from Esana. Ampa
Badji was concerned about his sons being captured and inducted, but he was

far more concerned about the other (perhaps more pressing) consequences of his sons not finishing their schooling and returning to Esana to take up the *bujandabu*. As we will see in subsequent chapters, his concerns to keep his children in school and away from what he increasingly considered to be a dead-end life in the village have gone far beyond the initiation shrine.

*   *   *

Nho Keboral

"My father was a great hunter," Nho Keboral told me many times. The rafters of his veranda were lined with the skulls of all of the animals he had killed. By Nho Keboral's telling, her father's hunting prowess seemed to shape the trajectory of her parent's lives, and by extension her own. This was encapsulated by two central hunting stories that she regularly recounted to me.

One day, before she was born, Nho Keboral's father, Bontai, was out hunting and, although he usually killed gazelles, he came across a hippopotamus eating rice in the paddies outside Bukekelil, and he shot and killed the hippopotamus. For Jola hippopotamuses are sacred animals, especially for one particular lineage, and are not meant to be killed by a single individual. If a hippopotamus was disturbing rice paddies, as they often did, then a group of men was organized to chase it off or, on some occasions, collectively kill it. But Bontai killed this one by himself, and as soon as others in the neighborhood found out they scolded him for doing so. From that moment forward Bontai's children kept dying. As soon as another child was born he or she would die and be buried. He began the process of cleansing himself of the wrongdoing of killing the hippopotamus, but more importantly, he decided to move from his natal neighborhood of Bukekelil, where he believed his misfortune lay. This, as explained previously, was a common strategy to deal with misfortune, usually assumed to be the work of witchcraft in one's own lineage. In Bontai's case, he moved to his mother's brother's house, and once there his reproductive success improved and Nho Keboral was born.

Many years later, when Nho Keboral was working as a domestic in the Gambia, her father went hunting again and he came upon two wildcats mating. He only had one bullet so he could not kill them both, but he was afraid that if he killed just one the other one would come after him. He was also afraid to kill a wildcat because of the suffering that ensued after he killed the hippopotamus. But his most pressing fear was that the wildcats would soon see him. Jola believe that animals, especially wildcats, get vexed when a human comes upon them while they are mating. So he took aim and shot the male wildcat. The female escaped from underneath the male and Bontai quickly hid in a tree until she finally left the area. After returning to the village for more bullets he went to collect the dead wildcat, skinned him, and took the pelt to sell in Dakar (although sometimes Nho Keboral said he sold it in the Gambia, and other times in Ziguinchor, still other times she combined the various faraway places as "Dakar-Gambia"). With the proceeds he bought a new gun, which is still in use in Esana.

Sandwiched between these two hunting stories was Nho Keboral's childhood. Her own birth was understood as the result of her father's move from his natal neighborhood to his mother's brother's neighborhood, but, especially for her mother, this change could not undo all of the misfortune that preceded it. Nho Keboral's mother, Apekua, had given birth ten times, and Nho Keboral was the last, and only, child remaining. "My mother would just bury and bury her children." Like Ampa Badji, Nho Keboral was the only child who escaped what seemed like an endless cycle of births and burials. Her mother had reached her limit: after Nho Keboral was born her mother insisted that she did not want to be near her because she was afraid that being close to any of her children would kill them. "So, from that point, my mother said that she didn't want me, and she went away, she went away and stayed. . . . Since she rejected me, she said she didn't want me, because if she had me, I would also die. Well, I stayed put. My mother would come and go, come and go."

Although her life as a girl rejected by her mother and fostered by her father's brother's wife was clearly filled with disappointments and hardship, Nho Keboral also consistently pointed out how, in general, childhood was better in her time than it is now. Many Jola adults expressed the same kind of evaluation on the change—and always the worsening—of childhood experiences between "then" (broadly glossed as the era of their own childhood and the previous few generations) and "now" (the era of their own children). The consensus among Jola adults was that, because of the decline in rain and rice, children now have to work harder, and start working earlier, whereas previously children had a relatively carefree existence until they took on the responsibilities of their own families as mothers and fathers. Nho Keboral, Ampa Badji, and others of their cohort often reminisced about their playful childhoods. As Nho Keboral recalled,

> My life as a girl was good because at that time you didn't have to be concerned about anything, you go off and wander, play, wait for your mother to cook, as soon as she was done, you relaxed. Nothing was the

matter in those times; work wasn't as hard as it is now because in those days it would rain all the time, so there was lots of rice. Those of us who grew up at that time, we didn't even know the paddies. We would sit around the house, dry the rice, pound it, we would take the rice and wet it and put honey on it, because at that time there was lots of honey in the forest, but now there's no honey, there's no rice, you work until you're exhausted and still you have nothing to show for it. At that time, there was lots of rice, there were fish in the paddies. But now there's no fish. If our mothers went fishing in those days, they would get a lot of fish, but now you wouldn't get much fish. In those days, we would go out, we would go to the forest and look for cockles and sometimes we would gather them. But it wasn't like little children went to work, like now. The water's finished, it doesn't rain, there's no water, there's no rice. That time was better than now. At that time we would just play in the paddies. But now, even very little children go to work to help their mothers. Everything her mother does, she goes along to help.

Many Jola women lamented the fact that children start working in the forests and paddies at increasingly earlier ages. Although they painted a rosy picture of their own childhoods as relaxed and carefree, they certainly learned to master the essentials of Jola agricultural labor in their youth, mostly alongside their mothers who demonstrated transplanting techniques and other tasks involved in rice cultivation. It was their mothers who taught them not only the technical aspects of massaging the rain-drenched paddy soil with their feet and punching the seedlings into the moist earth so they stood up straight, but also the value of hard work itself. "If you fool around," Nho Keboral explained, "she'll catch you and say, 'if you don't do this, I'll hit you.' And you start acting right by listening to your mother. Children are hit at work, but not in any which way. If you know that your child is not interested in the work, you can hit him. If he or she doesn't want to work, you can hit him."

Nho Keboral learned such lessons in her foster home and occasionally from her mother when she returned to visit. As she grew in size and strength she began to accompany her adult female relatives more often in their work and she became known as a competent and hard worker. It was around this time that Ampa Badji began to notice Nho Keboral as he passed by the house where she was being raised on his way to the paddies. Before long she followed the path of most young women from her generation and crossed the Senegalese border to find work as a domestic in the Gambia. In general, Jola from Guinea-Bissau have long been oriented northward, toward Senegal and the Gambia, for all kinds of purposes from trading to seasonal work to occasional refuge. It is only very recently that they have become more connected to Bissau, their own country's capital, as an urban center to fill some of these needs. But in Nho Keboral's time travel to Bissau was very rare, although travel across the Senegalese border was quite common. This is partly because of proximity and infrastructure—it is far easier to walk across the Senegalese border than to make the two river crossings necessary to get to Bissau, which, until the 2009 completion of bridges across both, still required crossing by erratic and often broken-down ferries.[20] But orientation to the north was also because of extended Jola kin through the Casamance and even into the Gambia, as well as the relatively better-off economies of both countries compared to Guinea-Bissau. So Nho Keboral followed a well-worn path among teenaged girls and found work with a Mandinka family (washing, ironing, cleaning, and other domestic tasks) so that she could earn money to buy the clothes and cooking implements she would need for marriage.

Jola used to mark various stages of maturity visibly on the body with particular headpieces for boys that showed their progression through the four main phases from boyhood to manhood (cf. Chapter Five) and specific cloth skirts for girls. Once a girl was declared she wore a black-and-white cloth wrap painstakingly decorated with geometrical patterns of beads. These days only very old women know how to sew such skirts, and while many women Nho Keboral's age keep theirs tucked away as nostalgic items from their own young adulthood, they are no longer used by their own adult daughters for the purpose of marking their marital status, or for that matter, for any purpose at all.

Kuji-kuji

Even though Nho Keboral lamented the loss of an easier life "back then," by her own telling, her first several years of marriage and motherhood were by no means easy. Her first child was born soon after marrying Ampa Badji, and her second child just two years after that. Nho Keboral's memories of these years are full of hardship: of the weighty responsibilities of taking care of two young children while working hard in the paddies and forests; of the struggle with sicknesses; of the lack of help because of her lack of extended kin. "I would get so worn out," she told me. "We turned ourselves inside-out to get money. . . . It was so much work." By the time her second son was born Guinea-Bissau was a newly independent nation state. Nho Keboral never expressed any emotions or strong opinions about colonialism or any of the political changes—from independence to the ongoing turbulence of a fragile nation-state—she had witnessed in her lifetime. Although there were vague references to the challenges they faced during the liberation war, especially given the fighting in the forests that surrounded Esana, what Nho Keboral experienced most was a change in access to basic commodities. Newly independent Guinea-Bissau was struggling to set up a socialist economy in the aftermath of an eleven-year war that had ravaged much of the country. Rural agrarian populations had been deeply disrupted, especially in the country's south, and the war exacerbated what was beginning to feel like a general decline in rain. "It still rained a little bit then," Nho Keboral recalled, but many rural communities had already become dependent on some amount of sack rice. Nho Keboral and Ampa Badji had gotten by reasonably well with Ampa Badji's allotment of 50 kilos of sack rice per month as a teacher. But with national independence came a long-lasting dearth of imported goods, especially rice (see Forrest 1992). Nho Keboral remembered this as a time with no sack rice within the borders of her own country, and she would go to the Senegalese border to barter for rice. Ampa Badji tapped palm wine or cut palm fruit, which she processed into palm oil and carried to the border in exchange for rice. Sometimes Nho Keboral traded palm oil for tobacco, which she brought back to Esana and sold for a small amount of money in order to buy basic necessities. Other times she bought sugar-cane liquor and re-sold it in small cups to older men who gathered around her veranda. In this way she was able to raise a little money to cover her growing family's basic needs. This was the beginning of her long-term effort to *kuji-kuji* by engaging in small exchange activities in an everyday effort to make ends meet.

Many of Nho Keboral's complaints from this period centered on the fact that she did not have a mother or sisters who could help her with her small children. Even worse, since Ampa Badji came from a similarly sibling-less family, the kinds of support most young Jola families receive from their kin were lacking in their case. Rather than leave her small children with a grown sister, Nho Keboral carried them to the forest, tying her eldest child, Sabina, on her back and hoisting her young son, Gregório, onto her shoulders. Children kept coming in an ideal Jola succession of equal sons and daughters. After Gregório came Marina, then another son, Angala, then another daughter, Noelza, then a sixth and final child, a son, Tiago.

By the time Marina was born, Sabina was old enough—probably around seven—to help around the house and Nho Keboral had some relief. But her general account of her many years of childbearing and childraising is characterized first and foremost by sickness. "The life of a mother," she would often say, "means taking care of sick children. When your children

are sick, which is always, all of your senses are scattered." The small amount
of money she was able to make by selling tobacco or sugar-cane rum more
often than not went to treatments and medicine for her constantly sick
children.[21] "We wore ourselves out for those kids," she told me. "We've
worn ourselves out. All of my kids have been sick. . . . All of the money that
we had, we've spent it on treatments for our children."

Nho Keboral, herself, battled with persistent illness and recurrent miscarriages. During my residence in Esana in 2001–2003 she was often severely sick, although she maintained her rigorous work regimen in the
forest and paddies and continued to expand her *kuji-kuji* endeavors. Once,
during my first year in the village, she prepared palm oil in several large
jerry-cans, which she planned to carry across the Senegalese border where
she could get a better price for it. She told me she would be gone for a week
or more, but a few days later she came back while Ampa Badji and I were
sitting on the veranda and several of the children were playing in front of
the house. "*Nukailoh* [You've arrived]," Ampa Badji greeted her, without
glancing up. "*Nikailoh* [I've arrived]," Nho Keboral responded. Nothing
more was said, but I later learned from Nho Keboral that she had a miscarriage *en route* to the Senegalese border while carrying her heavy jerry-cans,
and she had to abandon her palm oil in one of the villages to the north. She
had lost a significant amount of blood and she was later diagnosed with
severe anemia, but she was mostly concerned that she would be unable to
recuperate her losses in palm oil exchange. It was much later that same year,
after more miscarriages and increasing weakness, that she approached me
for help in securing birth control across the border. "I just need to rest a bit,"
she told me. "I can have more children later, but for now I need a break."

Jola women regularly compose short songs about themselves that
become a kind of abbreviated anthem associated with a particular individual. Their friends—generally the women in their work association—all
know each other's songs and often sing them while working in the paddies
or gathered around a collective rice bowl and some palm wine after a long
day's work. Usually only two lines, these songs encapsulate a moment or
episode in each woman's life, often encoding a rebuke to someone who has
offended them or cryptically revealing that they have overheard gossip
about themselves. Nho Keboral's song from this time (and it continued to
be her song even many years later) was:

> Oooh nahote, cupalal kigiradelo yo, inje [Nho Keboral] niponyue
>   nilañe;
> Oooh nahote, cupalal kigiradelo, inje [Nho Keboral] iyetua ekonomi.

"Nahote" is the Jola word for someone who is constantly sick; not a hypo-chondriac, but someone who is actually plagued by recurrent illness. The song roughly translates as:

Oooh sick-one, friends are playing, but I [Nho Keboral] have had
   enough and I'm going home;
Oooh sick-one, friends are playing, but I [Nho Keboral] have no
   money.

The last line refers to Nho Keboral's regular lament that any small amount of money she had managed to *kuji-kuji* was consumed by paying for medication and treatments for her (and her children's) various ill-nesses. Nho Keboral told me that she composed this song ("I felt the words in my heart") when she was in the midst of a period of constant sickness and her workmates mocked her lack of participation in their collective social gatherings. Even though Jola men tend to use various nicknames for each other more than women, "Nahote" became a kind of teasing nick-name for Nho Keboral; it defined, in a way, a dimension of her life's experi-ence and—like the hard work of rice farming—she wore it as a badge of both pride and punishment.

*   *   *

Many Jola today will tell you that life was easier for their parents and grand-parents. They insist that, in times past, their ancestors did not have to worry so much about rain and rice, as there was plenty of both. Although they acknowledge that Jola have always worked hard to cultivate their sacred crop, their general assessment of the past is that it was a time of abundance, a time when people were "rich with rice."

This selective history of a generally better past with respect to the present does not bear itself out in the specific life histories of Jola individu-als from one or two generations ago. Ampa Badji's account of the life and times of his parents and grandparents revealed that Jola villagers were beset by problems of internecine war, colonial brutality, constant sickness, premature death, the precarious life of orphanhood, a high incidence of infant mortality, and the constant struggle to bear more children in these vulnerable conditions. Perhaps there was indeed more rain and rice, but the relatively recent past was not quite as rosy as most Jola often portray it in their casual assessments of "then versus now."

Such a seeming flattening of the past also appeared in many contem-porary Jola portrayals of themselves. Although Ampa Badji had a wide range of personal and professional skills and qualities—he has been a teacher for many years, he served as the first director of Esana's community radio station, he is a devoted father, an avid reader (when he can find anything to read), the next-in-line for an important initiation shrine, and a member of one of the first cohorts of baptized Christians in Esana—he identified first and foremost as a rice farmer.

Although Ampa Badji, Nho Keboral, and others in their generation have undoubtedly changed in response to the many new institutions—late colonialism, the PIME Mission, the state—that have played a part during their lifetime in rural Jola-land, they have also remained steadfast in their commitment to their life's work in the rice paddies and their identities as rice farmers. Framing these externally driven institutional shifts and the internal transformations in socialization, gender, work, knowledge, and religion that they have brought about was the slow and steady but irrefutable evidence that Ampa Badji and Nho Keboral's (and their kin and neighbors') devoted efforts in the forest and paddies were bearing increasingly frustrating results. This realization and the anxieties that came with it, as well as the re-orientation it required for the parents of children who will likely not identify—at least primarily—as rice farmers, shaped their characterizations of the past, their sometimes paradoxical practices in the present, and their projections of the future.

CHAPTER 3

"We Work Hard"

[T]illing the soil not only procures means of subsistence but
in this process prepares the earth for building the world . . .
the cultivated land is not, properly speaking, a use object,
which is there in its own durability and requires for its permanence no more than ordinary care in preservation; the
tilled soil, if it is to remain cultivated, needs to be labored
upon time and again. A true reification, in other words, in
which the produced thing in its existence is secured once
and for all, has never come to pass; it needs to be reproduced again and again in order to remain within the human
world at all.

—Hannah Arendt,
The Human Condition

Ampa Badji's maternal grandfather was so committed to his work in
the rice paddies that he snuck away from his Senegalese healer's
home, despite the healer's admonition that Jola "hard work" would
make him sick again. He returned to Esana, picked up his *bujandabu*, re-
immersed himself in the hard work of rice cultivation, and, sure enough,
became sick again and died soon after. Ampa Badji's paternal grandfather
and his peers attempted to till their fields and tap their palm trees while
dodging Portuguese bullets. Eventually they joined their wives and children in refuge across the border (where Ampa Badji's grandfather died
soon after). But his peers were so concerned to get back to their paddies
and reclaim Esana and its environs from the encroaching bush that they
negotiated an uneasy truce with the colonial troops in the Esana barracks
and returned to their work. Cooperation with Portuguese soldiers was the
price they paid to get back to work.

Despite constant sickness and continued colonial violence, notwithstanding high infant mortality and premature death, the "time of our grandparents," many contemporary Jola insist, was a time of relative ease and abundance because they had plenty of rain and rice. Despite the dangers—disease and bullets—they fulfilled their side of the contract with *Emitaï*: to work hard in exchange for *Emitaï*'s rain. And they inculcated their own children into the same work ethic.

Ampa Badji learned the techniques of rice cultivation and the ethic of hard work from his parents and the older boys in his work group. He was the first in his family to attend school, be baptized, and have a salaried job. He had Portuguese "amigos," learned to love olives, and lived through the War of Liberation and the birth of the independent nation-state of Guinea-Bissau. And he identified himself throughout as a rice farmer. He taught his own sons how to wield the heavy *bujandabu*, and he instilled all six of his children with the ethic of hard work. But something had changed in his lifetime beyond the influence of schooling, the Mission, and the new state. Although he continued to work hard in the paddies, he had less and less rice in his granary. His response was to work harder. During my own residence in Esana from 2001 to 2003, most Jola villagers were doing the same as Ampa Badji: working hard in the paddies and forests and teaching their children to do so, too. They acknowledged the changed environmental conditions but, like Ampa Badji, continued to expend most of their time and energy in the parched rice paddies.

Why did Jola villagers in Guinea-Bissau uphold such strict adherence to their notion of work, even—or perhaps especially—when they admitted that their work was not actually working for them? This chapter follows up on the particular details of Ampa Badji's and Nho Keboral's life histories to explore, at a more general level, why Jola saw their agricultural work not simply as a means of sustenance but also as integrally bound up with social relations, ritual obligations, and collective cultural identity. I focus primarily on my 2001–2003 fieldwork period in order to elucidate Jola norms around work and how they were tied to notions of personhood, morality, socialization, and social organization. When I returned to Esana in 2010, Ampa Badji, Nho Keboral, and their peers were still spending most of their time cultivating rice. Many of them (especially the women) were working even harder than before. But the way they talked about this work had changed; the tone had shifted, if not the actual substance. Even more, the way they envisioned their children's lives, and how they invested in their children's futures, had also changed considerably. Toward the end of this chapter I begin to discuss how such longstanding norms around hard work in the rice paddies were reaching a breaking point and starting to unravel, although even their unraveling was happening in a very Jola way.

*   *   *

I was introduced to the centrality of Jola notions of work immediately upon my arrival in Esana in late 2001. On my second day of fieldwork I went to harvest rice. Nho Keboral and I joined her work association in a member's paddy and I spent a long, hot day cutting ripe rice with a small blade. By midday an older woman demanded that I take a break under a shady tree, but I already sensed that I was being evaluated on my ability to stick it out, so I continued cutting, tearing, and gathering the rice stalks into large bundles. It was early evening by the time we returned to the village, each woman carrying several large bundles of harvested rice on her head, and I was exhausted. But as we wended our way back along the village paths my coworkers animatedly told curious passers-by that I had stayed the whole day to harvest rice, refusing to take a break. For the next several days, wherever I went in the village I was greeted enthusiastically by my workmates, and they would repeat their narrative of my participation in the harvest to whoever happened to be around. It was work—especially the willingness to work hard—that provided entrée into a group of women who would become my closest friends and confidants throughout my fieldwork.

Of course, the hard work did not stop after harvesting. I continued to spend most of my time for several months working in the forests and fields, both with my adoptive family and with the women's work association. We harvested dry rice in the forest groves and wet rice in the paddies. We clear-cut sections of thick bush with machetes and planted rice seeds in prepared forest nurseries. We transplanted rice seedlings from the bush to the rain-flooded paddies and carried heavy baskets of homemade fertilizer to feed the fragile seedlings. And when the dry season came around again we harvested rice once more. In between the primary labors surrounding rice cultivation, we cut and braided dried thatch for roofing, made salt on sweltering days out in the sticky mangrove flats, and carried heavy objects from the forest to the village and back. In the first flush of fieldwork I rarely knew what each day would bring. But I learned quickly that it would involve walking and hard work in the forest or the paddies. With Nho Keboral as my guide I joined in the day's activities, gradually grasping the rhythms of Jola life, learning just how much work it takes to grow rice, and trying to maintain the efforts that had won me camaraderie and a sense of inclusion from my first day in the paddies.

In fact, I often struggled throughout my residence in Jola-land to maintain a balance between participating in Jola agricultural work—with my adoptive family and work association—and getting any other kind of "work" done, like conducting interviews and surveys, or writing field notes. While my initial days and weeks of work in the paddies and forests provided me with a wealth of data and a sense of legitimacy among my neighbors in the village, they also set up a standard that became difficult for me to sustain for the following two years. I had shown myself capable of manual labor and I was therefore expected to show up for work association workdays, which I usually did. But on the days when I had scheduled other activities members of my work association chided me for missing work, and I felt the sting of their disapproval.

One of the central characteristics of Jola rice cultivation is the performance of arduous manual labor—"hard work." This chapter elucidates the significance of "hard work" as a cultural trait independent of actual productivity. But it also considers the consequences of Jola villagers' adherence to these practices given current environmental and social conditions. Because Jola have preserved a commitment to an exacting work regime in the face of its acknowledged inability to meet basic subsistence needs, and have disciplined individuals who seek alternate productive activities, I argue that Jola work has become increasingly detached from its provisioning purposes. The idiom of "hard work" and the emphasis on the practice and ritual mimesis of wet rice cultivation—regardless of its outcome— expose the ways that Jola work obscures its own embeddedness in a social, historical, and ecological frame. In this way, the experiences of Jola villagers in northwestern Guinea-Bissau touch upon Raymond Williams's (1977) concept of displacement: that is, how emergent categories shift away from the conditions of their emergence. In the short term, this shift has generally resulted in worsening Jola villagers' standard of living. But the tensions and disparities currently at the forefront of rural Jola concerns are provoking villagers to reconsider their relationship to "hard work."

The Right Way to Work

As discussed previously, Jola residents regularly articulated their predicament in clear terms and were fully aware that growing rice as a subsistence crop was no longer tenable. But they continued to spend most of their time in the parched rice paddies, and they disapproved of—and sometimes punished—their kin and neighbors who sought some measure of relief in other productive activities or wage labor. "Hard work," defined as manual wet rice cultivation, remained a significant attribute that they believed distinguished them as Jola. Unlike many others in Guinea-Bissau, Jola resisted adopting cashew farming as a replacement—or even a large-scale supplement—to rice farming. Until recently, the transformed landscape in the rest of the country—grove after grove of cashew trees and, for several months of the year, jerry-can after jerry-can of cashew wine—was notably absent in the Jola and Baiote villages that dot the dirt road between São Domingos and Varela. This was partly because growing cashews is much less physically demanding than growing rice; it was considered "lazy work."[1] Within the spatial confines of Jola villages in northwestern Guinea-Bissau, "work" referred specifically to manual wet rice agriculture and corollary efforts, and activities other than wet rice cultivation were not considered real work. Such attitudes were clear in Jola evaluations of their non–rice cultivating neighbors. A comment I often heard from Jola about the Fula merchants in their midst was: "They don't like to work, they just sit around and sell things." Linares (1987) noted similar attitudes among Senegalese Jola, although with important distinctions, given the more frequent and longer-standing migrant labor patterns among this population. "Being a full-time cultivator," she observed, "is a different matter from being a full-time salesman or middleman. When it comes to the Jola selling their labor power as salaried workers by migrating to cities, which they are doing in great numbers nowadays, the Jola see this as work (burok). On the other hand, they do not see funom (a word which means both 'to sell' and 'to buy') as work" (Linares 1987:139; see also Lambert 2002:35–36, 115, 122). Anyone engaged in alternate productive endeavors, whether as a teacher, mechanic, domestic, or even a cashew farmer—performed these activities in addition to, not instead of, wet rice cultivation. To be sure, some Jola residents in this area had planted small plots of cashew trees. But Jola men, women, and increasingly children spent most of their time engaged in the taxing activities that make up wet rice cultivation, although with ever-less rice to show for their efforts.

Jola attitudes toward work are particularly interesting not only because of the apparent incongruity between their convictions about hard work and the practical results of their labors, but also because so much scholarship on African notions of work has focused on the opposite attitude: that of perceived African "laziness." Most postcolonial scholarship in this vein addresses stereotypes of "native laziness" by revealing how local work practices were developed as a subversive tactic to resist menial or forced labor, or how cultural understandings of work, time, and pace conflicted with colonial notions.[2]

Although Jola work habits ran contrary to colonial and neocolonial stereotypes of "lazy natives," their approach to work also clashed with Western capitalist orientations to work. Not only did Jola have a counter-ethic to that of individual accumulation, but the hard work that Jola performed in the forest and the paddies was no longer tied to output. Rather, the "right way to work" among Jola involved each individual's adherence to the physically demanding set of activities required by manual wet rice cultivation, regardless of the ultimate outcome of these labors in terms of crop yield. Even the adoption of labor-saving devices such as draft animals or wheelbarrows was judged critically by kin and neighbors as "taking the easy way out." The Jola model of work emphasized individual strength and ardor and required participation in a labor regime that demanded autonomous discipline at the household level, as well as moments of cooperation at the lineage and neighborhood levels.

In the sections that follow I discuss the basic contours and inducements to compliance (Moore 1978) of the Jola wet rice labor regime. I then provide various examples of how the notion of hard work was expressed in Jola social and ritual life. Finally, after discussing the discourse and practices of hard work in the current context of environmental and economic transformation, I consider the ways in which contemporary Jola villagers were "caught in a custom of their own making" (Parkin 1994:61).

Rice Cultivation, Social Relations, and Spirit Shrines: The Inducements of Jola Work

The activities that make up Jola rice cultivation—as well as those of neighboring populations along the Upper Guinea Coast—have been thoroughly and richly described by many scholars and observers of their social life.[3] In fact, the repeated cataloging, in such meticulous detail, of Jola agricultural practices is a reflection of the dominance with which these tasks define Jola lived experience.

Nonetheless, it bears repeating just how strenuous this method of rice cultivation is. The tasks involved in carving out paddies, erecting and repairing dikes, lifting heavy soil with the *bujandabu* to create the paddy's mounds, and then planting, transplanting, fertilizing, and finally harvesting rice all require rigorous physical exertion and diligence. Although the intensity of work increases during the rainy season, rice cultivation is a year-round endeavor, and most days involve some activity related to growing or processing rice, especially for women.

Most agricultural work is performed in a family's forest grove (*butat*) and paddies (*butonda*) in a mutually dependent, gendered division of labor.

A married man and his unmarried sons are responsible for preparing the *butonda* for rice planting (*ewañai*), and a married woman and her unmarried daughters are responsible for transplanting rice seedlings (*borokabu*) and harvesting ripe rice (*edjalai*). But there are certain moments in the agricultural cycle when household labor is not sufficient. Although there is an informal exchange of kinship-based reciprocal labor—for instance, a married man might help his married brothers in their *butonda* in exchange for the same service—this, too, does not adequately meet labor demands at the most intensive moments of rice production.

Such needs were met through neighborhood based, gender-exclusive work associations that could be contracted by a conjugal household for certain agricultural tasks that required more hands within a tight time frame.[4] In Jola villages just a few kilometers closer to the Senegalese border these collective work groups were called *societé*. Incorporation of Portuguese/Crioulo or French words into Jola typically followed this pattern of proximity to the Senegalese border. Jola in the forest villages where I resided most often used the Crioulo word *asosiason* when referring to these work groups, instead of the Jola word *awassau*. Men's groups were typically contracted for *ewañai* and women's groups for *borokabu* and *edjalai*. Given virilocality, female work groups within each neighborhood were divided between those comprising affines and those comprising agnates. Work associations could be contracted by anyone, and the contracted group need not derive from one's own neighborhood. Typically a fixed rate was established for a day's labor (whether the task took an hour or a full day) according to the size of the group.

Although they were primarily defined by their collective work activities, work associations were also important social groups and constituted the closest-knit set of relations beyond the family. Most Jola do not get deeply involved in one another's lives and troubles, but members of work associations take on a more active role in terms of providing advice and counseling for each other. When I became inducted into a work association I found that I had suddenly acquired a group of people who felt it was their right and duty to advise me on all kinds of things, often reprimanding me when they thought I had made a social error. They did this much more than my adoptive family ever did. In addition to pooling their labor to work one another's fields and pooling their earnings for a collective feast, work associations sometimes collected dues from their members, which they held for other purposes, such as purchasing matching cloth to wear at festive occasions to mark their members as belonging to the same association. (This is further explored in Chapter Six, especially with regard to the expansion and strengthening of these work groups—particularly for women—in the context of shifting labor needs.)

Villagers' participation in collective work regimes reflected, in part, the "regular reciprocities and exchanges of mutually dependent parties" (Moore 1978:63).[5] Beyond this, productive activities were linked in crucial ways to religious beliefs and practices. In her studies of Senegalese Jola, Linares has shown how Jola politico-religious concepts—especially their system of spirit shrines—operated to enforce cooperative labor through "fulfilling socio-ritual obligations" (Linares 1992:66). In essence, work associations were "corporate wage earning organizations" affiliated with specific shrines that enforced members' reciprocal contributions to the group (Linares 1992:67). The money earned, rather than being distributed to individuals, was collected, pooled, and used to hold a feast at the end of the rainy season to propitiate the spirit-shrine that facilitated their work.

> The purpose is to earn enough money with which to buy rice, sacrificial animals, condiments and palm wine in order to propitiate the community shrines. On these occasions, members of the association with their guests will feast amply. Unlike wage labor that is performed in the city, associative labor is directly under the supervision of the spirit shrine. . . . The association has practical, as well as symbolic, functions. Profits made from corporate activities are re-invested in rituals that ensure every person's productive, and hence reproductive, success (Linares 1992:69–70).

Social control, according to Linares, was thus exerted through the link between a work association and the ritual obligations it was meant to fulfill. To resolve the problem of how and why Jola adhered to such laborious work practices and overcame otherwise individualistic impulses to occasionally work cooperatively, all the while maintaining their largely decentralized political structure—that is, no one person or class was exerting its will, in a Weberian sense, to make them work this way—Linares demonstrated that social control can come from a different sort of politics, one rooted in religious beliefs and institutions.

> Legitimation is a political process. It can be achieved through consensus and shared ideals; it does not require outright coercion nor the use of force. In societies where bureaucracies are missing and there are no standing armies, as among the relatively self-sufficient rural communities of Africa, religious beliefs and ritual practices often reinforce many aspects of political economy. Cultural ideologies and symbol systems

usefully provide a legitimating idiom for the values and aspirations surrounding the economics of role behavior (Linares 1992:15).

Such an examination of social control through politico-religious mechanisms contributes to anthropological understandings of power as connected to "other aspects of the encompassing cosmological system" (Arens and Karp 1989:xiv–xv). It also corresponds to Sally Falk Moore's (1978) designation of a "semi-autonomous social field." That is, the Jola work regime reflects an internal generation of rules, customs, and symbols that serve as the "means to induce . . . compliance" (Moore 1978:55). As Linares observes, "politics is not solely about ways of dictating policies through the use of force, but also concerns how people may be directed, through mild forms of ideological persuasion and coercion, to perform socially-sanctioned tasks" (Linares 1992:10).

In this sense, I follow Linares's approach in emphasizing the inextricable connections among political, religious, and economic spheres in Jola social life—the trilogy of power, prayer, and production from Linares's (1992) book title. But my problem is a different one because current conditions have now changed, such that Linares's assertion that this all "works well" in the realms of production and reproduction can no longer be maintained.[6]

Environmental change and migration patterns are diminishing the viability of rice cultivation and threatening the economic underpinnings of Jola social organization. Furthermore, while religious ideals are expressed in various dimensions of Jola productive practices, the protective and punitive power of spirit shrines to enforce the social relations of labor has diminished in importance among contemporary Guinean Jola. The reasons for the waning power of spirit shrines in Jola social life include the increase of Christian missionary influence among a certain (although still relatively small) segment of the population, the influence of state and missionary schooling on the current and previous generation, and the impact of general economic decline on costly ritual activities and recruitment of adepts, each of which is considered in other sections of this book. Although work associations in Esana and neighboring villages operated in much the same way as Linares described for Senegalese Jola, and they still spent their season's earnings on a collective feast, these celebrations were not necessarily connected to propitiation rites. Given this break in the link between "prayer" and "production," what mechanisms of social control accounted for the continued cooperative practices of work associations?

In my experience among Jola villagers in Guinea-Bissau, the idiom and practice of "hard work" took on additional facets and expressions not

explored in Linares's otherwise resonant study of Senegalese Jola. Beyond
its place within the nexus of social and ritual obligations, "hard work" was
expressed as a cultural value in its own right, regardless of productive or
reproductive outcomes. In this context, Linares's concept of legitimacy is
not the best way to understand Jola conformity to their strict labor regime;
villagers enacted hard work even when they did not believe that such practices were necessarily legitimate. Building on Linares's important insights
into Senegalese Jola society, but based on the changing conditions and different context of Jola villagers in Guinea-Bissau, I re-examine this conundrum in Jola social life—why Jola villagers conformed to expectations
around hard work—particularly given the circumstances of ecological and
other transformations that made the fruits of their labor negligible.

"We Work Hard"

Jola villagers often claimed "hard work" as a distinguishing cultural characteristic. I once overheard a dialogue between two women drawing water
from a well that exemplified this point. One of the women, Segunda, was
Balanta—the majority ethnic group in Guinea-Bissau. The other was a Jola
woman named Aneki. As Segunda lifted a heavy, water-filled bucket on her
head to carry it home, Aneki teased her, "You're lazy. That bucket's not even
full." Segunda laughed off the insult and walked away. She returned a few
minutes later to refill two buckets. Aneki continued teasing her, "So, you
don't even work." Segunda replied, "Yes, I work." Aneki asked, "What work
do you do?" To which Segunda responded: "When I get up, I sweep. Then I
wash the pots and pans. Then I draw water." Aneki laughed: "You call that
work? You don't even go to the rice paddies. You just sit at home. . . . We
Jola, women use the machete, women even take up the *bujandabu*." Segunda retorted, "That's why you all get old so quickly," and Aneki proudly
agreed. "That's right. We get old quickly. We work hard. Balanta, they have
lots of money, so they can get people to work for them, and they just sit at
home. We Jola, we don't have money. We do the work ourselves." Segunda
left the yard and Aneki turned to me and explained: "You see, we Jola, we're
different. We work hard. We're just not the same as those others. We Jola,
our work is different. . . . We work hard."

Jola judged one another's work habits, socialized their children into a
life of disciplined manual labor, and expected adherence to a strict labor
regime. As Ampa Badji stressed, in his generation and that of his parents
and grandparents (and as far back as he could conjure), one would never
find a marriage partner if one did not "work hard." "If you don't know how
to do all kinds of Jola work," he told me, "like rice farming, tapping palm

trees, cutting oil-palm fruits, or perhaps you are lazy and you don't want to do this work, you will never—absolutely never!—find a woman to marry." A young woman's family always investigated a suitor to make sure he was a hard worker. Similarly, potential brides were evaluated on the basis of their capacity to work hard, and they would be unlikely to attract suitors at all if they were deemed lazy or reluctant workers.

The repercussions for those who did not adhere to this work ethic were severe. Take, for example, Ampa Bontai, a man who was universally disdained and shunned across Esana. He had once married, but his wife left him because he never worked, he left his children with nothing to eat, and he regularly stole household items to sell them for *sum-sum*, a potent distilled drink sold in shots in the small village shops. He would hobble down the village's main street complaining about his poverty, looking for charity, and usually finding none. He was ostracized from Jola social life, mocked and scorned by adults and children alike. When referring to him, most Jola villagers would shake their heads and say, "What can you do? He refuses to work." Although many villagers complained regularly about their own poverty, Ampa Bontai's grievances were dismissed; his lack of food could not be taken seriously because of his "refusal to work." Jola recognized others who had worked hard and gained little as "unlucky," and sometimes would help them with small donations of rice. But Ampa Bontai received no sympathy at all because of his rejection of the most fundamental of Jola tenets: hard work. Ampa Bontai's case and the attitudes of others toward him continually reminded me just how little room there was for any kind of nonconformity with regard to the Jola work regime.

Even elderly Jola continued to "work hard" at a time in their lives when similarly aged members of neighboring ethnic groups would typically be exempt from manual labor and supported by younger family members. I was often told that even grown children were not allowed or expected to work for their elderly parents. This assertion was typically backed up by various versions of the following story:

A long time ago, there was an old man who had several children. All of them had married and were living in their own houses or those of their husbands, except for one son, who had not yet built his own house. This son, seeing that his father was old and tired, spoke to him: "You should stay at home now. I will do all of the work. I'll hoe the paddies and tap the wine. You should not go to work anymore." The old man accepted, and the son worked hard, leaving nothing undone. This continued for several years, but in the fifth year the son died. The man returned to the

paddies, but when he picked up the heavy *bujandabu* to till the rain-
drenched soil he started to cry. He cried and wailed so powerfully that
people working nearby came to see what the matter was, and when they
saw the old man's pain, they helped him in the paddies. But the following year, when the same thing happened, people left him alone—they
had their own paddies to tend, after all—and the old man continued to
cry and was unable to work.

For Jola narrators, the point of this story was that providing help that
alleviated the labor of others—even that of the elderly—was actually a disservice, as it ultimately rendered the person incapable of toiling in the
fields and undermined the self-sustenance that is so crucial to Jola notions
of personhood.

This is not to say that Jola were unrealistic about the difficulties of their
lives or that they spoke of their work as pleasurable. Indeed, these attitudes
were mixed with complaint. During the course of my fieldwork I heard villagers sigh every day that Jola life was only hardship and drudgery. Once,
when I asked Ampa Badji about Jola notions of hell, he replied, "We cannot
believe that hell exists after death, because our life on earth is hell, so what
kind of god would make yet another hell after this one?" A typical condo-
lence offered to the bereaved relatives of someone who had died, or even in
consolation to oneself in anticipation of death, was: "At least she is resting
now. At least now she can relax." For Jola, the end of work means death, and
vice versa. Indeed, hard work was performed not only in the paddies, but
also in the context of ritual mimesis. For instance, at certain moments
during a funeral, dancers hold an object evocative of Jola work—such as a
stick, machete, *bujandabu*, or a bunch of unhusked rice—as they dance in
a circle around the corpse. This simultaneously signals honor for the dead
person's lifetime commitment to work and visibly distinguishes the living
from the dead. By carrying objects that represent work, funeral dancers are
performatively marking their status as living beings.[7]

A corollary to such ceremonial moments is the village-wide ban on
work during funeral proceedings. This ban is one of the key characteristics
of a Jola funeral, and it is often brought up by development workers and
urbanized Africans as one of the greatest obstacles to "modernization"
and "progress" among Jola. During a layperson's funeral the work prohibition lasts only for the day of the funeral itself, but for a shrine priest or
ritual elder it can last up to three months. The work ban applies to the
entire village and can have grave consequences for every family's crop
yield if it occurs during important moments of the agricultural cycle, such

as the particularly labor-intensive phase of the rainy season. This happened once during my residence in Esana, when the village's *ai* died in 2002 (cf. Chapter Four). At his funeral, the paramount *ai* from Karuay declared that residents of Esana could not work for six weeks. The Esana *amangen-i* later requested a reduction of the work prohibition to four weeks by paying a fine of cattle, but they were ultimately unsuccessful. The work ban included any kind of agricultural work in the forest or paddies. Men could continue to tap palm wine, as it was needed for dancers and ceremonies, but they could not sell it. Women could continue to gather cooking wood, but they could not stay in the forest all day as usual. Everyone was required to stay around the village in order to dance at the funeral grounds (*hukulahu*). Teachers continued to teach and came to the *hukulahu* only in the late afternoon, because, Ampa Badji explained to me, the laws around work bans pertained only to agriculture; new kinds of work, like teaching, were exempt.

It was precisely because work—in the form of wet rice cultivation and the collateral agricultural efforts that support and complement it—was such a defining feature of Jola lives that a funeral work ban set in relief the essential difference between life and death. The ways in which work was evoked, performed, or prohibited illustrated how Jola work was a complex of values that cuts across economic, religious, and social domains. For Jola, to be a living human being was to work.

Part of this emphasis on hard work was bound up with characteristics integral to wet rice cultivation. As we know, certain kinds of production regimes require certain kinds of workers (Chakrabarty 1988; Pandian 2009; Thompson 1963, 1993), and hard work was part and parcel with the particular demands of wet rice agriculture. It was simply not conducive to partial disengagement; one could not decrease one's participation in it or engage in it minimally or symbolically. As I have discussed before, wet rice cultivation required not only physically taxing individual labor, but also participation in a set of social relations—at the household, lineage, and neighborhood levels—that wove Jola together in a nested series of interdependent obligations. If individuals attempted to extract themselves by seeking out alternatives, their neighbors and kin sanctioned them partly because they relied on their participation in moments of collective labor.

Neighborhood work associations exemplified this dynamic. Although work associations have long been a central way of organizing labor needed for the most intensive and time-sensitive aspects of wet rice cultivation, they were becoming an even more important part of the agricultural workforce as the rainy season had become increasingly shorter, and the labor required to complete certain critical activities during the ideal period of time usually exceeded the capacity of the conjugal family or extended kin. But the increasing importance of collective labor coincided with the relatively recent phenomenon of urban migration of youth.[8] Since the local school stops at sixth grade, young people who are able to continue their studies must go to either São Domingos or Bissau. In 2001–2003, they more often than not returned to their home villages during the rainy season to help their families during this particularly intensive phase of wet rice agriculture. But within the past decade young people have started to stay in Bissau or other urban areas even during the rainy season.

Youth work associations in the villages have used their importance in the work system to force absent youth to return and do their share of labor. For instance, a man whose son has not returned from Bissau contracts a youth work group to work in his paddies. They give him his assigned day, but when that day comes they fail to show up. The family recognizes their absence as a form of punishment for the fact that the man's son is not among them, and is "taking it easy" in Bissau. The man, losing an important day of agricultural labor, puts pressure on his son to return home; when he does the youth group is contracted again, and this time it fulfills the commitment. Thus, in response to the challenges that increasing youth migration poses for both agricultural production and social solidarity, work groups have leveraged their crucial role in the cultivation cycle to compel their wayward members back to the rice paddies. In this way work associations have become an important mechanism for the social reproduction of Jola agricultural production, in some respects more so than the previous control exerted through the spirit shrines.

The Paradoxes of Custom: Uncoupling Production from Its Products

In many ways Jola incitements to and practices of "hard work" have become what David Parkin calls a "paradox of custom"—that is, "in the short term they seem to maintain the status quo of custom and authority and so are publicly approved, but in the long term they serve to mask the development of a fundamental cleavage" (1994:6). This cleavage separates the performance of hard work—and the social and ritual mechanisms that enforce it—from the realities of a changed physical and social landscape that make wet rice cultivation, as it is currently practiced, increasingly untenable as a way to provision Jola households.

The intrinsic characteristics of wet rice cultivation, the tightly woven and often tangled web of social relations and obligations involved in Jola agricultural practices, and the religious ideals with which they are linked reinforce one another and serve as powerful drivers of continuity. This gets expressed most clearly in Jola orientations to hard work, which refract across these economic, social, and religious realms. Jola villagers experienced and enacted this configuration as a kind of hegemonic lock; it was through the idiom of work that Jola villagers talked about being a member of this society. These notions of hard work as expressed through self-sufficiency, participation in a particular social organization of labor, and performative ritual evocations were the index of who was an accepted and acceptable member of their society. Like Ampa Bontai, one was essentially outside the social order if one was not participating in and reproducing this mode of work. Opting out of the wet rice labor regime required physically removing oneself from the spatial zone of rural Jola villages, and even then—as in the case of would-be urban migrants—pressure could be exerted to retrieve far-flung work associates at critical junctures in the agricultural cycle.

The particular process of wet rice cultivation, the social organization of labor, and the cultural ethic that values hard work were once elegant solutions to the challenging environment in which Jola have resided for centuries. But in the context of environmental change and the decreasing viability of Jola agricultural practices, these attitudes and practices around hard work become unyoked from the products they are meant to generate. Jola work was taken as given and fixed, rather than as a particular social form that arose under certain historical and environmental conditions. It was perfectly acceptable—even commendable—for Jola villagers to toil in the rice paddies for many months of the year with little or no yield in rice. As the constraints and limits in the natural world were more keenly felt, Jola were perhaps stressing the ways in which enactments of their work ethic and the moral obligations they reinforced might be all the more important. What was reproduced, though, was an increasingly detached social form—a commitment to arduous manual work—even while the conditions that it was meant to safeguard—the capacity of households to provision themselves—were disintegrating.

As noted in previous chapters, decreasing rainfall, increasing erosion, escalating urban migration, disadvantageous market conditions, and national political instability have coalesced to make it ever more difficult for Jola farmers to grow enough rice to sustain themselves. Although Jola residents in Guinea-Bissau acknowledged that their capacity to cultivate sufficient rice had diminished, their commitment to—and sometimes reinforcement of—their core agricultural practices signaled a growing separation of their work regime from the conditions of its emergence. In this way, Jola villagers in Guinea-Bissau were maintaining the very social forms that exacerbated—however unwittingly—their central problem.

*   *   *

In exploring these dynamics I have presented a rather uniform picture of the Jola work regime as a seemingly hypostasized system. I have minimized internal differences and emphasized conformity around these practices for the sake of highlighting the overriding dominance of this work ethic among the vast majority of Jola villagers. Although it is imperative to appreciate the normativity of these attitudes, they are neither completely consensual nor uniform in their practice. Even while villagers engaged in hard work and censured their neighbors and kin who attempted to resist it, they simultaneously, as we have seen, complained about such obligations. The appearance of consensus also masks differences along gender, generational, and other social distinctions, especially as changing conditions and new opportunities propelled individuals toward different trajectories and increased differentiation along these and other lines. Various competing activities— such as cashew farming, schooling, and wage work—did not replace the hard work of rice cultivation, but they increasingly took place alongside it. These parallel endeavors, as well as the increasing poverty of most Jola families, provided new opportunities and anxieties through which people were reassessing their beliefs and practices.

Hard work remains a central social value, but the widening chasm between Jola rice cultivation practices and the ability of villagers to provision their households, as well as escalating internal variation and the expansion of possible productive activities, all lead to a new set of questions and perspectives. As social relationships are reorganized on the ground and people continue to evaluate and reconsider this core ethic and practice in relation to new pressures and possibilities, key moments of ambivalence and fissures represented by variation are becoming sources of possible transformation. The next chapter explores another arena of Jola custom— their approach to knowledge in quotidian and ritual domains—and how it, too, is a form of "hard work" currently challenging (and being challenged by) Jola villagers' increasingly precarious circumstances.

CHAPTER 4

....

Cultivating Knowledge

If human sociation is conditioned by the capacity to speak,
it is shaped by the capacity to be silent.

—GEORG SIMMEL,
The Sociology of Georg Simmel

....

The Death of an *Ai*

During my second year of fieldwork, Esana's *ai* died. Ampa Kapeña had
been transported to the clinic in São Domingos when he had become very
ill, but fear over his dying away from Esana—an *ai* must always die in his
natal village—prompted several men to retrieve him from São Domingos
and bring him back to Esana, where his condition quickly worsened.

Jola burials are generally secret and secluded affairs (Davidson 2007).
When it comes to the death of an *ai*, many more layers of secrecy are
added. An *ai*'s death is supposed to remain secret, sometimes for many
months, with only *amangen-i* attending to aspects of his post-mortem
preparations and burial. Although everyone is buried in secret, with only
burial specialists (*batolhabu*) attending, an *ai*'s burial is conducted by only
the *batolhabu* among the *amangen-i*, and the location is kept secret from
the rest of the population. The top of the gravesite is made to look undisturbed; as one of my neighbors put it, "you would not even know if
you were lying on top of it and drinking palm wine." Furthermore, unlike
Jola buried in neighborhood-based cemeteries, *ai-i* are not disinterred.
Such practices correspond to the range of prohibitions surrounding *ai-i*—
that one may not see an *ai* eat or drink or urinate. These are all humaniz-
ing bodily acts that—when visible—diminish some of the *ai*'s elevated
spirituality. Death is, of course, the ultimate mark of mortality; hence the
secrecy and seclusion surrounding an *ai*'s death and burial.

When the previous *ai* in the neighboring village of Elia died no one was told for three months, not even his wives. When I inquired how it was possible to keep such a secret from his wives Ampa Badji insisted, "It's easy. When such a man gets sick, no relative is allowed to attend to him; only the *amangen-i* minister." Nho Keboral confirmed this later, but she was quick to note that things have changed in this respect. "Back then," she said, "we were not so savvy. If the *amangen-i* told you that the *ai* went on a trip, you would simply believe it. You would not question their authority. Now, everything has changed, and people tell even the smallest of secrets."

This was certainly the case with Ampa Kapeña's death, news of which spread rapidly around Jola-land the very next day. It was even announced on the newly installed community radio station that broadcast to Esana and several surrounding villages, although the announcer carefully avoided the same phrasing used in other death announcements, and instead told his listeners: "Children, your father has been lost." But even though Ampa Kapeña's death was not kept secret for the requisite amount of time my neighbors commented on this as a violation of norms, and gossiped about who messed up. Many of my interlocutors expressed concern that Esana's *amangen-i* had made an egregious error in divulging Ampa Kapeña's death so soon, and that they would be given a fine of cattle. They stressed that they should have taken Ampa Kapeña to another place when he returned from São Domingos, so they could care for him in seclusion; instead they left him at his house and when he died people found out immediately.

But events surrounding the funeral proceedings remained a mystery. No one knew whether there would be a funeral the following day or what the procedures would be regarding the normal funerary customs. Nho Keboral, who was related to Ampa Kapeña in such a way that it would normally require her to spend the night at his house (*harimanahu*), did not know whether she would be required or allowed to do so. As people drifted around the village after the news spread, they repeatedly confirmed that they did not know even the most basic aspects regarding his funeral— when the funeral would be held, whether there would be a corpse inquisition (*kasaabaku*), whether he had already been buried. "We're waiting for the *amangen-i* to tell us," they repeated. Ampa Badji summed up the state of affairs: "We are like women in this matter: we know nothing."

When the *amangen-i* finally did send messages regarding Ampa Kapeña's funeral procedures, people began to gather at the Bukekelil clearing (*hukulahu*), but they still did not know whether Ampa Kapeña's body would be there. By noon most of Esana's population of women was at the *hukulahu*; a small group of women were in the center of the clearing, pacing back and forth and chanting funeral songs, while a larger group of women remained seated in the shade of the cottonwood trees that framed the clearing. The typical platform structure for displaying the corpse had been erected, but instead of standing in the middle of the clearing, as it usually was, it was off to the side across from where the women were sitting and completely covered in cloths. It was impossible to see whether there was actually a body on the platform or not, but clearly the platform and cloths were there to suggest that Ampa Kapeña's body was hidden within.

In the early afternoon a procession of men entered and all of the women stood up. The procession was led by an elder man, followed by the paramount *ai* from Karuay and his second-in-command from Sukudjak, then a few *ai-i* from neighboring villages—Budgim, Edjaten, Djifunco—all of whom were dressed from head to toe in the signature red robes and hat of an *ai*. Ulandjebe (Esana's second *ai*) followed behind these *ai-i*, and behind him came two men carrying drums on which they beat a slow rhythm as the procession walked forward. A line of twenty or so men, most of them elders, finished off the procession. The men entered the *hukulahu* and circled it once, walking slowly and solemnly while the drums sounded. As they entered, the women greeted them with chants and dancing. Then the Karuay paramount *ai* and a few other *ai-i* sat on their stools at the foot of the cloth-covered platform.

Circular dancing commenced, and the funeral began to take on the rhythms by now so familiar to me, with the exception of the dignitaries present. People danced and sang funeral songs for a few hours. Later in the afternoon a man came to the group of seated women and told everyone to gather around the center. The drumming stopped and everyone made a close circle around the *ai-i* from Karuay and Sukudjak, who stood at the center of the clearing with Ulandjebe. Each spoke briefly, repeating and reinforcing what the previous one had said. They declared that residents of Esana could not work for six weeks and would have to bring enough palm wine to the *hukulahu* every day to quench the dancers' thirst and to provide for the appropriate posthumous ceremonies. After this pronouncement the dancing continued for a little while longer and then people began to disperse.

As I made my way home I discussed the *ai*'s proclamation with several people along the way. I asked a group of men affiliated with the Mission whether the work ban applied to their work within the Mission walls, and they told me that Mission work could continue as usual. The work ban included any kind of agricultural work in the forest or paddies (cf. Chapter Three). When I asked them what the reason for the work prohibition was, they insisted that they could not know the reason as they were not *amangen-i*. One responded, "Only *amangen-i* know such things, and everyone else simply obeys them. It is not for us to know the rationale." When I asked whether people would respect the work ban they said that some would and some would not, but that the Esana *amangen-i* would make a request and pay a fine of cattle in an attempt to reduce the work prohibition from six to four weeks. (This was ultimately an unsuccessful effort.)

At the time, what struck me most about the proceedings surrounding Ampa Kapeña's death was the widespread and general lack of knowledge about what would happen, both in terms of the immediate funerary rituals and of Esana's residents' work and lives and material circumstances in its aftermath. It was also a moment that crystallized the difference between certain kinds of anthropological and Jola ways of knowing. I was the only one asking questions; my Jola interlocutors, whom by now I knew well enough to discern when they really did not know something or when they were dissembling, were for the moment content to remain uninformed, waiting for the ritual authorities to provide them with information about the funeral and their own day-to-day activities for the following months.

Ampa Kapeña's death and funeral also manifested the complexity of Jola knowledge production and circulation. The many structures and performances surrounding his death—the cloth-enclosed platform that might or might not contain his body, the as-yet unrevealed obligations of his kin, the location (or even occurrence) of his burial, even the violated secret that he did, in fact, die—all served to uphold a "public secret" in Taussig's (1999) sense, a secret that is not really a secret. Everyone knows that an *ai* must eat, drink, urinate, and ultimately die. So why the pretense of secrecy around such acts? Other ethnographers have discussed the ways in which shrouding banal occurrences with mystery gives them potency (Lurhmann 1989), but the explanation that so much effort went into preserving or even fabricating a sense of mystery and divinity seemed too transparent. What was significant here was not the content of the concealed information itself—of course the *ai* urinates, and dies—nor the pretext for such content being, so to speak, secreted, but the energy, effort, and complexity of the secret-keeping process, as well as the real material consequences of the funerary rituals surrounding the *ai*'s death. In Esana's case, villagers were prohibited from engaging in agricultural work for six weeks. In other instances involving more important *ai-i* the work ban could last as long as three months, and if it coincided with the rainy season an entire village could lose its rice crop for the year.

What broke down in Ampa Kapeña's case was the secrecy shielding the fact of his death, the untimely exposure of this "public secret." And this violation was met with anxiety about the consequences, demonstrating that it was recognized as a breach of moral conduct around information flow. But the work ban itself was never questioned; even the failed effort to bargain it down to four weeks did not challenge the prohibition itself, just its duration. In the previous chapter I demonstrated how committed Jola are to hard work. So why would they cooperate in a work ban that not only seemed to contradict their core work ethic, but had significant detrimental material consequences in terms of their ability to sustain themselves? I have already suggested that the funerary work ban enacts the key difference between life and death: Jola lives are defined by work, so death is marked by a temporary cessation of that fundamental activity. Now, I want to go further and understand this within a system of knowledge production and information flow.

In this chapter I demonstrate that efforts to manage knowledge, erect structures that conceal information, and maintain control over who can know what and when is also a kind of work. But unlike the wet rice cultivation work regime that tends to level Jola villagers in socioeconomic and practical domains, the work involved in producing, delimiting, and circulating knowledge differentiates people along various axes, including gender, generation, lineage, and other kinds of status distinctions. Furthermore, unlike the natural world with its inherent limits of land and water, there are no natural limits to what one can do with information. This is an enormously productive realm of Jola social life. Amid material poverty, the abundance of cultural information in both quotidian and ritual realms makes some Jola villagers   perhaps all Jola villagers, to some extent—rich. And the range of ethnographic examples that follows suggests that this world of information is as important to till, cultivate, and harvest as the natural world.[1]

But first back to Ampa Kapeña's funeral. Knowledge about and decisions regarding the proceedings were kept closely guarded by a small group of elders, and everyone else in Esana was kept in ignorance. They did not ask about any matter related to the funeral itself or how it might impact their own lives, especially regarding the work ban; they waited for the elders' proclamation. With reference to the untimely disclosure of Ampa Kapeña's death, Nho Keboral's comment is important to unpack. "Back then," Nho Keboral said, "we were not so savvy. If the *amangen-i* told you that the *ai* went on a trip, you would simply believe it." On the face of it, this seems to imply an association between secrecy and naïveté; that is, contrary to a previous era modern Jola could not be so easily duped. But Nho Keboral's comment did not so much index the "wisening up" of the lay population that made such secrets no longer tenable as the need to respond to changed conditions for complicity. The leakage of information that would, "back then," have been kept under close wraps reveals the necessary joint nature of maintaining "public secrets," and the orchestration involved in upholding such secrets is not static. This was less a matter of belief and more an instance of "ritual collusion" (Moore 1976) that had been ruptured and needed repair.

Controlling Knowledge: "Jola Have Lots of Secrets"

One of the most persistent and stereotypical characterizations of agrarian peoples pertains to their communicative restraint, often glossed as secrecy (Bellman 1984; Piot 1993; Richards 1985). Jola are no exception to this portrayal and might even represent an extreme. "Jola have lots of secrets," people in Bissau would tell me just as frequently as they observed that "Jola work hard." Even the scant ethnographic accounts from Portuguese colonial officials stated that Jola were probably the most closed and guarded of Guinean ethnic groups and that plumbing the depths of their world was no easy task (Lehmann de Almeida 1955; Taborda 1950a, 1950b). And, just as they acknowledged their work ethic, Jola themselves voiced such characterizations. Many villagers told me, "We Jola have lots of secrets."

When my interlocutors told me that "Jola have many secrets," they generally collapsed at least three different kinds of secrecy into one category. First, the flow of information and access to certain kinds of knowledge is highly regulated. That is, women and men know different things and are prohibited from knowing each other's "secrets." Also, information and esoteric knowledge about history, ritual, and various aspects of religious practice is circumscribed by those who have either been born with or earned the right to know such secrets.

Second, Jola have secret powers and capacities that reside in the supernatural realm, such as shape-shifting and trading souls. Such assertions were often offered with a contradictory mix of respect and denigration that typically textured Guineans' perceptions of the more "traditional," "tribal," and "authentic"—though simultaneously "backwards" and "superstitious"—members of their society. Colonial and postcolonial characterizations of Jola as both "secretive" and "resistant to change" generally came in the same breath, as if the very practice of secrecy—particularly in the form of supernatural beliefs and practices—posed an obstacle to modern rationality and progress (Lehmann de Almeida

1955; Taborda 1950b).[2] As I will elaborate later in this chapter, such an assumed divergence between secrecy and modernity did not only apply to practices such as shape-shifting, but also to the more quotidian ways in which secrecy was deployed around concealing possessions and various domains of knowledge.

Third, Jola are secretive people in the sense of being reserved and restrained in their interactions and not revealing more than what is absolutely necessary (and usually dissembling even that) in a given encounter. As one resident in Esana—a Mandinka soldier stationed at the army barracks—put it: "Almost everything is kept secret. Even if you ask someone, 'Do you know Joanna?' and they definitely know Joanna, they will respond, 'No, I don't know Joanna.'"

Contemporary ethnographers of the Jola and neighboring groups have richly explored various aspects of secrecy. Baum (1999) considers secrecy in relation to Jola ideas about history and esoteric knowledge within their system of spirit shrines, and the ways in which knowledge of a supernatural and/or ritual nature is closely guarded by those who have rights to it. Schloss's (1988) ethnography of the neighboring Ehing touches on secrecy in the realm of spirit shrines. Geschiere and van der Klei (1988) consider how the Jola "obsession with secrecy" relates to political authority and the emergence of the Casamance separatist movement. Both Mark's (1992) study of Jola-Fogny male initiation and de Jong's (2008) ethnography of Jola masquerades cover many aspects of secrecy in male initiation (bukutabu) practices. As a complement to this focus on male initiation, van Tilburg's (1998) more humanistic approach discusses the ways in which secrecy surrounds pregnancy and childbirth, not just from men but among women. Her own experience as a pregnant fieldworker in a Senegalese Jola village led her, in a complicated and ultimately tragic way, to understand the depth and layers of secrecy enveloping reproductive matters. My immersion among Guinean Jola largely confirms these ethnographers' discussions of circumscribed information in terms of history, specialized knowledge, and ritual. Even more, in the first flush of fieldwork, secrecy seemed to texture most aspects of Jola social life; there was, simply put, a pervading ethos of secrecy among Jola villagers with each other and with outsiders.

Studying Secrets

Secrecy is an intrinsically difficult topic for ethnography: how does one study secrets if they are just that? Anthropologists have long struggled with the methodological, political, and ethical challenges posed by this subject matter. One approach has been to view secret knowledge as a key to indigenous worldviews, which has led some ethnographers to focus on uncovering and representing secret content, usually in formalized ritual domains. The quest for "secret knowledge" operates at both theoretical and methodological planes; not only would a cultural group's secrets explain their "way of being," but the very process of uncovering them would demonstrate an ethnographer's prowess at getting beyond the surface and exposing the supposed core of a culture.

Anthropologists critical of this approach on moral and methodological grounds have questioned ethnographers' right to expose—or even ask about—information deemed by their informants as not appropriate for public consumption, as well as probing the presupposition that really important "cultural stuff" necessarily lies concealed in secret or esoteric knowledge. Gable (1997), for example, provides a particularly compelling critique of this penetrative aspect of the ethnographic endeavor. He discusses how ethnographic narrative generally follows the dumbfounded or perplexed ethnographer as he or she probes and prods his or her way into becoming the ethnographer with insights into the workings of indigenous worldviews. Not only does this approach place too much emphasis on unquestioned ethnographic authority (Clifford 1988), but it assumes that "the secret" of a given society's inner workings requires digging deep. Perhaps what seems hidden and secret to the ethnographer is actually the most obvious thing to his or her interlocutors:

> It is all too easy for the ethnographer to project his or her initial befuddlement and emerging understanding as a model for the surface and depth of an indigenous culture. Fieldwork may feel like a kind of penetration, but crucial cultural truths are as likely to be obvious as hidden or esoteric (Gable 1997:227).

Responding to these critiques, as well as to anthropology's increasing interest in questions of process and power, contemporary ethnographic approaches to secrecy have largely taken their cue from Simmel (1950) by shifting from an emphasis on content (the secret itself) to form (the dynamics of concealing and revealing information). Simmel's seminal essay suggests that what is significant about secrecy as a sociological technique is the way information is shared or not shared in a given society. The content of the secret is secondary, or perhaps even irrelevant; it gains value *because* it is secret, rather than being secret because it is valuable. What ensues from this proposition is an examination of the differentiating power of secrecy independent of its specific content. The focus on form over content has spawned a great deal of literature that examines the dynamics of concealing and revealing information in various contexts (Barth 1975; Lurhmann 1989; Ottenberg 1989) as well as analyses that stress secrecy as a social form imbricated in sets of power relationships (Bellman 1984; Murphy 1981, 1998; Taussig 1999).

In my own case, I did not go to Guinea-Bissau to study Jola secrets, or even the dynamics of Jola secrecy. In fact, I was particularly concerned to distance myself from such a problematic approach. When my interlocutors—both Jola and non-Jola—regularly told me that "Jola have lots of secrets," I always responded by expressing my disinterest in—and respect for—areas of cultural content they deemed secret. I insisted (to myself and others) that I was not interested in prying, in digging for secret cultural knowledge through pesky questions or sneaky methods of selective self-disclosure and participation, of conducting penetrative ethnography.

While my self-presentation was quite sincere, I soon found out how naïve such a stance was. I quickly ascertained the contours of gendered domains of knowledge and secrecy, as well as the basic rules governing access to—or silence around—esoteric and religious knowledge and practice. I learned that only certain people were privy to certain kinds of knowledge, and to know something not within one's purview was a breach of moral conduct and potentially dangerous. But beyond gendered domains of secrecy and arenas of religious-esoteric knowledge, Jola were guarded (with outsiders and with each other) about even the most seemingly mundane information. Secrecy regarding one's movements, possessions, and opinions seemed to be embedded in almost every instance of quotidian social interaction. There was often a deliberate effort to shroud even the most seemingly pedestrian matters. For Jola, the idiom of secrecy was very much on the surface, was claimed daily by villagers, and was staked out—both internally and externally—as a form of ethnic distinction. But, although secrecy seems to have become a reified marker of Jolaness, the performance of this disposition toward dissembling for its own sake was not the primary driver of these dynamics. As I discuss later in the chapter, the reasons for maintaining—and even reinforcing—such practices from a Jola perspective were less a matter of protecting an aspect of their endangered cultural patrimony than they were about their understanding of the leakages and links among the supernatural, social, and natural spheres.

My experience during an old man's funeral made me more aware of the impossibility of ignoring secrecy as a central aspect of Jola social life. During this funeral I was temporarily "adopted" into a small cohort of dancers. I had observed these small groups who took on special roles during a funeral, often dancing in the opposite direction as the long line of dancers around the circular clearing and engaging in antics and frivolity, especially at the funerals of old men and women. I had learned that the groups were made up of the cohort of men and women who had declared their brides (or been declared as brides, in the women's case) at the same time. The men and women (those who declared and those who were declared) remain a cohort (*buyabu*) even if the marriages end. They formed a tight-knit social group on certain ritual occasions, and the women often wore a distinguishing article of clothing, like matching cloth skirts or the same color cloth tie around their waists. During this particular funeral I was swept up into a *buyabu*, given a matching cloth tie for my waist, and taken everywhere they went for the day. At one point one of the *buyabu* members told me, "Now that you are part of us, you will learn all the secrets of our '*buyabu*.' We will tell you everything." Each time he or one of the other members told me a "secret," they did so with a conspiratorial bearing and a great deal of gravity in their tone. But the content, such as what bound them together as a buyabu, was hardly a secret. Each time one of them offered an "ah-ha" explanation to either a question I asked or an unsolicited piece of information I felt disappointed that I had not learned anything new at all, or that the "big secret" they were revealing was completely banal. What I missed at the time was that the content of the secret was irrelevant; it was the performance surrounding its concealment and revelation that was significant. Following Simmel, I re-oriented my thinking about secrecy not as a body of facts I was desperately trying to avoid but as a process of social interaction inextricably intertwined with the very questions animating my larger research goals.

This realization signaled my own shift in understanding that it was not "the secret" that I was after (or, rather, trying to avoid being after), because "the secret" itself would reveal nothing new. Of course the *ai* dies, and of course this kind of *buyabu* is made up of contemporaneously declared brides and their spouses. The fact that such effort went into making these prosaic facts secrets was the fact worth pursuing. Who could know such things? When and how could they access this information? How was such knowledge revealed? In this sense, neither penetrative ethnography nor the protesting-too-much stance against it was a useful methodological guidepost. The possibility that there might not be any *there* there—that the *ai* might not be within the cloth covered platform, or the *buyabu's* supposed secrets might be quite commonplace—makes a wild goose chase out of penetrative ethnography.

Beyond the emphasis on form over content there is another aspect of the secret that has implications for its epistemology: its inevitable disclosure. Simmel discussed the secret as "a form which constantly receives and releases its contents . . . the secret is full of the consciousness that it *can* be betrayed" (Simmel 1950:333, 335, emphasis in original). In ethnography, this is often discussed in terms of formal structures or pivotal moments of revelation, such as initiation (Kratz 1990; La Fontaine 1985; Ottenberg 1989). But I also found that there is an informal, spontaneous desire to reveal. Interestingly, my explicit insistence that I was not concerned with secrets *per se* opened up the possibility for people to share with me—not the esoteric knowledge of the spirit shrines, but their own stories and anxieties and interpretations. This was unintentionally facilitated by establishing a residence separate from my adoptive family's house; a private space in which my friends and neighbors could visit and talk—increasingly freely— out of earshot of their kin and neighbors. Jola customary behavior around secrecy, especially in quotidian social interaction, is enmeshed within the tangled social relations of village life. As an outsider I became an impartial repository of information generally kept close when among kin and neighbors. As I developed different kinds of relationships with residents in Esana and became more aware of the multiple threads—beyond obvious ones like kinship—that textured their relationships with each other, I began to observe various levels of sharing and withholding information depending on the context and composition of each gathering. I became better at discerning when people were being guarded or dissembling—either with me or others—and more adept at recognizing subtle forms of managing the flow of information.[3]

Moreover, what was continually glossed as secrecy—by Jola and their observers—started to overflow this conceptual category. Secrecy as a term is neither big enough nor precise enough to adequately contain all of the attitudes, behaviors, and examples generally lumped under its rubric. Nor is it robust enough for discussing the consequences these different approaches to knowledge and communication have within the current context of changing internal conditions and the potential (or even hypothetical) arrival of external change-agents. Thus, continuing the analytic shift from *content* (the secret itself) to *form* (the dynamics of concealing and revealing information), I consider the processes of producing, controlling, and transferring knowledge among Jola villagers in Guinea-Bissau.

What follows is an attempt to understand Jola communicative strategies as they are manifest in both formal and informal arenas and to consider what bearing these have on the key questions in this book. I want to distinguish two kinds of knowledge here: The example of Ampa Kapeña's death touches on *ritual* knowledge and the ways in which information flow is wrapped up in explicit cultural forms like funerals, initiations, and spirit shrine ceremonies. Ritual secrecy organizes access to religious and esoteric knowledge along gendered, generational, and lineage lines. The other category of knowledge, which I discuss first, I call *interactional*. It is at play in everyday forms of social intercourse around consumption, possession, and action. Ultimately, however, the codes of the former leak into the latter, and quotidian communicative practices bear the mark of formal principles regarding religious knowledge (see Bellman 1984).

Interactional Knowledge: Concealing Actions and Possessions

"Ukai Beh?"

During a certain phase of fieldwork I found myself reluctant to go outside the confines of my own or my host family's house, even on a short walk around the village. When I did venture out, I had to gear myself up for the inevitable barrage of seemingly innocuous questions that people would yell at me as I walked past their verandas. After the appropriate age-based greeting, my interlocutors would ask "*Ukai beh?*"[4] (Where are you going?), followed quickly by "*Ubei bukayemih?*" (Where are you coming from?). Simple and apparently friendly questions, but by the time I had walked a hundred yards I had answered them many, many times and always felt poked and prodded and scrutinized a bit too closely for comfort. I usually provided a brief response, such as "*Inje mikai beh butat*" (I'm going to the forest) or "*Inje mikai beh huyungorahu*" (I'm going for a walk). Later, I found that Jola typically provided even more obtuse responses to such inquiries. I observed my neighbors field the same questions with "*Mikai beubeh*" (I'm going over there), not indicating where, in particular, with any further words or gestures. Or, even more vague, "*Inje muh*" (Here I am). And after having found out nothing from their initial inquiry people would rarely pry further. A question had been asked, it had been answered with no real information, and everyone seemed satisfied with the exchange.

Other tactics involved avoiding the observing eyes and ears altogether. Early in my second year of fieldwork, one of the pregnant members of my women's work association was approaching her due date. She was expecting her eighth child, and she had always experienced very difficult births. She was afraid that she would die in childbirth if she delivered in the village, and she asked me if I would take her to Ziguinchor, across the

Senegalese border, so she could give birth in a hospital with better medical conditions than those available in Guinea-Bissau. I made arrangements with her to meet at my house at mid-morning, but when I woke at dawn on the morning we were to leave, I found her on my back veranda. She said she knew we were not leaving for several hours, but she had left her house early, before dawn, and come to hide out at my house and wait. If she left her house with a bag when people were already awake, they would ask her where she was going. "Ukai beh?" they would demand. "You see," she explained to me, "people here are tiresome. They ask and ask and ask."

In a similar occurrence, I agreed to take Nho Keboral and a few other women to Karuay the next time I visited the paramount *ai* there. They were eager to cross the Senegalese border at the river in Sukudjak to sell their palm oil, and it was a long journey from Esana to Karuay, especially when carrying heavy jerry-cans. When we made arrangements to go, Nho Keboral suggested that instead of meeting at my house, they would walk ahead past the village and wait near Ampa Badji's forest grove. When I passed there in the car, I could pick them up. She said that if people saw them getting in the car at my house, they would ask where they were going, ("Jikai beh?") and she did not want to have to explain. "You see, Joanna, people here wear you out. They want to know where you're going, for what reason, and so on and so on. Better that we leave them behind here."

As many ways as Jola have to "ask and ask and ask," there are methods to counter or avoid such attempts.[5] The preceding examples demonstrate the lengths to which villagers go in order to avoid the inevitable and predictable surveillance of their own neighbors. But why bother? Why not reveal where one is going or what one is doing in a straightforward manner? Why all the effort to evade, dissemble, and conceal?

First, these tactics provide a sense of insulation in the face of constant observability. To some extent, they can be understood as "simply a way to preserve a sense of autonomy or privacy in the close world of the village" (Gable 1997:217). Such interactional dynamics have been documented and accounted for in a similar way by others studying contexts in which one's every move can be seen by those in the immediate vicinity (Coser 1962, 1979; Pitt-Rivers 1971). Providing evasive or empty responses about such matters as where one is going or what one is doing can be partly understood, then, as a response to the intrusive aspects of living in a fishbowl.

Beyond the drive to maintain some measure of privacy for its own sake, these interactions encode a particular type of power relationship. Not a Weberian coercive power over others, but a productive kind of power that has the effect of both maintaining a connection between individuals and making manifest their very autonomy. In the seemingly fruitless structure of greetings, what gets expressed is a kind—or, as Michael Jackson (2013) would have it, a *sense*—of agency. It would not be appropriate to follow an *"Ukai beh"* with silence; there is a script that one follows, even if it seems to lead nowhere. *"Ukai beh"* becomes an invitation to assert one's power to withhold, to conceal where one is going and where one has been. It is precisely because Jola villagers are so enmeshed with one another in the small and tightly woven world of village life that dissembling and evasion become meaningful forms of social interaction. As Fabian contends, "Secrecy, far from being non-communication, is a cultural practice of communication" (Fabian 1991:184). The daily repeated performance of *"Ukai beh"* and *"Inje muh"* acknowledges that people have a kind of power not only to decide where they are going but whether or not to reveal or conceal that information.

Likewise, in higher stakes moments, concealing one's actions and movements also enables individuals to navigate around the more oppressive structures of surveillance, particularly when their actions might be judged as non-normative or suspected as a breach of conduct. Obtaining special medical care in the context of childbirth is not an outright violation of Jola norms, but it is certainly grist for the gossip mill, and gossip, in turn, could lead to leveling disciplinary measures.

Beyond *"Ukai beh,"* which, as described earlier, does not actually lead to any further knowledge, Jola do not engage in direct questioning into people's lives or about any specific body of knowledge. Regarding religious or ritual practice, Jola do not ask *amangen-i* or others with ritual authority how and why certain practices are observed. When I asked such questions—like how one became a corpse carrier at funeral divinations (*kasaabaku*), or why *ai-i* wear red—lay people not only did not know, but most had never thought to ask those who might.[6] Beyond ritual and religious matters, Jola do not tend to acquire knowledge through direct questions, but through observation and first-hand experience.[7] My own process of learning how to harvest rice and transplant rice seedlings came through quick demonstration and then practice, and I sensed my work associates' irritability when I tried to ask questions about how best to cut the rice stalks or punch the delicate seedlings into the mud.

This pattern points to an important distinction in epistemological assumptions. When we ask, we assume there is an answer and that we have rights to it. But for Jola, neither of these principles can be assumed. Not only are certain kinds of knowledge restricted in terms of who can and cannot access it, but Jola assume an essential unknowability to some things. Such a view is encoded in the Jola word for their supreme deity—*Emitaï*—the root of which is a condensed form of "*irit*,"—which means "that which cannot be known."

As my own sensibilities regarding appropriate decorum meshed with those of my Jola friends and neighbors, I felt ever more awkward and self-conscious about asking pointed questions. Like many ethnographers, I had framed my objectives for residing in Jola-land as a search for knowledge. I repeated to my interlocutors that I was there to learn—about language, culture, history, daily reality, current conditions, and so forth. But learning among Jola is not primarily a process of asking questions. My approach to learning about these and other arenas of Jola social life by asking questions felt increasingly at variance with my acculturation into Jola customary behavior.

Beyond "*ukai beh*," then, direct questions are not appropriate, whether regarding religious practice, basic household or agricultural tasks, or other people's lives. Regarding this last realm people are particularly concerned with not asking about—or displaying—material conditions.

Out of Sight

Paulo, the newly arrived Protestant evangelical missionary in the village, once made the mistake of walking on the main road from his house at one end of the village to the resurrected baking ovens at the other end of the village. He bought six loaves of bread for his family, but by the time he reached his home again, he had only half of one loaf left and he looked bewildered. He had carried the loaves in plain sight and everyone he passed along the way asked for a piece of bread. He quickly learned to carry his purchases concealed in a bag or backpack. People would still glare at it, trying to divine its contents, but—just as in their attempts to divine a passer-by's destination—they would not pry further.

No one buys anything at the small shops in Jola villages without putting it in a bag, preferably a dark one. One of the most universally coveted objects among rural Jola is a black, opaque plastic bag, used in the central market in Bissau and much preferred over the more ubiquitous but transparent blue striped plastic bags. Once obtained, these flimsy bags are treated with great care, as they can be used to conceal any objects one might need to transport around the village. Even better than a bag, many people hide items in their shirt or other clothing. Many times, older men came to my house and sat on the back porch, seemingly carrying nothing. Then they would reach deep inside their long shorts and extract a liter of palm wine, or take off their hat and uncover a leaf of tobacco, or search in the recesses of their robe and pull out a papaya. Once, I gave one of the members of my women's work association a t-shirt she had asked for. Hearing other people approach, she quickly folded it into a tight bundle and tucked it under her cloth wrap skirt.

Early in my stay, I was instructed on basic norms of privacy, such as yelling out "*kon kon kon*" when approaching someone's house, to let them know well in advance that someone was coming. Or, when approaching anyone talking in the dark, always saying "*Inje muh*" (Here I am) to warn the talking people that someone is nearby and within earshot and if they are saying something private, they should stop. Likewise, in the forest, when approaching someone's grove where men sit and drink and talk under the sheltering fronds of oil palm trees, one always announces oneself with "*Inje muh*" from a reasonable distance. Such norms indicate a respect for privacy and reveal the complicity involved in acts of secreting objects or information from intruding eyes and ears by announcing one's imminent arrival. I saw people in Jola villages exhibit these behaviors regularly, but of course I also saw them being violated.

Jola household organization also reflects similar concerns. Rice, for example, is stored in a separate room in one's house, out of visitors' view.[8] Although I lived in a Jola village for more than two years and ate at my adoptive family's house every day, I never saw the inside of the granary, nor did I see anyone else in the household enter it besides Nho Keboral. The only household objects on public view are those possessions that everyone has—straw baskets, worn-out eating bowls, well-used aluminum pots, a *kandaabaku* (belt for climbing palm trees to tap wine), and a *bujandabu* propped up in the rafters. Anything besides these common objects that members of a household might possess is kept out of sight.

Once, while sitting on Ampa Badji's veranda, I had a discussion with him about different books we had read. Having completed fourth grade, Ampa Badji was one of the few literate Jola residents in Esana, and he was eager to discuss his love of reading. He said he had collected many books from his days as a teacher in Canchungo. Later that night, when we were behind closed doors, he disappeared into the room he shared with Nho Keboral and their youngest son and brought out a 50-kilo rice sack filled with his books, most of them termite-ridden Portuguese translations of American westerns. We were looking through them when we heard someone approach with a "*kon kon kon*." Ampa Badji rapidly put the books back in the sack and brought them to the interior room before the visitor entered. On another occasion I offered to give Ampa Badji a suitcase for his books, to help protect them a bit from the ubiquitous destructive trio of termites, dust, and mold. He said he would come to my house, just around the corner, to pick it up, which he did late at night, when no one would see him. Villagers regularly used the cover of darkness—even better than an opaque plastic bag—to achieve the closest thing to invisibility when transporting objects to and from their homes. One of the women from my work association came deep in the night to collect two large logs—leftover from repairs to my house—that she had asked for. Once, I went with Nho Keboral on a midnight errand to the other end of the village to one of Ampa Badji's relative's houses where we fetched a pig that they were giving her to raise. It was pitch black outside, and I had to navigate carefully not to trip over tree stumps and other obstacles on the path. But by that time I knew it would have been unheard of to fetch the pig during daylight hours, when everyone would see Nho Keboral walking all the way across Esana with a new pig.

One of the clearest examples of this attitude came very early in my stay in Esana. During my first few weeks, I discussed with Ampa Badji and Nho Keboral how I could best contribute to their household in order to compensate them for feeding me every night. I offered to pay them a monthly sum and buy a sack of rice each month. Discussions such as these take several days (weeks in this case), and I learned not to bring it up when neighbors or other kin were visiting the house. Finally, Nho Keboral and I were walking to the forest one day and she said—once we were out of earshot of anyone—that she and Ampa Badji had discussed the matter and decided that it would be better if, instead of arranging for the sack of rice, I just gave them the money that I would have spent on the rice. I agreed, of course, and Nho Keboral went on to explain that they did not want people to see me bringing a sack of rice to their house every month. People would think they were better off, she said. It was safer to just give them the money; no one else needed to know about it, and they would arrange for the extra rice.

In a similar vein, when a neighbor once stayed for dinner at Ampa Badji's house he commented that he never ate so well at his own home. Nho Keboral responded that this was unusual fare for them too. We were, in fact, eating the same food as always: rice with *bagiche* (cooked hibiscus leaves). But Nho Keboral took pains to express that we were eating lavishly that night. She said: "Ask Joanna. She eats here every night. She sees our poverty." I nodded, playing my part as expected. Nho Keboral was concerned, again, about her guest reporting to others that her household was better off than others, a clear example of "keeping behind the Joneses" (Gable 1997:215).

Again, why all this effort to conceal? Just as Jola develop evasive responses and tactics to avoid the omnipresent surveillance of their neighbors, so too do they have imaginative ways to skirt the obligation to share. If you possess an item—especially food—in plain sight, it is quite appropriate for others to ask you for a piece, and it would be rude to deny them. Children are brought up to offer whatever they happen to have to those in their immediate vicinity. The only way around this imperative to share is to remove such objects from view by concealing them in a bag, a hat, or the recesses of a house. If you are foolish enough, like Paulo the missionary, to show too much there are consequences.

Some Jola found the imperative to share so oppressive that they removed themselves entirely from the context of such norms. I once met a young Jola man from Caton—an outlying Jola village—who was making a living as a fisherman in another part of the country. When I asked him why he left the fish-abundant waters of Jola-land, he said he could never get anywhere if he fished in his natal land. "Every time I would return from a day of fishing, I would walk through the village and my fish would disappear. I'd have to give some to this person and that person and this person, and soon enough I had no fish to sell or even eat. No, I had to get away. We Jola, we make it so difficult."

Such tactics for hiding possessions are, of course, quite common in contexts where one is not only obliged to share whatever one has, but material wealth—and a loaf of bread or a t-shirt certainly count as material wealth in Jola villages—arouses enmity or suspicion among one's neighbors. Not only do methods of concealment help protect the object from being consumed by others, but they also protect the possessor from jealousy-inspired actions by those who seek to undercut others' wealth. And, in a related logic, they protect the possessor from accusations that they acquired the object in some ill-gotten way. Jola concern with concealing possessions, then, seems to fit within the general framework of "nightmare egalitarianism" (P. Bohannan 1963; L. Bohannan 1964; Foster 1965). Such views contend that in egalitarian societies,

> People share equally in material poverty. Or, if some are richer than others, they hide their good fortune. . . . Usually, the implication is that the "less prosperous" are motivated by a fundamental belief that the equality of conditions (as opposed to the equality of opportunity) is a moral good. To be rich is to be morally reprehensible (Gable 1997:215).

Gable's (1997) study of the Manjaco—an ethnic group just south of Jola-land in Guinea-Bissau—effectively pokes a hole in the logic of nightmare egalitarianism by demonstrating that it is not the fear of having something that motivates Manjaco secrecy, but the fear of being found to have nothing worth inciting jealousy. Gable's essay—a parallel critique of nightmare egalitarianism and ethnographic authority—is worth exploring in some depth. Just as I assumed in the case of Jola behavior, Gable at first saw Manjaco secrecy around possessions conforming to conventional anthropological wisdom regarding egalitarian societies. That is, it is a dangerous prospect to reveal or be public about one's possessions because of either inciting envy—and hence repercussions in the form of witchcraft—by others who have less, or by being accused of using witchcraft oneself to acquire such possessions. This, at least, is what Gable assumed was going on in the Manjaco village in which he observed his neighbors concealing their possessions. But it gradually dawned on him that this motive was actually a façade, and, from a Manjaco standpoint, it was better for one to be assumed to have power and possessions—even if that might attract envy—than for it to be revealed that one had nothing. Thus, older men seemingly concealing objects in their ever-present satchels actually had empty satchels. It was better, according to Gable, to seem to have something worth concealing than to be found to have nothing at all.

> For much of the time I operated under the assumption that the Manjaco were concerned with hiding the full sack, the full granary, the full bottle. . . . It was not until late in my stay that I came to believe that "hiding" or "secreting" had as much to do with concealing an empty bottle as it did with hiding a full one. While it may be true that Manjaco inhabit a world of limited goods where one person's gain must be paid by another's loss, many of them . . . are nevertheless more afraid of appearing unworthy of envy than they are afraid of being accused of injuring others to further their own interests. It is the empty sack or granary, not the full sack or granary, that they wish most to conceal (Gable 1997:227).

Gable came to understand that, even in a supposedly egalitarian society, individuals often aspire to have the upper hand—to be the winner—even at others' expense. His argument corrects long-standing anthropological representations of egalitarian societies that do not account for the "will-to-power" of their individual members. Gable's understanding of the particular features of Manjaco secrecy challenges a depiction of egalitarianism devoid of this image of the individual who admires—and strives to be, or at least appear to be—the one who has power and possessions rather than hiding this.[9]

In the Jola case, I would not go as far as Gable to assert that Jola are more concerned with hiding what they do *not* have than what they have. Some aspects of Jola behavior and communicative practice genuinely are caught up in a "keeping behind the Joneses" dynamic, and, at least as Jola experience them, their actions and interactions are very much oriented around concealing what they do, in fact, have and know. But the link between *possession*—whether of information or goods, and even if performed as an absence—and *power* in the context of a so-called egalitarian society is instructive in the Jola case.

The relationship between Jola work ethic and modes of concealing information and material goods is revealing here. In the previous chapter I demonstrated how Jola maintain a particular work regime and sanction those individuals who deviate from long-established wet rice cultivation practices. Jola work is public and visible and can be maintained through sanctions and admonishments that are likewise public and visible. Concealment as a pervasive mode of social interaction provides a counterpoint to the conformity demanded by the work regime and enables a measure of autonomy and differentiation. The Jola wet rice cultivation regime allows people to uphold the appearance that everyone does and has the same things. Carefully scripted modes of dissembling and concealing also protect the image and idiom of equality, but they simultaneously provide a sphere for individuals to store up a little extra and do or be something a little different. Concealment preserves the appearance of an egalitarian society, while at the same time providing an arena for individual variation. In a society generally emphasizing conformity, keeping one's opinions and actions under wraps enables individuals to gain some measure of autonomy without openly disputing the smooth veneer of public consensus. It allows for differentiation—or even for accumulation, as we will see in the more formal domains of ritual—without disrupting the outward display of equality.

Furthermore, like the evasive responses to "*Ukai beh*," concealing possessions affirms one's power to keep a secret, and, hence, provides a modicum of agency and autonomy within the structures that generally require redistribution. It is worth emphasizing that all the effort to conceal—shrouding objects in dark bags and under dark skies, insisting on material poverty, and so forth—does not actually obscure the understanding that people buy things in shops and raise pigs and maybe even give birth across the border. This is neither about the content of what is being concealed nor about maintaining the illusion that such "secrets" are in fact quite public. Rather, these dynamics indicate a complicity in and deference to a particular scheme of information flow. Extending Sally Falk Moore's (1976) concept of "ritual collusion," this is not a matter of belief but is a kind of interactional collusion.

The experience of Jola widows further elucidates this economy of information and sheds more light on the inadequacy of the concept of nightmare egalitarianism. Despite the large proportion of widows in Jola villages, widows remain a largely invisible and silent population.[10] Because of Jola land tenure arrangements, widows have no direct access to either paddy or forest land, and even those with young children are in extremely vulnerable positions regarding their livelihood. Once a deceased husband's rice paddies are re-absorbed into his lineage his widow is reduced to borrowing her kin's unused paddies, a fragile and tenuous arrangement at best. If she does not have grown sons or benevolent uncles who will hoe the paddy for her, she will wield the heavy fulcrum shovel herself and perform what is considered quintessentially male labor. If she cannot borrow paddy, she begs for rice. Sometimes her grown children provide her with a small quantity of rice, sometimes neighbors take pity on her and send over some rice. But, in the past several years, bad harvests make it extremely difficult for anyone to be generous. When the average members of the population are anxious about having enough rice to feed themselves and their families, widows are left even more on the margins.

But in my many discussions with widows they stressed to me that they do not talk with others, even other widows, about their hardships and struggle to survive. After getting to know several widows independently and becoming increasingly aware of and concerned about their extreme conditions, I asked one widow with several young children in her household whether she spoke to other widows about their similar situation and whether she thought about joining them together to collectively address their common problems. She looked at me blankly. I tried to explain that there were many women who were dealing with the same problems— women whose husbands had died, who had no access to land, who struggled to feed themselves and their children. I asked if they talked about such things, perhaps when visiting each other or when attending the same event, like a funeral. Her response was unequivocal: "We do not talk about such things. . . . For us, it is a secret." "Poverty is a secret?" I asked. "Yes," she responded. "For you to tell someone, 'Today I don't have this or that,' he'll listen to you, but won't give you anything. That's why, in this sense, I stay alone with this poverty. That's why I don't tell anyone."

What is revealing about the foregoing examples and the predicament of widows is that, for Jola, concealing possessions is not about celebrating poverty, as nightmare egalitarianism would have it, but about performing a kind of equality in self-sustenance. By displaying only objects that everyone else also has and secreting those that might distinguish them, Jola perform a lack of difference in the material world. The ideal is to be—or at least to create the image that one is—in a middle zone of self-sustenance. If one rises above this level, diffuse leveling sanctions come into play. Likewise, if—like widows—one falls below, the consequences are mockery and shame. Displaying or performing poverty is kept very much within the realms of expected and normative material conditions. But widows fall out of this norm. They are silent about their particular kind of poverty because speaking of it would expose the shameful fact that they are unable to sustain themselves. And they are invisible to their kin and neighbors because—as a consequence of their extreme conditions—they have become non-persons.[11]

Simmel's seminal essay on the sociological character of secrecy suggests that secrecy offers "the possibility of a second world alongside the manifest world" (Simmel 1950:330). This insight has typically been applied to realms of magic, esoteric knowledge, and secret societies (see especially Bellman 1984; Lurhmann 1989; Murphy 1980; Zahan 1979), but it is equally apt in the domain of material possessions and quotidian acts of dissembling and concealing. In the manifest Jola world, everyone conforms and has the same possessions. In this second world, people have and know different things. This "secret" world of differentiated individuals exists in a complicated but ultimately convenient way alongside the manifest world of equality, conformity, and consensus. This is even more clearly the case in the formal realms of gender-based knowledge and rites of initiation. And, as Simmel notes, "the latter is decisively influenced by the former" (Simmel 1950:330); that is, the codes that govern the formal world of ritual knowledge leak into the everyday world of concealment and silence.

Ritual Knowledge

Gendered and Generational Spheres of Information and Influence

In addition to the ways silence and dissembling around a range of quotidian interactions serve to differentiate individuals while maintaining the appearance of conformity, more formalized arenas of knowledge and secrecy differentiate Jola in terms of gender, generation, and various statuses that ultimately preserve a very different kind of impression. The gendered division of labor in Jola cultivation practices is carefully reproduced in the realm of cultural knowledge. One of the first rules I learned among Guinean Jola pertained to the gender-specific prohibitions around women's and men's spheres of knowledge. As discussed in previous chapters, men were not supposed to know anything about women's reproduction, and women were not supposed to know anything about male initiation. Uninitiated members of both genders were not supposed to know anything about either.[12] As I discussed previously, when Catholic missionaries set up the first school in Jola-land in the 1950s and started forcibly matriculating students, one of the most frequent parental and community-wide objections to schooling was the possibility that children would learn about the "secrets of reproduction."

Beyond distinct men's and women's knowledge, information is strictly organized *within* each gender. Van Tilburg's (1998) essay on her fieldwork experience as a pregnant ethnographer among Senegalese Jola is instructive here. Van Tilburg discusses how she unwittingly learned the rules of secrecy and silence surrounding pregnancy and childbirth through the constraints on her own access to information about these domains. She confesses: "I hoped that my fieldwork while pregnant would initiate me into Jola womanhood and help me acquire the knowledge of the Diamat Jola women of Youtou" (van Tilburg 1998:180). But quite the opposite occurred. "I found that there were different lines, those that separate women from men, those that separate women from various statuses, and those that separate Jola from all others" (van Tilburg 1998:185).

Access to different knowledge about reproduction organizes women into a hierarchy. Women gradually learn more and more "secret knowledge" based on their experience and success in childbirth As van Tilburg explains,

> As time went on, I started to learn the categories to which Jola women belonged according to their stage and success in reproduction. These categories formed a hierarchy. On the lowest rung were women pregnant for the first time; next in order were the women whose babies did not survive; then women who had given birth only to girls; mothers who had given birth to and raised both sexes; culminating in mothers who had passed menopause (van Tilburg 1998:183).

My research among Guinean Jola confirms and expands upon van Tilburg's analysis of Senegalese Jola secrecy around pregnancy and reproduction. For Guinean Jola, giving birth marks a woman's initiation into adult status. Interestingly, while male initiation is highly collectivized and rare (once every 30 years), female "initiation" in the form of childbirth is highly individualized and frequent. But both male initiation and child-birth are moments of complete gender-based seclusion, as well as realms of total secrecy within each gender.

Each neighborhood has a maternity hut, enclosed with thick palm branches, thus distinguishing it from every other building in the village. Men are not allowed to go near the structure. Although many Jola women in Esana now give birth in the state clinic with the assistance of the male (non-Jola) nurse, some women continue to use the neighborhood maternity huts. Until about twenty years ago, all women went into seclusion in the maternity hut when they were about to give birth. If it was their first time, they were supposedly ignorant of all proceedings until they unfolded, just as men were meant to be ignorant of circumcision until the moment they felt the knife. Older women assisted as traditional birth attendants in the maternity huts, and some continue to assist at births in the state clinic.[13] After giving birth, a woman stayed at the maternity hut for a few days and was then moved with the newborn to a nearby older woman's house. She could not go home—and her husband could not see her or the baby—until the umbilical cord had fallen off and the wound had healed. The reason given for this extended stay was that if the husband saw the umbilical cord wound he would ask what it was, and that might lead to revealing information about the "secrets of birth."

During the late stages of my extended fieldwork, women in Esana collectively built a separate building behind the existing clinic for the exclusive use of women with obstetric needs. The construction of a separate maternity center provided a compromise between the secrecy of women's reproduction and the need for improved health services. Such a move represented women's recognition of the decreased rates of mortality during childbirth at the clinic, but simultaneously demonstrated their desire to create the conditions that maintained long-standing practices of secrecy and seclusion around childbirth.

A similar compromise occurred during an NGO-sponsored training for Jola traditional birth attendants I attended in May 2003. A Portuguese NGO that had recently become involved in the region organized the training in which each Jola village selected two or three women—most of them recognized for their experience in attending births—to participate. The training was conducted by three non-Jola nurse-midwives from other cities in Guinea-Bissau who spoke to the participants in Crioulo. Some of the older women needed translation, so a young Jola man who was helping the Portuguese NGO with various tasks around the region was called in to translate. Because the topics on the first day pertained to general health and hygiene, his participation was not a problem. But at the end of the day the women decided that no men were allowed in the room for the rest of the training because the group would be discussing female reproductive matters. So the translator was sent home and the more competent Crioulo speakers among the women took on the task of translation, although this often resulted in much confusion.[14]

At another point in the same training, also in the absence of the male translator, the nurse-midwives asked the Jola women what they knew about methods for preventing pregnancy, and several of the younger women mentioned birth control methods they had heard about (although very few had access to) such as Depo Provera injections, intra-uterine devices, and the pill. The nurse-midwives pressed them to discuss what kinds of methods they used before such modern means, or what other options they knew about from "traditional medicine" to prevent or abort a pregnancy. They were met with blank stares and shrugs. "Come on," one of the nurse midwives pushed, "You must know ways to do these things. Every ethnic group has these methods." When asked again what plants would help a woman avoid conception, the Jola women demurred; several of the participants around the room insisted, "Jola don't do such things."

It is impossible to know whether the women actually did not know such methods or they were unwilling to divulge such "secrets" to the younger women and non-Jola attendees. There was a rather stringent pro-natalist ethic among Jola that some women confessed to finding oppressive. Once I had become closer to several women in the village, I was often asked to fulfill a somewhat clandestine role pertaining to birth control or other aspects of childbirth. On several occasions, I shuttled women across the Senegalese border to Ziguinchor, where they could receive both birth control and childbirth assistance unavailable to them in rural Guinea-Bissau and far from the watchful eyes of their neighbors.

Nho Keboral's case is particularly illustrative. I should note that my discussions with Nho Keboral on this topic were extraordinarily open, probably due to both the unusual intimacy of our friendship and, more importantly, her recognition that my outsider status—not to mention resources—would be of service to her. Nho Keboral had six children, and several of her pregnancies after her last child had ended in miscarriage. She had become quite weak and anemic and suffered from persistent abdominal cramping. She often told me that she would "like to take a break" from pregnancy and childbirth. I asked her whether there were any ways of preventing pregnancy that other women in the village knew. She said that there were, that the elder women knew ways and that her ancestors had long used "traditional medicine" to prevent pregnancies and perhaps induce abortions. I asked why she did not try one of these methods, and she said that the women who knew would not be willing to tell her. "This knowledge is secret," she shrugged.

It is not clear how elder women eventually come by such knowledge, but Nho Keboral (and others) insisted that they would not readily part with it, even to women who had given birth many times. She reinforced this point when I asked her whether such prohibitions applied even to women like her, who had given birth to six healthy children—boys and girls—and who were clearly sick and might compromise their health further with another pregnancy. Nho Keboral shrugged again. It did not matter, she said, whether she had "six or ten or twenty children. You are still expected to give birth, just keep giving birth. They tell you it's better to die giving birth than to avoid getting pregnant."

In a parallel fashion, women are not supposed to know anything about male initiation and circumcision. There is a great deal of secrecy surrounding what happens in the sacred forest, where initiates are secluded for three months. Women are not allowed to walk beyond a certain point in the direction of the sacred grove, and the food they prepare each day for the initiates and their male kin in the forest is carried by other men—usually the most recent initiates from the last village to have undergone the rites—into the bush. I was often told a cautionary tale about a man in the neighboring village of Elia who, having drunk too much palm wine, told his wife when the initiation proceedings would begin. As it is strictly forbidden to reveal such information to women, the man was severely disciplined; residents of the village raided his granary and took his rice, then tore the thatch off his house and broke down the mud walls. He was expelled from the village and he now lives in the Gambia. What is important here is the emphasis with which Jola refer to the secrecy of male initiation, both in terms of the actual proceedings and the "secret knowledge" revealed to initiates by the elders in the forest.

Jola men also emphasize the instructional aspects of male initiation. Just as women in the maternity hut gain knowledge previously inaccessible to them, elders in the sacred forest instruct male initiates in oral history, songs, and norms (see Mark 1992; de Jong 2008). When several Catholic families desisted from attending the last male initiation one informant told me, "The initiation forest is our library. Those that did not go will never really know the true meanings." And "those who did not go" are regularly reminded of their ignorance of and exclusion from these realms of Jola cultural knowledge.

Interestingly, gendered domains of secrecy tend to institute power relations and hierarchy within the same gender rather than between genders. The parallel secrecy between genders regarding reproduction and male initiation both minimizes and emphasizes difference between genders. It establishes a structural difference between men and women, without that difference necessarily leading to a position of domination and subordination between them. In fact, such measure-for-measure practices around gendered domains of secrecy could be seen as maintaining some sense of equality between men and women: we know some things, you know others. But secrecy about such matters within the same gender tends to lead to status distinctions laden with power and control between elders (the initiated) and juniors (the un- or less-initiated). Elder women, in the case just discussed, maintain control over a realm of knowledge that helps give them power over their juniors. Until recently, women in labor depended entirely on their elders for assistance in the maternity hut during their most vulnerable moments. Such differentiated knowledge and modes of secrecy give elder women power not only over the fate of particular women but over maintaining and enforcing norms regarding high parity. Likewise, uninitiated men are entirely at the mercy of their elders when they enter the sacred forest, and their status as full Jola men who "know the true meanings" can only be attained through submission to elders' authority, both in the act of circumcision and in the acquisition of cultural knowledge.

Such dynamics resonate with scholarship on the technologies of control over the flow of information, particularly in the realms of religious and other esoteric knowledge (Keen 1994; La Fontaine 1985; Murphy 1980, 1981, 1990, 1998). Murphy (1980, 1990), for example, asserts that the performance of secrecy is always part of a larger play for power. Scholars in this vein tend to follow a largely Marxist and/or Foucauldian formula in which knowledge equals power and differences in access to knowledge lead to particular kinds of hierarchy. As Appiah encapsulates, "Secrecy generates differences in what people know. These differences matter; knowledge is power" (Appiah 1985:15–16). I suggest that these differences matter more in some instances than others. In the Jola case, such power is exerted within the same gender, but the differentiating aspects of secrecy between the genders seems to distinguish without specific ensuing power implications.

What is perhaps most interesting about the insistence on gender-based secrecy and knowledge is just how much effort goes in to preserving

these exclusive domains of knowledge. The process of generating, concealing, and eventually transferring cultural knowledge sometimes seems as
laborious as do Jola efforts in the rice paddies. And the content of such
carefully guarded "public secrets" is, again, largely irrelevant. Of course
men know about reproduction and women have a generally good idea
about what happens in the initiation grove. Maintaining separate spheres
of knowledge and secrecy differentiates women from men and is important enough to require elaborate preservation mechanisms, both through
jural consequences—as in the case of the Elia man who revealed the date
of the initiation's commencement to his wife—and through *batolhabu*
burials. It is both an instance of ritual collusion and a manifestation of
how cultural energy is expended to reproduce social forms that cannot be
taken for granted (see Arens and Karp 1989). In the case of gendered domains of secrecy, such regulation of knowledge serves as a mask to separate, in a structuralist sense, along the lines of sex and status, an artificial
distinction that enables differentiation on the basis of access to particular
kinds of knowledge and practice.

Spirit Shrines and Esoteric Knowledge

Another institutional domain structured around a strictly regulated flow of
information is the realm of spirit shrines (*ukinau*) and the religious knowledge involved in attending to the spirit world. What bears emphasizing is
the way in which knowledge regarding religious practice is maintained and
transferred within a very small, exclusive segment of the population. Knowledge about rituals and shrine ceremonies is not just restricted from nosy
foreigners; most lay Jola do not know much about spirit shrines beyond who
officiates at each one and which animals can be sacrificed there. Esoteric
knowledge is strictly forbidden to those who do not have rights to it—either
through birthright or selection as a shrine priest. It is deemed dangerous to
know something beyond one's purview.

As with Ampa Kapeña's funeral, elders and ritual officers (*amangen-i*)
possessed and controlled all information regarding the funerary rites and
posthumous mandates, and laypeople neither did nor could question their
authority in these matters. Such was the case in most ritual occasions I
observed. Even when participating in ritual activities, lay Jola had very
little idea of the reasons for ceremonies and religious practices and, unlike
me, would never ask for such explication. When I would inquire about the
significance of religious or symbolic acts—such as why *ai-i* carry their own
stools and wear only red, or why the *ai-i* light a fire to commence a wrestling match—my questions were met with shrugs. Often my interlocutors

would tell me, "It is not for us to know such things. Only the *amangen-i* can know." Whether or not they did, in fact, know and could not (or would not) reveal this knowledge to me is irrelevant. What became clear in these interactions is that they were not *supposed* to know, and it would have been a serious breach if they admitted to such knowledge.

Gaining the rights to such knowledge—even if one inherits the role of a shrine priest—involves a long and often expensive process of initiation and ceremonial inductions. As we have seen in the case of Ampa Badji, not everyone who has rights to a ritual office is eager to exercise them, and some go to great lengths to avoid them. In many instances, shrine priests have to physically catch a would-be adept and force him or her (although usually him) through an ordination process. Ampa Badji regularly escaped the clutches of his ritual elders by running away to the capital city at certain moments in the ritual cycle during which he could be forcibly inducted. Thus, the active refusal to become a member of an exclusive class of ritual officers who control valuable knowledge about the natural and supernatural world demonstrates that, for Jola, the pursuit of knowledge is not always an unqualified benefit.

*   *   *

Alongside the manifest world of material constraints, then, Jola inhabit another world rich in ideas and information. It is a world free from the limits of natural resources, intricately managed in its production and reproduction, and potent with the capacity to differentiate and cohere. Knowledge is a kind of currency. One can possess it, it flows among people, and it has hidden power. In the Jola case, the production and circulation of both informal information about oneself (where one is going, what one might have in a bag) and more formal knowledge about the natural, social, and supernatural worlds are inflected with subtle configurations of power, autonomy, and differentiation. In more stark terms, information as a kind of currency that one can generate, amass, and withhold provides a contrast to the experience of material limitations in the manifest world.

Efforts to manage knowledge, conceal information, and maintain control over who can know what and when is, for Jola, a kind of work. But, while the rice cultivation work regime upholds at least the performance of commonality and equality among Jola villagers, the work involved in cultivating knowledge distinguishes people along gendered, generational, lineage-based, and other lines. Perhaps even more importantly in the current context of perceived environmental decline and material hardship, the world of cultural knowledge has no natural limits, like land and water, and it provides an arena for abundant production, whether in day-to-day social interaction, important stages in the life cycle, or ongoing efforts to engage the supernatural.

Taking this one step further, from a Jola perspective, the power that resides in certain knowledge does not just pertain to the world of interactions and ideas, but it coalesces in the "interaction between natural, social, and supernatural realms" (Arens and Karp 1989:xviii). It is precisely because Jola recognize their precarious circumstances, and in a more general sense, have always acknowledged the fragility of the natural and social worlds, that they invest so heavily in maintaining control over the forces— often mediated through particular forms of knowledge—that order both of these realms. Jola adherence to these modes of knowledge production and circulation proscribe, in powerful ways, what they can and cannot do in their daily lives. For Jola, the world of circumscribed cultural knowledge ultimately shapes—or, more importantly, they hope it will shape— the manifest, material world. As they more keenly feel the constraints and limits inherent in the natural world, similar to their adherence to a particular work regime and—as we will see in the next chapter—to participation in male initiation, Jola are perhaps accentuating the ways in which controls over and enactments of various forms of knowledge might be even more important.

Some Implications of Speaking and Silence

Jola encode the insight offered in Simmel's observation quoted in this chapter's epigraph in their very conception of what it means to be human. The Jola word for human is *anau*, the root of which—N—means "to speak." But the words for each particular type of person—a man, a woman, girls and boys at different levels of maturation, and so forth—add to this root N a range of conditions and constraints. A human being, then, is one who speaks, but becoming a person involves understanding when and how and with whom to be silent. Learning how to manage information—who can know what, when knowledge can be revealed, how to dissemble in everyday forms of social interaction—is all part of Jola socialization processes. The capacity—or sometimes the imperative—to be silent refracts across Jola social organization along many dimensions, such as gender, generation, lineage, ritual roles, and life course. The interplay of speaking and silence, concealing and revealing, textures Jola social life, organizing axes of difference and shaping human sociation in powerful ways.

Simmel hailed secrecy as "one of man's greatest achievements" (Simmel 1950:330). From a developmental perspective he saw secrecy as a sophisticated social form that contrasted with the "childish stage in which everything is expressed at once" (Simmel 1950:330). At one level, Jola communicative practices are a "great achievement" in terms of the elaborate structures of knowledge into which people sort themselves (Simmel 1950:330). Information flow is partly organized in formal domains of social structure—widely understood categories of gendered, generational, and status-based access to knowledge—and partly in individual choice. This is a sophisticated and elaborate system of producing and transferring knowledge that is highly complex and differentiated.

Gaining a better understanding of how Jola manage information and strategize around concealing and revealing knowledge enables a more appropriate engagement with the central concerns that motivate this book: how Jola are responding to their own acknowledgment of profound economic and environmental changes that make their lives—individually and collectively—precarious.[15] Faced with the dilemma of increasing and intensifying food insecurity and generally deteriorating economic conditions across Jola-land, one might assume that Jola villagers discuss these problems and potential solutions among themselves. But, as demonstrated in the extreme case of widows and the general situation of Jola villagers more widely, norms that regulate the circulation of knowledge and the habits of concealing information about oneself and the conditions of one's household texture the ways in which Jola confront such changes in their ecological and economic landscape.

Among other implications, this presents thorny challenges to contemporary development policies and practices. For instance, recent efforts to transform Africa's agricultural sector have emphasized the need to "learn from farmers" (Alliance for a Green Revolution in Africa 2009). Such an approach reflects a general shift in international development thinking and practice that engages would-be beneficiaries in collaborative endeavors to improve their conditions. In particular, it serves as a corrective to previous agricultural reform initiatives—notably the Green Revolution of the 1960s and 1970s in Latin America and Asia—that tended to denigrate or ignore traditional methods, tools, and seeds of indigenous farmers in favor of modern science and technology.

Jola farmers exemplify exactly the kind of people with exactly the kind of problem that architects and planners of recent rural development initiatives—notably those under the rubric of the Alliance for a Green Revolution in Africa (AGRA)—want to address.[16] Engaging rural Jola in this process would begin, according to AGRA's stated approach, "in the fields alongside small-scale farmers, to learn from them and to understand their most pressing problems and the potential solutions" (AGRA 2009). But what would "learning from Jola farmers" really look like? Assuming for the moment that AGRA's objective to derive insights about pressing problems and potential solutions from African farmers does indeed reflect their sincere intentions to incorporate indigenous knowledge and small-holders' concerns into agricultural development projects, such a goal assumes that indigenous knowledge is ripe for the picking, readily available to whichever plant geneticist or grant portfolio manager might ask for it. But as we have seen throughout this chapter, rural Jola, like many agrarian people, have deeply ingrained formal and informal communicative strategies that make access to agricultural knowledge—or really any relevant knowledge regarding farmers' circumstances—extremely difficult. Through an analysis of Jola approaches to knowledge and communication, this chapter has exposed some of the challenges that would likely confront and confound AGRA officials and other development practitioners eager to "learn from farmers."[17] What this adds up to—whether regarding information about possessions or problems—is a mode of communication that tends to obscure what is really going on. To be sure, anyone working "in the fields alongside small-scale [Jola] farmers," as AGRA program officers propose to do with agrarian groups across Africa, would learn a lot about the rigors of their wet rice cultivation scheme, the contours of their social organization of labor, and the ingenuity of their longstanding irrigation and other agricultural practices. But understanding their "most pressing problems and potential solutions"—or even some of the most basic aspects of their current circumstances—is, as demonstrated herein, not a straightforward endeavor.

Jola approaches to knowledge also open up questions that extend beyond the confines of agricultural (and other) development initiatives. "Learning from farmers" is a metonym for a wider preoccupation, not only of learning any local knowledge seemingly pertinent to development purposes, but of embedded assumptions about the pursuit of knowledge writ large. Development practitioners espouse many of the same assumptions that undergird scientific inquiry and progressive politics more broadly: that knowledge is an extractable resource, that more knowledge is better, and that democratized knowledge leads to progress (Adams and Pigg 2005; Habermas 1972, 1979, 1989; Latour 1993). Jola approaches to knowledge not only challenge developers' goals and expectations, they remind us that the assumptions supporting and sustaining such epistemological orientations are not universal.

In a general sense, it is a rather Western commonplace to see openness, broadly conceived, as beneficial on both individual and social planes. Modern psychological theory and practice rests on an assumption that openness—with oneself and others—is the crux to restoring and maintaining a healthy mental state. Not only is openness assumed to be essential to the health of the individual body and psyche, but openness and transparency are seen as the hallmarks for a healthy (democratic) society. Simmel was clear on this point, too:

> Every democracy holds publicity to be an intrinsically desirable situation, on the fundamental premise that everybody should know the events and circumstances that concern him, since this is the condition without which he cannot contribute to decisions about them (Simmel 1950:337).

Many scholars have focused on the presumed antithetical dynamic between secrecy/concealment and democracy, discussing how state secrets and "public secrets" challenge or undermine the relationship between citizens and state actors, or generally subvert supposed democratic values (Bok 1979, 1982; Masco 2006; Shils 1956; Taussig 1999; Tefft 1980).[18] Simply put, there is something disturbing about secrecy to the Western, modern mind. The teleology of the Western version of its own history of knowledge is that transparency replaces other forms of knowing, such as secrecy and witchcraft.[19] Secrecy is often cast as the bedfellow to such irrational, antiquated, and reactionary projects as magic, witchcraft, and authoritarian power. The free pursuit of knowledge and transparency in the relations between citizen and state: these are the values that define a democratic and open society. And these cast secrecy in the shadows of the anti-modern and the sinister. When we uphold the values of "truth and reconciliation," secrecy becomes conjoined with conflict, chaos, and backwardness.

In Jola approaches to the production and circulation of information, knowledge is often conceived of as dangerous and is sometimes actively avoided. Given this orientation, secrecy and silence are seen as protective strategies, as van Tilburg acknowledges: "I learned the rule that speaking makes one vulnerable and silence makes one strong. Silence not only increases the value of the knowledge it protects; it also protects people during periods of vulnerability" (van Tilburg 1998:178). The efforts to conceal possessions, opinions, and actions; the habits of social interaction that emphasize reserve, restraint, and evasion; and the seclusion of the initiation forest and the maternity hut all stand quite a long way from Habermas's (1989) public sphere.

Furthermore, within the Jola framework, patience becomes more than just a virtue: it is a dominant cultural feature. Jola individuals spend a lot of their lives not knowing things, secure in the understanding that waiting until they reach the appropriate age or status will yield knowledge at the apposite time and place. The prolonged initiation cycle means that some men wait over 30 years to acquire what is deemed to be the bulk of valuable cultural knowledge. Beyond that, it takes a great deal of time and effort to acquire the knowledge that comes with a particular ritual office. And beyond even that, there is an entirely ineffable realm—that of *Emitaï*, the supreme deity whose ways are, as the root of the word indicates, "unknowable." Although the lived experience of patience can be an anxious state, it comes with a general confidence that things get resolved with time, according to their own norms, not according to an outsider's sense of urgency. This can be frustrating to observe, and it can look like no one is doing anything to address problems, even when many residents in this region—like other agrarian groups across Africa—are acutely aware that they are living in a moment of extreme difficulty.

This chapter and the preceding one have demonstrated that the production of rice and the production of knowledge both entail rigorous work. These are arenas in which Jola expend a great deal of physical and cultural energy. The adherence to these particular regimes of work and knowledge has significant consequences for the ways in which Jola villagers confront their current predicament of environmental and economic decline. As we have seen, the boundaries that get maintained and the domains that get reproduced and reinforced operate at the level of values and social forms that are often detached from the provisioning needs that these are meant to support.

CHAPTER 5

Of Rice and Men

Not only are the weather, the crops, and the soil complex
and variable; the farmer is, too. Season by season and frequently day by day, millions of cultivators are pursuing an
innumerable variety of complicated goals. These goals and
the shifting mix between them defy any simple model or
description.

—JAMES C. SCOTT,
Seeing Like a State

[T]hough we are organisms and our unique genes are so few,
the greater part of our waking time, and even of our dreams,
is taken up with worries ... bearing on the rights and
wrongs that we feel have touched our sense of personhood.

—WENDY JAMES,
Key Debates in Anthropology

....

I n 1998 Esana held its once-every-thirty-years male initiation. Jola male
initiation— *bukutabu*—is a massive undertaking during which novices
and their male relatives remain in the initiation forest for three months,
healing their circumcision wounds, dancing, and learning the bulk of what
is deemed to be important male cultural knowledge from their elders.[1] Because of its prolonged cycle an entire generation of Jola men—aged roughly
three to thirty-three—is initiated during the same proceedings.

Several years before the 1998 Esana *bukutabu* Padre Luigi had engaged the nascent Jola Catholic community in an effort to analyze *bukutabu* and determine whether attending would violate aspects of their
Christian faith. The discussions took place during catechism and, at first,

only adult males participated. Shortly after the process began, Padre Luigi insisted that their wives (the mothers of prospective initiates) participate as well, since, as he said, "Christian families are a united front." According to Padre Luigi, after many years of discussion the group reached an apparent consensus that attending male initiation would indeed violate basic Christian tenets, and certain ceremonies would require them to "put Christ aside." Jola Christians agreed not to attend.

Despite this seemingly collective conclusion, when the initiation proceedings began the majority of Jola Catholic families participated. Only a small minority refrained. Ampa Badji took his three sons to the initiation forest, the youngest just barely three years old.

The ensuing division—between those who *did* and those who did *not* attend the initiation proceedings—continues to be felt as a significant rupture in Esana's social and religious life. The immediate post-initiation fallout was severe on both sides. Physical violence erupted on several occasions between members of each group, and several deaths in the village have been linked to the dispute. Jola Catholics who participated in *bukutabu* subsequently left the PIME Mission, although whether they were expelled by Padre Luigi or left of their own accord depends on whom you ask.[2] Those families who did *not* participate had their borrowed and pledged rice paddies reclaimed by their original owners. Every Jola family depends on a mixture of inherited, borrowed, and pledged land, and the reclamation of paddies had serious repercussions for these families. Finally, the disagreement over *bukutabu* caused a rift in what was a tight-knit Jola Christian community and reorganized alliances strictly along the lines of those who *did* and those who did *not* attend. Work associations, youth clubs, soccer teams, and social events all split along the pro- and anti-initiation divide, each side claiming its members to be the "true Christians." As one anti-initiation man explained to me, "When one is baptized, one is asked: 'Do you reject all the ceremonies and fetishes of traditional religion?' And one responds, 'Yes.' Those who attended simply broke their pact made at baptism." But those who attended insisted that there was nothing anti-Christian about the proceedings; as one of my neighbors reasoned, "Even Jesus was circumcised."

Conflicts over male initiation were not limited to Esana. Each of the outlying Guinean Jola villages that have Catholic communities went through a similar process, but since the Catholic communities are much smaller there the proceedings caused less commotion. Another factor that led to the particularly intense turmoil over Esana's initiation lies in the way male initiation circulates from village to village each year, causing a kind of snowball effect of accumulating tension and problems that culminated in Esana's 1998 initiation rites.

Even though the dispute was largely framed in theological[3] terms, and might be seen simply as a clash between traditional Jola and Catholic missionary religious mandates, the question remains: Why did the conflict occur over male initiation? In its sixty-year existence in Guinean Jolaland, the Catholic Mission has challenged and reshaped much of what its Jola converts believed and practiced regarding gender norms, family organization, and religious acts. But changes such as monogamy and rejection of sacrificial spirit-shrine ceremonies went largely uncontested in the Jola Catholic community. When it came time for male initiation, though, things turned out differently. Why was male initiation and not another traditional Jola practice the locus of debate and ultimately division in the Jola Catholic community?

Discussing religious change in Africa typically entails an analysis of the encounter between African traditional religions and universal salvation religions—particularly Islam and Christianity—in terms of the ways in which this encounter both reconfigured the indigenous social order and indigenized the newly introduced religion. What are the processes of conversion (Baum 1990; Engelke 2004; Horton 1975a, 1975b)? How are different metaphors and codes assimilated and transformed in these processes (Fernandez 1978, 1986; James 1988; Werbner 1989)? How are community organizational structures—or even the notion of community itself—altered (Beidelman 1982; Bravman 1998; Ranger 1987)? Among other themes, Africanist scholars have examined the collusion between missionaries and colonial authorities (Jean Comaroff 1985; John L. Comaroff and Jean Comaroff 1991, 1997; Etherington 1983), as well as the instrumentalist motives of Africans who seek membership in religious communities or brotherhoods (Long 1968; Parkin 1994). Although the Jola initiation case can also be explored along many of these lines, and it does, in part, bring to the fore the ways in which missionary Catholic and traditional Jola approaches might diverge, in this specific case I argue that we gain deeper insights into these dynamics when we embed them within the framework of traditional male socialization processes, as well as within the context of the decreasing viability of rice cultivation. The dispute over *bukutabu* took place within a wider context not only of missionary pressure but also of pressure on Jola livelihoods that challenged many customary Jola beliefs and practices.

In order to examine this question more fully I first provide a picture of boyhood as it looked in Ampa Badji's time, emphasizing its largely blithe nature and its involvement in mastering both the techniques and the ethics of rice cultivation. I also elaborate on some of the symbolic aspects involved in making a Jola man as they are inscribed on the body in particular ways that lend insight into Jola ideas about masculinity. I then explore how the increasing involvement of the PIME Mission in Esana— particularly through its school—disrupted many of these socialization processes and introduced new (and often conflicting) ideas about gender and knowledge. This may have gone uncontested if not for the simultaneous impact of environmental changes that challenged Jola efforts—and, by implication, Jola masculinity—in the rice cultivation complex. Building on previous chapters, I draw out connections among agrarian culture, conceptions of personhood, current environmental conditions, and missionary mandates to understand the *bukutabu* incident not just from within a purely (or primarily) theological domain, but as enmeshed in contemporary dynamics of environmental change.

Learning to Labor

As discussed in Chapter Two, boyhood for Ampa Badji and his peers was a generally carefree time, punctuated by particular age-specific tasks and ongoing efforts to become inculcated into—and ever more competent at— a life of cultivating rice. Beyond their relatively minimal herding duties, boys were generally left alone to amuse themselves for most of the day. They would organize wrestling matches, mimicking the adults by pretending to "capture" one of their friends and make him an *ai*, and declaring the wrestling match in his honor. They would dance *konkon*—the most widely performed male dance—in the afternoons, practicing the songs that spoke of various valiant deeds of their forebears. They would go to the mangrove estuaries and gather crabs and mussels and oysters, or occasionally scoop up fish in their nets. They would make arrows and hunt game in the forest, like guinea fowl, partridges, and monkeys. They would gather bananas and papayas, and sometimes even oil-palm fruits that had been cut down from the tall trees and left on the forest floor to be carried home by the women. But there were always rules and limits to these games, a kind of understood code of moral behavior in which making off with bananas was a generally permissible sort of mischief (as long as you weren't caught), but taking an entire oil-palm fruit was unthinkable. They would simply pick as many pods off the fruit as they could stuff in their pockets or hold in their hands and run away. Likewise with palm wine. Sometimes, as they wandered through the forest on the way to the paddies or the mangrove banks, they would come across a liter of palm wine in a man's forest shelter, and as long as it was sweet and had not fermented into the more potent variety, they would help themselves. But when they returned, they would stop by the same shelter, and if the owner was there they would tell him what they had done. Or, perhaps, if he was not yet there, they would leave some of their catch—a fish or some mussels—tucked away in his shelter and stop by his house in the village to tell him. "We passed by your shelter," they would say, "And we saw wine there and we drank it. But when you go back there, some fish is there, you should take it."

Often these activities took on a more organized and educative form, called *hubohu*, with older boys taking the lead in instructing the younger ones on everything from *konkon* songs to work techniques (and ethics) to wrestling. The older boys would gather the younger ones from their homes and take them out into the paddies, where they had erected a large platform. While the older boys would work in the paddies, the younger ones would sit under the platform and prepare rice to feed their older peers. Or perhaps they would be in the forest pruning palm trees, and the younger boys would attend to them there. After they had eaten together, the older boys would lecture the younger ones on the importance of hard work, and the impossibility of laziness. Sometimes they would organize the boys into teams and send one team off to find fish in the river or another team to hunt for small game in the bush, and the teams would rotate the following day. Nowadays people in Esana lament the lack of fish and often eat just plain rice with nothing on it. But when Ampa Badji was a boy it was easy to catch fish: "There was lots of rain, there was lots of water, so there was lots of fish. Sometimes you couldn't even fit all the fish you could catch in your basket," he reminisced. They would carry the fish back, grill it over a fire, and place it on top of the rice they had brought from home in large shoulder baskets woven by their mothers and kept warm by the sun while they went about their work.

Although he spent much of his time with his peers and in the *hubohu* group, Ampa Badji insisted that it was his own father who really taught him how to farm rice.

> Overall, I can tell you that the person who taught me how to cultivate rice was my father. He taught me the work of rice cultivation. So, once your father taught you how to farm, not like it is now, but in the olden days it was like this, if you don't know how to do all kinds of Jola work, like rice farming, tapping palm trees, cutting oil-palm fruits, or perhaps you are lazy and you don't want to do this work, you will never—absolutely never!—find a woman to marry. That's why, in those times, our fathers would teach us all of these things.

Like most boys at the time, as soon as he was old enough to wield the heavy fulcrum shovel (*bujandabu*), Ampa Badji accompanied his father to the paddies and the forest to learn the quintessentially male task of manual tilling. Soon after, he joined his friends and the older boys in his neighborhood work group. Younger boys honed their skills by watching their older peers and often competed with each other to see how fast they could till a row across a stretch of paddy, or how many rows they could complete before taking a break. There was enormous pride in mastering these skills and in demonstrating prowess, not only because, as Ampa Badji indicated, it put one in good standing for finding a bride, but because, as described in the previous chapters, Jola value hard work—defined principally by manual rice cultivation—above most other attributes.

Working in the paddies was not only tiring, it came with certain dangers. Often the water reached above Ampa Badji's knees, and there was no way to see under the water to make sure he was farming in the right place and in the correct manner. It was only by feeling his way through that he got a sense of his progress, and sometimes it was only when the paddy eventually dried out that he was able to verify that it was, indeed, the correct spot and tilled in the appropriate way. Not only does the water-filled paddy obscure one's work, it also obscures dangers lurking within it, especially snakes. Often, men knee-deep in a rain-filled paddy would be bitten by snakes and have to rush over to Kugelh, where the lineage that specializes in removing venom resides. Sometimes, if it was a highly poisonous snake, a man would die before he could reach the healer's household, but if he made it he would be instructed to inhale the steam from particular boiled plants that would make him vomit the venom until he was cured. Once he was cured, he would head back to the paddies and continue work as usual.

Embodied Personhood: Making and Marking Jola Male Maturation

In addition to demonstrating his growing proficiency in the paddies, a boy's progress toward maturity was marked physically on the body to signal the stages that led from boyhood to manhood. In Ampa Badji's time (and in his father's and grandfather's times) a Jola boy passed through four stages that marked his maturation, signified by adornment and activity. Jola do not count their years, and even ten years ago it was rare to find someone who knew their numerical age unless they had frequent contact with bureaucratic institutions that require this kind of information. But age—especially a boy's age—was marked physically on the body with various kinds of adornment, and through various kinds of work, educational, and recreational activities.

The first age grade—*apurau*—typically included boys around eleven or twelve years old, but could also include boys as young as six years old. This was the age of cow herders, when young boys took responsibility for their family herds (or were lent to another family with herding needs). The adornment used to mark this age grade, worn typically at large public gatherings like wrestling tournaments or dances, was a hairpiece with small shells sewn as a circle into the boy's hair at the back of his head. The next stage—*aruntchikau*—included boys in their late teens to early twenties. An intermediate phase—*aruntchikau arau*—encompassed boys who were not quite big enough to be full *eruntchikai* but had outgrown their *epurai* status (usually fourteen-year olds). At this stage, the headpiece no longer had shells but several buttons scattered on back of head to make a star-like shape. This was first phase of various *ebongai*, the headpiece progressions that distinguished male age grades, each phase with its particular name. This first one, *badjolidjolabu*, was comprised of white buttons threaded onto the back of the boy's head. The ash from a burnt jackfruit shell was mixed with palm oil and spread on the back of the head until everything turned pitch black except for the white buttons. At wrestling matches *eruntchikai* were not distinguished by any particular clothing, as they were in later stages. During the late *aruntchikau* phase a boy started to explore his options for betrothal. When he was ready to declare a girl as his wife he added another ring to the headpiece, turning it into a *kugabaku*, with two buttons tied together around the star on his head. It was at this point that the boy and his family began to raise pigs for the *ebandai* marriage ceremony.

During the next phase—*adjadjau*—more emphasis was placed on wrestling and *konkon* participation. *Edjodjowai* wore white skirt-like cloth wraps when wrestling, and their *ebongai*, now called *bapendabu*, was thread around their entire head with three or four buttons in a row on each part of the star. Later in this phase, the headpiece was transformed into a *hungómahu*, in which the buttons from the previous phases were removed and an *embelengai* (pl. *bambelengabu*), a type of copper-like metal, was sewn into the hair covering the whole head. At this point, the young man waited for the elders in his neighborhood to give him the go-ahead to build his own house. Much of this depended on his wrestling ability; if he was an exceptionally skilled wrestler, elders sometimes decided to delay his house-building activities for a couple of years in order to keep him in the wrestling circuit (once married, he must retire from wrestling). The final *ebongai* phase was *ehendjekurai*, in which the *embelengai* was removed and the young man's entire head was tied with shells. This signified that, during the following year, the man would begin to build his own house. At this stage, young men traded in their white skirts for black ones, which they wore at wrestling matches and *konkon* dances. They also removed the red tail worn by all boys at wrestling matches from *apurau* to *hungómahu* phases. They replaced the red tail with a *hurirahu*, a white cloth with beads sewn on it, twisted until it was hard and reaching to the back of the knees. The year that young men built their own houses they became *esubangilai* (*asubangilau*, sing.), the final youth phase. They no longer wrestled, although they usually took on supervisory roles at wrestling matches and *konkon* dances. After this final youth phase one became an *adjamurau* (pl. *edjamurai*), a married adult with an autonomous household.

Although many of these adornments are no longer worn by Jola boys, it is instructive to explore how the changes in *ebongai* and wrestling wear encode several key insights into longstanding Jola ideas about masculinity, personhood, development, and knowledge. First, a young, pre-pubescent boy wore a circle of shells on his head, and did not have any distinguishing clothing below his waist. The shells contrasted with the later use of buttons in their naturalness, and the circle suggested self-containment, both of which mark this phase as one of undisturbed, intact boyhood. It was only with entrance into the *aruntchikau* phase that change was signaled by opening up this circle into a multi-armed star, and by replacing "natural" shells with "artificial" white buttons.[4] The progression of the star shape suggested incompletion—there will be more buttons and the headpiece (like the boy himself) will grow outwards. The openness of the star image conveyed this sense of growth; as buttons were added, the star radiated outward, mimicking, on the one hand, the body's transformation from the inside out, while suggesting, on the other hand, the multiple directions of possible growth. It was still unclear how the process would end, and Jola indicated the potential for following multiple paths simultaneously through the many arms of the star, each of which represented a possible area of growth and a possible path toward manhood.

The contrast between the black ash and white buttons symbolically set up a meeting of opposites that marks most liminal moments, and that has to be worked out and ultimately resolved through a transitional process. These next several stages coincided with ages that marked growth and transition in the boy's physical and social life; it was a vulnerable period in which the previous state of an unmarked and largely ungendered child went through the gradual process of becoming more visibly marked as a man. The use of artificial (e.g., "man-made") buttons as opposed to naturally found shells suggested that Jola recognized the ambiguity of gender, and had a clear sense that gender difference must be socially and symbolically (not just physically) worked out. The final stage of a full head of shells marked the completion of this process, and a return (although somewhat differently configured) to a natural state—that of a fully completed man. All of this symbolic work happened on the head, again emphasizing that this was an imaginative process. Jola see the head not only as the site of intelligence, but as a source of potentially creative or destructive power. A witch, for example, is said to "have head," meaning his or her capacity to perform extraordinary feats (for good, but more often for evil purposes) resides in the head. That *ebongai* also resided on the head implied an attempt to imprint and guide the still vulnerable youth into each next stage by symbolically demarcating both growth and the working out of contrasts (in this case, male and female encoded by black and white) on the site where creative and destructive power dwell. Moreover, locating this process of adornment on the head revealed how Jola thought about knowledge as tied to maturation. Again, the transition to manhood was not just about growth and physical change, but importantly included the acquisition of different kinds of knowledge (represented by the multi-armed star) necessary to become an autonomous head of household.

The seemingly incongruous *hungómahu* stage, in which the buttons are removed and a type of metal is tied around the head, can be better understood when we think about the properties of metal. As a material object, metal represents the ultimate in potential; it requires human intervention in order to transform it into something useful. Among Jola, metal is most often used at the tips of the long fulcrum shovel that men depend on for hoeing the rice paddies. Blacksmiths must transform a block of metal by exposing it to fire, which, for Jola, simultaneously encodes male chiefly power and female creative power. *Ai i* are said to have firepower, which they use for punitive purposes. An *ai's* link with fire is manifested in his clothing, which is red from head to toe.

Hungómahu, as the penultimate stage, dramatically encapsulated this extreme transformative process by moving from the gradual accumulation of buttons to a headdress of metal, suggesting at once the joining of male and female power (through fire) in the making of new people,[5] and the consolidation of this new person as a man, most importantly distinguished by his trademark instrument of labor in the rice paddies.

Jola *ai-i* at an inter-village wrestling tournament, Karuay 2002 *(photo by Joanna Davidson).*

While all of this symbolic work was happening on the young man's head, we might also glean insights into Jola notions of gender by examining what changes were happening on the lower half of the body. Once a boy entered into the liminal and transitional phases demarcated by *ebongai*, he also began to wear a white cloth with a red tail at wrestling matches.

Again, the contrast of these colors hinted at some level of gender confusion—or at least ambiguity—marked, not coincidentally, around the sexual organs. *Eruntchikai* and *edjodjowai* were not yet fully sexualized

Jola wrestlers, Karuay 2002 (photo by Joanna Davidson).

beings; in other words, their sexuality was still indeterminate as indicated especially by the red tail. Red, like fire, is a polyvalent symbol among Jola, sometimes signaling male ritual leadership and other times encoding female fertility.[6] Its use during these transformative stages suggested again the blending of gender archetypes that needed to be worked out in the ultimate reconstitution of a fully sexualized man. We see this happening at the final stage of *chendjekurai*, when the metal headpiece is removed and the young man's head is covered with shells. At the same time, the white cloth and red tail are replaced by a black cloth and *hurirahu*.[7] The symbolic work that has been conducted on the head is no longer necessary, because the accumulation of knowledge necessary to become a man is now complete. Instead, the final symbolic gesture was located around the sexual organs, as the young man removed the ambiguous red tail and wrapped himself in black, publicly displaying himself as a fully sexualized man about to embark upon an autonomous life by building his own house. (The Jola word for house and family is the same—*eluupai*—and the building of one always already encapsulated the building of the other.)

We can see, then, that the key elements in a Jola male's maturation involve an ever more refined distinction between male and female spheres, an emphasis on knowledge as constitutive of manhood, and a sense of the multiple directions that growth and development can entail. These elements are epitomized in male initiation, during which initiates are

Youth Age Grades for Jola Males

GRADE NAME AND APPROXIMATE AGE	ACTIVITIES	ADORNMENT
Apurau (pl. *epurai*): eleven or twelve, but can include younger boys	Cow herding	A hairpiece with shells on back of head
Aruntchikau (pl. *eruntchikai*): late teens to early twenties (*Aruntchikau arau* = mid-teens)	Wrestling, dancing, betrothal process	*Ebongai* stages begin (headpiece comprised of buttons in star shape on back of head): 1. *Badjolidjolabu*: Mix of burnt jackfruit shell and palm oil spread as black ash around head; white buttons sewn into hair. 2. *Kugabaku*: After declaring a wife, another row of white buttons is added to the star shape.
Adjadjau (pl. *edjodjowai*)	Wrestling and dances	3. *Bapendabu*: Three or four buttons in a row on each part of the star. 4. *Hungómahu*: Buttons from previous phases are taken off; *embelegai* (pl. *bambelengabu*), a type of metal, is sewn onto hair over all of head. 5. *Ehendjekurai*: Take out *embelengai*; tie whole head with shells. At this stage, white skirt is switched for black skirt at wrestling matches, and a *hurirahu* replaces the red tail.
*Asubangilau** (pl. *esubangilai*)	Build autonomous house; retire from wrestling	

* The phases from *aruntchikau* to *asubangilau* generally take seven to ten years.

separated from their female kin and secluded in the forest for three months, women and girls are forbidden to go near the site or even know about the proceedings, initiates are instructed in the bulk of Jola cultural knowledge, and the dangers of circumcision leave open the question of the young man's (or boy's) very survival.

Boys, Interrupted

The process of passing through each age grade, as well as the more informal peer education practice of *hubohu*, were both disrupted during Ampa Badji's boyhood: first by the newly arrived Catholic Mission in Esana and then, after independence, by the state school system. Schooling slowly moved in to structure children's—and especially boys'—activities during the day in a different way. But the shift did not only transform daily rhythms of work, education, and play. The precepts enmeshed in the *ebongai* cycle butt up against Catholic notions of gender, family, knowledge, and development in significant ways. Moreover, pressures from the PIME Mission were being exerted contemporaneously (and coincidentally) with other pressures coming from the decline in rain, challenging Jola farmers to work even harder in their paddies, often with frustrating results. The combination of these pressures helps explain the conflict over the 1998 male initiation in Esana.

Ampa Badji entered the initiation forest in 1968, the same year his younger brother and sister died from measles. After his seclusion in the forest for three months, he came back to the village and found that several of his peers had started attending school at the PIME Catholic Mission, and he was desperate to join them. He was uninterested in the religious aspects of involvement with the Mission, or rather, at the time, he was unaware that Mission involvement entailed a religious dimension. But he was obsessed with the idea of attending school, in no small part because he saw the other schoolchildren—his peers—wearing shorts and t-shirts that he coveted. Once Ampa Badji came home from the initiation forest he told his mother that he wanted to register for the Mission school, but she refused. He would go to the Mission compound anyway, and one day as he was entering the grounds he saw the priests and several young boys carrying heavy sacks filled with cockles that had been gathered along the saline river banks. The priests had begun to sell the cockles to other missionaries, Portuguese colonial officials, and military personnel who came to visit from their posts around the country. This was before independence, in the middle of the liberation war, and missionaries often had to be quite creative in their financial dealings given the precarious status of the waning colonial regime. When Ampa Badji noticed the priests and other children carrying the bags of cockles he saw his opportunity and joined them. Padre Marmugi welcomed Ampa Badji. After they finished the task Padre Marmugi gave Ampa Badji a pair of shorts and asked for his name, which he wrote down. Ampa Badji was instantly entranced. No one he knew could write, and he was determined to learn how. He kept returning to the Mission and joining in whatever task was underway, week after week, until one day, just as the children were preparing to go back home, Padre Marmugi made an announcement: "Every child who has registered for school will be allowed to stay in the Mission for another week." Ampa Badji went home and implored his mother to enroll him. "I'm going to go to school!" he insisted. "I'm going to go to school." But she continued to refuse. He screamed and cried so much that their neighbors intervened. "Let him go," they told her. But she still refused because, she explained, "If he goes to school, who will help me pay? Who will pay for those school supplies?" In these early years of the Mission school, parental sentiment in Esana was generally against it for both economic and moral reasons. Like Ampa Badji's mother, most parents were concerned about what obligations they would become entangled in once the Mission ensnared their children. And, as mentioned previously, they were even more concerned about what their children would hear in the classrooms, especially regarding reproductive knowledge that is strictly safeguarded from Jola children. They saw the Mission school—*kajanayaku*—as the place where their children's ears would be poisoned with forbidden and dangerous knowledge.

Despite his mother's refusal, Ampa Badji was absolutely set on the idea of school, so he started to attend in secret. Each morning he would feign leaving his parent's house to play with his friends, as was his custom throughout boyhood, but would instead rush over to the Mission. Early one morning, as he was preparing to leave, his father called him over. "Where are you going?" he asked his son. "I'm just going to join my friends over there," Ampa Badji lied, and ran off to the Mission. After he had finished a week of school, his father caught on. But by then he was hooked. It was only later that the new pupils began receiving catechism along with their basic schooling. Their recess was replaced with a catechism class, and the conversion process began. Ampa Badji's cohort of peers who entered the Mission school around the same time comprise the bulk of current Jola schoolteachers in the region, as well as the majority of Jola Catholics, although their relationship with the Mission has been a rocky one since those early school days.

As described previously through Ampa Badji's experience, Jola boys have traditionally enjoyed an untroubled childhood with minimal parental interference. They were, in many ways, an ideal target population for the Mission. Girls were expected to perform extensive domestic work at a young age, and Jola adults were busy in the forests and rice paddies throughout the year. Boys did help out in the demanding rainy season labor in the rice paddies, but during the dry season they had plenty of free time, and much of this was spent in their *hubohu* groups in the paddies. Padre Marmugi was aware of this, and was also convinced that elders would be unlikely converts, so he focused his attention on the boys. Padre Luigi explained to me,

Little by little some of them would come to understand. And he was in
no rush. If he could get just a few of the youth to enter, then they would
grow up and have autonomy and think about which direction to send
their own children. Because among Felupes, youth have no autonomy;
they cannot make autonomous decisions. Now it's a bit different because they go to school, but in those times, absolutely. . . . For Felupes, as
soon as they build their house and marry, that's when they gain authority. The minute he marries, he gains a voice to speak. That's why Padre
Marmugi waited until they [the youth] had their own houses and gained
autonomy to make their own decisions. He waited 17 years to baptize
anyone. He left them until they matured, until they gained autonomy,
independence. . . .

By the time they grew up, of course, they had already been inculcated
into a new system of thought. As Baum noted for Senegalese Jola, "In the
schools children received religious answers at an age when they had not
yet begun to formulate religious questions" (Baum 1990:390). This is a
particularly effective strategy for Jola, who do not receive religious instruction as children; as discussed in the previous chapter, shrine priests
and elders maintain access to religious and spiritual knowledge, and one
can only earn the rights to such knowledge through the long (and sometimes inaccessible) process of becoming an adept at a particular shrine.
Most Jola remain quite ignorant of specialist religious domains, and hence
Jola children certainly could not counter Catholic teachings from an in-
formed and solid position in Jola religious (or *awasena*) ways.

Immediately after independence, the PAIGC government took official
control of all schools across the country, and Esana's Mission school was
shut down and eventually replaced with a state-run school shack near the
entrance of the village. Even though other Missions across the country
have since re-opened and expanded their schools, Esana's Mission school
building remains vacant to this day. But even in its short-lived history it
managed to have a major impact on a cohort of Jola men—now heads of
households in Esana—and their families. The Mission school certainly afforded new opportunities to Ampa Badji and his peers, and many of them
continue to be involved in schooling as state-employed teachers in village
schools throughout Jola-land.

Each member of the Jola Christian community in Esana has a unique
story about his or her initial involvement, ongoing interaction, and general relationship with Catholicism and the PIME Mission. In Ampa Badji's
case, although he was enthusiastic about schooling, his relationship with

the Mission—and particularly with Padre Luigi—deteriorated over the years and he became increasingly uncomfortable with the tensions between Mission mandates and Jola mores. For example, he was not happy with the way Padre Luigi spoke openly about sex during Mass, especially since attending children would hear references to sexual matters of which they were supposed to be ignorant. According to Ampa Badji and others, Padre Luigi would call out specific names of people and accuse them of having extra-marital affairs, discussing sex openly in "vulgar words." Jola are quite careful when it comes to sexual references; as one of my friends put it: "It's fine to speak of sex, but one must do it in evasive, hidden language, so the children would not understand." Congregants complained to Padre Luigi about his inappropriate public references, but, as Ampa Badji complained, "Padre Luigi took no heed and continued doing so." In this sense, Ampa Badji and his similarly Mission-educated peers continued a line of thinking that their own parents had expressed regarding knowledge and open communication of sexual and reproductive matters.

By far the overwhelming majority of current Jola Christian families are those who were captured as schoolboys during Padre Marmugi's early years and were essentially separated from traditional socialization in village life and brought up within the Mission walls, often being sent off for more schooling and teaching positions elsewhere in the country. They were taught to disbelieve spirit shrine ceremonies, and their baptism vows included a commitment to forgo attendance at "idolatrous ceremonies." But the majority of missionized Jola who rejected spirit shrine ceremonies did not, as we have seen, reject *bukutabu*, and many of them have rejected Padre Luigi—as the embodiment of the Esana PIME Mission—over and above any theological or other religious inclinations. Never mentioning Padre Luigi by name, but alluding to him in a typically coded Jola way, Ampa Badji sums up,

> Well, but at the Mission, these years, I don't go there. Like I've told you, the Mission used to be good but not now. Now the Mission is damaged, the Mission is damaged. Now the way the Mission is damaged, the difference is both more immediate and bigger. Because you want to go to the Mission, and you think about two things: you will arrive there and you won't be respected, because "I said, I said," or "They said, they said. . . ." So-and-so says you did such-and-such thing and it so happens you didn't do it. That same person [encoded reference to Padre Luigi] who tells you such lies there, like, "So-and-so did such-and-such . . ." . . . he is the worst person. He is the worst person because he does those very

things that you yourself have not done. So one says, 'Better that I sit here
and take my own path . . . rather than taking that Christian path.' That's
why now you see lots of folks are joining these new religions that have
entered. You see? So that's how it is. As for me, I left early, I converted to
the Christian religion, so I'm there until now. Because even these ceremonies that are done, very rarely do I attend those ceremonies. We took
our sons to the 1998 initiation but there are no ceremonies there.

From the perspective of most Jola Christians—even those no longer
active in the Mission—being both Christian and Jola is neither a contradiction nor particularly difficult. Many people explained to me that there
are not many differences between Jola and Christian beliefs: they both
have a supreme deity (and the word "*Emitaï*" is used in PIME Catholic liturgy to refer to God) and the Ten Commandments are already inscribed
in Jola mores. One man who, like Ampa Badji, had defied his parents by
attending the Mission school insisted to me that Christianity had changed
"only a couple of things from the time of our fathers," namely, no more polygyny and no more war. Jola used to have a "problem of war," he explained,
with villages fighting each other all the time, but Christianity had taught
them to resolve problems by talking them through rather than killing each
other. On the marriage issue, he was quick to qualify that Jola never practiced egregious polygyny, like some other ethnic groups; generally, polygyny
resulted from the levirate system. Still, Christian doctrine insisted on only
one wife, which he said was better for everyone because it "prevented problems and confusion." He and many others left out a range of other changes
that were quite obvious to me—the rejection of spirit shrine ceremonies, the
shift in gender norms and birthing practices, the disruption of the male age
grade *ebongai* progressions, and the *hubohu* peer-education system, to name
a few. But most adult Jola Christians did not mention such shifts, and perhaps more to the point, Mission-educated men continued to identify not as
Christians or as Mission affiliated, but primarily as Jola farmers, spending
most of their time—even when employed in the Mission *uficina* or as teachers in village schools—tending to their forest groves and rice paddies.

But when it came time for Esana's adult men to bring their own sons
to initiation, thirty years after their own circumcision and forest-seclusion
in 1968, the Mission's disruption of Jola male-making processes seemed to
finally come head-to-head with Jola ideals.

Becoming a Jola adult is defined, in many ways, by what one knows—
or, equally important, what one cannot know—about being a man or a
woman. The significance of distinct gendered spheres of knowledge reaches

its peak at male initiation and women's birthing, each of which are gender-segregated affairs and are marked by the attainment of knowledge that must be guarded within the exclusive realm of the initiated. The idea of a Christian family as "a united front," as Padre Luigi insisted when he included women in the catechism discussion of initiation, was the first intrusion by the Mission into the sanctity of gendered domains of knowledge and secrecy. A Jola family is, in fact, "a united front" when it comes to household provisioning, but this is only the case because of gender specialization of knowledge and practice that makes the family deeply interdependent. In the complex system of wet rice cultivation, men command knowledge over the irrigation techniques and women know the differences among a vast array of rice seeds and are in charge of choosing which varieties to broadcast. Men prepare the paddies by tilling the soil; women transplant and harvest the rice. This interdependence of the husband-wife pair is so strong that divorce—normally a straightforward and uncontested affair—is not permitted during the rainy season, when the husband-wife team depends on each other for the vital work of wet rice cultivation.

As we have seen from Ampa Badji's experience, aside from the initiation forest and a young man's head, the other site of "man making" is in the rice paddies. The strenuous manual labor of hoeing the heavy mud to prepare the paddies for rice seedlings is a quintessentially Jola male act. Adolescent boys often brag to each other about how fast they can hoe a rice paddy, and members within the neighborhood-based work groups of unmarried men often compete with each other during the rainy-season weeks of tilling to see who can reach the end of the row fastest. The intricate system of Jola nicknames—*kasaalaku*—is a testament to Jola ideals of manliness. Most men have multiple *kasaalaku*, some invented just for them, others inherited or temporarily borrowed from others. But almost all nicknames encode references to wrestling prowess and hard work in the rice paddies. Two of Ampa Badji's many *kasaalaku* are illustrative of this general theme: Ampa Badji was often called "Amisabangeh," a combination of the Jola words for "small person" and "hard worker." Even though he is small, this nickname expresses, he works hard in the rice paddies. Another even more cryptic nickname conveys the same sentiment from a different angle: "Kudjunto di kudjal" literally translates to "If they stand, they cut." But the phrase encodes an allusion to abundant rice in the paddies, suggesting that even if women simply stand still, they will be surrounded by rice to harvest. It is essentially a praise name for having abundant and fertile rice fields, an empirical reality long passed since Ampa Badji first acquired the nickname.

Similarly, eulogistic couplets composed at a man's funeral typically emphasize his cultivation expertise. Funeral grounds are meant to be decorated with bouquets of stored rice from the dead man's granary, although such displays have become more difficult. Rice abundance is also tied to increased ritual authority. I was often told the story of Kassompa, the man who presided over more spirit shrines than anyone else in the village. He had single-handedly irrigated and cultivated a large tract of paddies and produced enough rice to offer sacrifices at several of the most important (and costly) shrines, eventually gaining rights to priesthood over them.

But now even the most able-bodied and perseverant men are not able to produce much rice. As a result, domains in which "being a man" is proven are on the wane and increasingly threatened. Jola are no longer able to eke out a living in the rice paddies, and previous accolades that attested to masculinity—whether through nicknames or eulogies—are becoming rare. Now that these sites of establishing, demonstrating, and performing masculinity are declining, others are becoming even more significant. *Bukutabu* gains in importance as one of the last purely male and man-making venues. Men's knowledge, what makes a man, and what maintains the gendered division of knowledge and secrecy, can only be preserved through participation in male initiation rites.

The making of a Jola Christian man—at least under Padre Luigi's missionary leadership—involved disrupting Jola ideas of gender, and particularly distinct gendered spheres of knowledge and secrecy, beyond the point where most Jola men were willing to go. Especially given recent ecological shifts that make it increasingly difficult for Jola men to be made in the rice paddies, male initiation has become an increasingly important site to maintain male exclusivity to certain kinds of knowledge. For the majority of Jola Catholic families, these factors trumped Mission mandates prohibiting initiation, even though their actions ultimately resulted in their removal from the Church and deep divisions among Christian community members.

Customary practices such as male initiation are accentuated in part because of the very precariousness brought about by the decline in rain and rice. Jola Christians who participated in the *bukutabu* proceedings despite Mission directives to abstain chose to do so within the contemporary framework of generalized problems concerning social change and continuity at the level of livelihood. In the Jola context livelihood is intimately and intricately bound up with concepts of personhood and gendered domains of knowledge and practice. Given their removal from the age grade system, Jola Christian boys no longer wear *ebongai*. Given the decline in rain, Jola men are now hard-pressed to earn praise nicknames and eulogies based on their cultivation prowess. The drums that called Jola Christian men and their sons to the initiation forest proved louder and clearer than the church bells beckoning them to stay within the Mission walls.

The decision of *bukutabu* participants can perhaps be taken one step further if we consider Fortes's (1966) notion of "prehending the occult" (see also Gell 1974). Understanding ritual as a way to influence conditions— often environmental—that enable one to make a living, Jola men's insistence on participating in male initiation might encode their hope to affect their natural world and regain the opportunity to become men in the rice paddies once again.

....

CHAPTER 6

Transgressive Segregation Revisited

Many of our children scorn us. . . . But deep down in us we are glad that our children feel the world hard enough to yearn to wrestle with it. . . . Always our deepest love is toward those children of ours who turn their backs upon our way of life, for our instincts tell us that those brave ones who struggle against death are the ones who bring new life into the world. . . . We watch strange moods fill our children, and our hearts swell with pain.

—RICHARD WRIGHT,
12 Million Black Voices[1]

....

This chapter updates and complicates some of what I have presented in the preceding ones. It does so particularly through Nho Keboral's perspectives as a mother and an increasingly active member of a women's work association, and also through Ampa Badji's hopes and dreams for his own children. Relying heavily on their own reflections and somewhat muddled comments, I try to convey this transitional and anxiety-producing moment in Jola social and family life by providing a candid account of one Jola family's dilemmas, and by opening up more questions that do not necessarily have clear answers, at least not yet. In this sense, this might be a frustrating chapter to read for those looking for a clearer theoretical package or exegesis. I have intentionally left this out. Even though the content is framed by the architecture of the book's overall narrative, I want to provide some sense of the confusion and uncertainty that most Jola experience in their current lives and in their attempted assessments of the future. But I will also indicate some of the perhaps hopeful (or at least new) trends that have emerged—especially in the arena of women's work associations—in response to these changing and challenging conditions.

*   *   *

In 2002, one of my closest friends in Jola-land, Bulorim, expressed his own version of a "paradox of custom" when he came to visit me from his neighboring village. It was a humid day at the end of a rainless rainy season, just before *agoto*, the only named month in the Jola calendar, a month that signifies hunger as it marks the time in the agricultural cycle when the dry rice has been consumed and the wet rice has not yet ripened. Even though *agoto* is a typically tough time of year, the suffering seemed more severe that year. Although the rains had come the previous year, a plague of insects had devoured paddy after paddy of delicate rice seedlings before they had a chance to mature.

It was the hottest part of the day, and I was taking a break from filling up my plastic buckets with water from the well, so I was grateful for Bulorim's visit. We sat down together on a low, wooden bench. My heavily thatched roof afforded good shade, and we kept our movements to a minimum in order to cool down a bit.

Perhaps it was inevitable—given the time of year, the heat, the cloudless sky—that Bulorim and I became involved in a familiar script. Shaking his head and sucking his teeth, Bulorim commented on the lack of rain, the lack of rice, and the struggle to continue what had clearly become an untenable way of life. I was having the same conversation over and over again with my Jola friends and neighbors in the village, and I had become rather frustrated with this predictable and seemingly dead-end discourse. When Bulorim repeated the habitual complaints of dearth and destitution I simply went through the motions of reciting my requisite lines about *Emitaï* being everpresent and all-knowing. Rather than agreeing with me by murmuring his own stock phrases about *Emitaï*, Bulorim surprised me by saying:

> If you put your foot in a fire, you feel it burn and you are quick to respond by taking it out. But here we are, all of our feet are in the fire and we don't do anything about it. We keep our feet in the fire and complain about how much it hurts, and no one takes their foot out and no one arranges to get water to put the fire out.

Bulorim had put his finger on the central Jola dilemma that I had been trying to puzzle out during my residence in the village. But it remained a puzzle, as most Jola adults in 2001–2003 kept their "feet in the fire" by maintaining their work regimes in the forest and paddies and insisting that they should not only "work hard," but, given the challenging environmental conditions, they and their children should work even *harder*.

When I came back to Esana in 2010, most of my friends and neighbors—including Ampa Badji, Nho Keboral, Bulorim, and their peers—were still working harder in the forests and paddies. In fact, Nho Keboral and the other members of my women's work association had increased their workload significantly, and although many of them had aged and had taken on additional childrearing responsibilities for their grandchildren, they very rarely sat still. Something had changed though: they no longer extolled the virtues of hard work. They admitted that they had no choice but to continue—this is what they knew—but there was an increasing sense of futility rather than nobility when talking about their own work, and a quite dramatic shift when they spoke of their own children's future.

On my second day back in Esana, I asked Ampa Badji how his work was going. "Well," he said, "farming doesn't have   it doesn't have anymore, well, farming has lost its strength. It has lost its strength because of the lack of rain. You can cultivate every paddy in Esana but when you transplant seedlings and you finish, the rain has already left and you won't see any rice, because rice needs a lot of water, a LOT of water, you see. Now, if there's no water, now what? There's no other way."

In Chapter Three I discussed the Jola work ethic both in terms of the particularities of Jola work and its increasing paradoxical nature. But how, from a parent's perspective, does family socialization around work fit into the current Jola world of decreasing rain and increasing schooling? Even more, how do shifts in the realities of work impact the ways in which Jola link hard work to their most strongly held social and moral proscription against theft? During my residence and return visits to Esana, the only time I witnessed physical discipline—whether adults disciplining their own or others' children or peers disciplining members of their cohort—was in response to not working hard and stealing. But the principle behind this—that hard work yields a full belly and thereby obviates the need or desire to steal—was no longer true.

Nonetheless, this formulation was still very much the basis on which Nho Keboral discussed her own parenting, even while she observed its unraveling. "It's mothers who educate the children most," she told me.

Fathers also educate them, but mothers are with them more because they take them to the forest, to the paddies, to every place. Mothers tell their children, 'Come to work, because one day, you will have your own children and you won't have anything to give them and you'll steal.' This is the truth. This is the truth our mothers told us. I tell my children, 'Whoever doesn't work hard like me, we're not going to get along. Because tomorrow you'll go steal something and people will say, 'It was Nho Keboral who gave birth to that one.' . . . It will damage my name, and I don't want that. I don't steal, and that's why my children always have to work.

Nho Keboral's own work ethic developed within the context of her relative lack of immediate and extended kin; as the only surviving child of her parents, fostered by her father's brother's wife, self-reliance was simply a fact of life from a very early age. Given her lack of adult siblings, she extended this self-reliance and "work hard" ethic to her own children.

All my life, it's been just me, just me. . . . That's why I tell my children that a person who doesn't have relatives has to work hard because you don't know where you will be tomorrow. . . . You punish yourself so you won't have to bother anyone else. . . . I *kuji-kuji* but I've never stolen anything from anyone to put in my mouth. Since we don't have family, if my children refuse to work, where can I go to beg? There isn't a place I can go beg, so that's why every time if I do something and my children don't get up I get mad at them.

The inextricable link between hard work and no theft comes up over and over again when Jola discuss parenting and socialization more broadly. There is so much emphasis on teaching children not to steal that I used to tease Nho Keboral and Ampa Badji (but especially Nho Keboral) that every story they told their children led to the same punch-line: that's why you should never steal. But much of the instruction also came through instilling a kind of fear in children about the consequences of theft. "If you hit them when they do these things," Nho Keboral explained, "they won't do them anymore. That's what we do with our children." Early in my residence in the village, Nho Keboral's youngest child, who was around six years old at the time, was caught stealing from an old man's net of fish. The man beat him with his shoe, and when Nho Keboral found out later that same day she said, "Good, now he's learned. But just in case. . . ." And she beat her son again, repeating over and over her various admonitions regarding theft. "I am not quick to hit children," Nho Keboral told me. And it was true; as I said, I never saw Nho Keboral or anyone else in Jola-land physically discipline their children except in the case of theft or lack of hard work. So children learn early that stealing comes with the immediate consequence of a beating, but there is also the threat of more dire consequences. "When it comes to stealing," Nho Keboral said,

Mothers tell their children, 'if you go steal something, someone can shoot you and kill you. Someone can put a curse on you at a spirit shrine and you will die. Someone . . . well, thieves are killed. If you don't work, you won't have enough to eat, and you'll steal. Those who refuse to work are the same ones that steal. . . . Parents tell their children, 'you go to work because if your belly is full you won't steal.' . . . Here, in Jola-land, we kill thieves. If someone tells you that's a lie, he's fooling you. Because thieves here are killed.

Perhaps thieves used to be cursed and killed and excommunicated, but not anymore. Whether the power of spirit shrines has decreased or the power of the state has increased enough to dissuade such forms of local justice is unclear. Nonetheless, such assertions are still made, and perhaps more relevant to contemporary circumstances, the lack of hard work which might lead to stealing will also lead to a lack of help when you might need it most. As Jola increasingly recognize the futility of their labor in the paddies and forests, they also insist that hard work is a precondition to mutual assistance. "Because now," as Nho Keboral affirmed, "you go to work and you don't get anything. You can work for a long time, but you won't get anything. . . . But if you don't work, no one will give you anything, no one will help you." (Recall the case of Ampa Bontai, and how his "refusal to work" made even his relatives and neighbors completely unsympathetic to his plight.)

Jola recognize that their ethic against stealing is a mark of ethnic distinction, both self-ascribed and externally assessed.[2] Many times, when traveling along the dirt road that winds its way from São Domingos to Varela, dotted with Jola villages along the way, I would see a shirt hanging from a tree branch or a flip-flop perched on a palm-frond fence, or once even a few CFA bills balanced on a cashew tree. This, my Jola companions would tell me, is what we do with found objects, even money. Once placed somewhere visible near where they were found, their owners would be sure to come back for them. And non-Jola passengers on the flatbed trucks would exhale and shake their heads. "Only here," they would say. "That only happens here." One year, during the height of the rainy season, a truck broke down along this same road. This was not an unusual occurrence by any means, but in this instance the driver had no way of towing the truck back to São Domingos, and as the terrain became muddier over the following days and weeks it became impossible to extract the truck.

So there it waited, through the entire rainy season, untouched. A Balanta soldier visiting Esana commented in disbelief, "If that truck had gotten stuck anywhere else in this country, there would be nothing left. First they would take the windshield wipers, then the tires and wheels, then all of the glass, then all the internal parts, and so on. There would be nothing left; you wouldn't even know that truck had been there. But not here. No one's even touched it." To which an Esana resident responded, "That's just how we are. That truck can stay there until its owner finds a way to take it away and fix it. No one will touch it." And no one did. Once the dry season came, the truck's owner came with a mechanic and towed the truck from the dried and rutted dirt.

When I discussed this with Nho Keboral and other Jola friends and neighbors, I asked if they thought such behavior regarding theft would continue. Their answers were unequivocal: No. The two most often cited reasons for the erosion of anti-theft norms were the increasing presence of non-Jola populations in Jola-land, and the scattering of their own children to *prasa* (towns), where they would learn (and bring back) the stealing habits of other ethnic groups. "It used to be that there was just one ethnic group in Jola-land," Nho Keboral told me.

> People mixed, but not very much. And it wasn't like our children didn't steal, but if you stole, people would know that it was you who stole. . . . If I, for example, go steal, within two days they will know me; they will say, 'there is the thief.' I'll be ashamed and I won't do it again. But the day that . . . all ethnic groups are here there has to be theft. And as for our own children, well, now they stay in Bissau and they go around with their friends. And those friends, maybe some of them are bandits . . . and so they want to enter into thievery.

Even with children scattered around the country and across the border to continue their schooling, and all the risks of "banditry" that come with it, many Jola parents still manage to bring most of their children home to help with agricultural work in the rainy season. This is aided by a school calendar that recognizes the needs of a still mostly agrarian population; as soon as the rainy season commences, school children flood back to their rural families and join them in the rice paddies. I have already discussed how peer groups help enforce the return of their members. Parents also exert their own pressures. Children are told that if they do not return to help their parents till and transplant, the small amount of money they have saved during the dry season meant for their children's school fees will have to be spent on hiring a work group to make up for the lack of their children's labor. Desperate to continue their schooling, most children are more than willing to acquiesce. As Nho Keboral confirmed, "My kids, they don't stray far from me. Just in the dry season. But during the holidays, they come to help me. They come back as soon as it rains. They'll help me here and then they'll go back. They know all of our Jola work, and they can do it: they can do *ewañai* [till a rice paddy], they can *pabi* [cut and clear a forest grove], they can climb palm trees. They know how to do all this work because they've done it together with us. We showed them."

But even when Jola school children return to help their families in the paddies there is no doubt that the meaning of work, and the links among a certain kind of work ethic and the social and moral foundations of Jola-ness, are undergoing significant transformation. "Because it doesn't rain anymore," Nho Keboral observed, "that's what made kids get up and go."

> For us, in those times, you would see a girl grow up and dance so she could go get married, but now that doesn't happen. It doesn't happen, and our time was better. It's work that kills us. Just look at me. These days, I go *pabi*, another day I go cut thatch, I carry compost to put in the paddies. . . . I would rest, but here I am, getting up at dawn every day to do this, to do that. . . . Who is going to bring you rest? It doesn't exist, there's no rest here, there's no rest here these days. If you arrive here in Esana, Esana is totally quiet. You won't hear a thing because all the women have gone, gone, gone. Every one of them is gone. . . . This kind of work kills a person inside. That's why some feel it in their bones, others feel it in their bodies, because of this work. You leave at dawn and go work but that work that you do from dawn for the whole day is brutal work . . . you don't eat and you don't drink water. Then you stay there working until late in the afternoon. This is the kind of work that explodes your head. . . . Our work is nothing like that of our mothers and fathers. Our parent's time was lighter and ours is heavier. . . . That's why children refuse and they go off. . . . Because today's world is nothing like that world before.

One of the changes in the Jola relationship to work is not so much in type but in tone. Even during the past ten years I have observed a shift in attitudes toward hard work, still valued in and of itself but talked about with less pride and accomplishment and more complaint and hardship. Jola have long recognized their particular agricultural practices as onerous, but this was often—even in 2001–2003—expressed as a matter of honor and dignity, or even superiority. Increasingly, though, rural Jola complain that their work has become too much of a burden. The twin realities of the sheer increase in labor hours and the simultaneous decrease in the fruits of that very labor have challenged, to the core, Jola conceptions about work. What was, in 2003, a paradox of custom has now begun to strain Jola understandings of where work fits into their ideas and practices around socialization and social life more broadly.

One of the responses to this increasing strain that Nho Keboral herself has helped spearhead is the increasing role of collective work, especially among women. Work, as Nho Keboral repeatedly pointed out, is not like it used to be. The generation of women preceding Nho Keboral and her peers would go to work in the morning and come back by noon. Now, women cannot complete their ever-increasing labor needs by themselves or with the occasional assistance from their daughters. So, while gender-based work associations have long existed in rural Jola-land, in the past ten years I have seen their importance increase in many arenas.

"We Work Together Now"

When I joined a women's work association in 2001 I began to understand the importance of neighborhood-based, gender-specific work groups in terms of the collective labor they provided for members at crucial moments in the agricultural cycle, the camaraderie they instilled among members who became, even for me, a close-knit group of friends, and the income-generating potential they had as they were contracted to complete specific cultivation tasks. None of these functions was new. In fact, as I explored the history of work associations among Jola, I found they had long played these roles across Jola villages, not just in Guinea-Bissau, but in Senegal and the Gambia as well (see Baum 1999; Carney 2001; Linares 1992; Mark 1985). Although Jola social organization in general is characterized by strong household autonomy, and the household-based family has been the primary labor unit for rice cultivation, work associations have long played a part in complementing household and reciprocal family labor, as well as providing a forum for social interaction and organization outside the household unit.

When development groups working in this region in the late 1990s and early 2000s identified the presence of work associations and saw them as a ready-made vehicle for collecting and saving funds that could be funneled into participatory, group-generated improvement projects, they were flummoxed time and again when an entire rainy season's funds—sometimes quite considerable—were spent on a pig and cashew or palm wine for a social celebration. To development workers this looked like a big (and wasteful) party; sometimes the funds were spent on renting a sound system to blast music for dancing, other times—especially for the women's and girls' groups—their hard-earned money was spent on cloth for matching skirts they could wear to a celebratory event. I had many conversations with exasperated development workers who were trying to "change the Jola mentality" from "wasting their money" on parties, rather than funneling it into small development projects, like collective gardens or pump wells or health posts. What work groups were doing with their money at this time was, in fact, a slightly modified continuation of what work groups had been doing for as long as anyone could remember. The end-of-season party echoed work association's ritual practice to funnel their funds into propitiation rites for the spirits in order to ensure continued favorable conditions for another growing season (Baum 1999; Davidson 2007; Linares 1992). Even Catholicized work groups maintained this tradition with their own parties and palm wine, and although they were not officially engaged in propitiation rites, there was undeniably a resonance with this aspect of maintaining the relationship between the natural and supernatural world.

But during the past ten years the dependence upon work group labor, the specific functions of work groups' collective activities, and, perhaps more elusively, the tone of work associations has shifted. By 2010 work associations—especially women's work associations—had already altered their ideas about themselves, as collective entities, and their practices around labor, money, and development. The seeds of this change began during my residence in Esana in 2001–2003, and Nho Keboral was a central player in these transformations. And, as I witnessed upon return visits and learned by talking with her and others, she continued to play a protagonist role in transforming Esana's women's collective work. The vocabulary for this had not quite kept pace with the practices and transformative attitudes that had emerged, and many residents in Esana were at a loss for describing or naming precisely what was going on. This is partly because there are no specific words in Jola for what was emerging as a collective treasury and insurance fund, and the Crioulo words for such things still rolled uncomfortably off people's tongues, even those who spoke fluent Crioulo. As Nho Keboral once told me, "I've seen that lots of things have changed here in Esana, lots of things are changing. Because now if you tell women, come close to me, they'll come. . . . Our mothers didn't do this, and we, now, we have more of this thing." As is clear from her rather abstract references, "this thing" did not yet have a name. Even more so, after she had helped form an association of her peers and established a weekly contribution of

1500 CFA that was to be kept as an emergency fund that members could borrow during a crisis, some young Jola men living in Bissau came to Esana and wanted to support the nascent group. "They took the name of our association," Nho Keboral recounted, "and they made us a card that made us 'statutu' or maybe you say 'estatutu' or, well, I don't know what. But they made us officially the Women's Association of Esana."

The small women's work association that I joined in 2001 had now become a strong core of adult women, dedicated to their collective work and committed to pooling their labor and meager resources to help each other. This might not seem like such a remarkable occurrence, as the same time period (and long before it) saw the marked increase in such mutual aid societies, especially among women, often facilitated by Grameen-style micro-financing and savings account schemes in the world's poorest countries. But such attempts at collective pooling of cash resources had been tried by development organizations—and even the PIME Mission—in the past in Jola-land, and had always frittered away. Jola were assessed, by development workers and Mission personnel, to lack the basic sensibilities required of mutual aid and collective savings, and Jola themselves, when I discussed such matters with them in 2001–2003, were quick to agree that one of the aspects that characterize Jola society is a "fend for oneself" attitude, and a lack of trust for collective efforts beyond the household.

Something, however, had changed, and Nho Keboral was at the center of it. The combination of work getting ever more hard with fewer results, the loss of their children to schools in São Domingos and Bissau, and perhaps the palpable sense of fed-up-ness that so many Jola—especially women—brought up even more in 2010 than they did ten years before had led to a shift in ideas around work, the social organization of labor, and the practice of collective efforts. Even the expression of "helping each other" would have been rare in 2001, and more likely than not scoffed at as either a ruse or as empty Mission-speak. But ten years later many women insisted that they could not have continued with their difficult lives if not for the help of their work association members. "Our association, our little association, we work together now," Nho Keboral told me. "We all have to pay [1500 CFA] when it's our turn to receive help." That is, the group works in each member's forest tract and paddy, and the member whose turn it is to receive group help pays into the collective fund. In addition to paying for labor, each member of the group contributes a small sum, usually 200 CFA, to the collective fund every week. "With that money, whatever problem, whatever crisis, whoever has a crisis in her house, like in the rainy season, like in sick times, like anyone who lacks the means to send their child to school, you come to me, because it's me who has that money of our little association. Afterwards, after you've gotten treatment for your child until he's healthy, you *kuji-kuji* and return the money to my hands." Even though none of the members of the women's group can read or write, they decided that Nho Keboral would be their secretary and treasurer. I initially helped her set up a notebook for recording contributions and other payments, and returning schoolchildren continue to maintain these records, even though they quite quickly get confused.

Many members of the women's work group commented on how much their participation in it has alleviated their work burdens. Nho Keboral's closest friend, Marijai, remarked,

> We've seen that this kind of work lightens us. It lightens us because if you have wood, you go with your friend and she'll help you carry it; if you have thatch you go with your friend and she'll help you carry it, if you have . . . like this year, we took on a lot of houses. An old woman built her house, she doesn't have any children here, her children are all in Bissau, but our little group helped her draw water, we went to draw water and helped make the mud to build her house. Afterwards, she will pay us, but it's not very expensive.

Such help would have been extremely rare if not nonexistent a decade before. Many times, back then, I saw old women, often widows, building their own houses without any help. When I asked people why no one helped them, they would shrug and say, "We're Jola. Who would help her? Everyone has to fend for themselves."

Not only are work associations helping each other and even nonmembers, they are using their collective funds in different ways. Nho Keboral explained that, "Now the money stays put. At first, in those days, when a celebration came, we would gather the money and buy pigs to eat; we would have that party and sit around and play. But these years, no one buys anything. No one buys a thing. Because the money that we have, we leave it there in the fund. Whoever has a crisis can borrow the money."

Again, even though this seems quite basic, I cannot emphasize enough how much of a shift this is within Jola attitudes and practices. It has not, of course, been without its bumps along the way, and Nho Keboral and others have been accused, in what I would have once called typical Jola fashion, of "eating the money" collected on behalf of the association. But whereas before that would have put an end to the collective efforts, this time (so far) the association has continued despite such accusations. "Even up to now," Nho Keboral explained, "we continue to struggle, we refuse to leave each

other, we continue to work for this fund. . . . Some people still don't understand, but we keep trying to make them understand that this money isn't
for anybody, it's for all of us. . . . Here, we talk a lot. Talk is all people know,
but they don't tell the truth. I got the women together and spoke to them.
I told them all, and then we continued to work."

"School Is the Path Now"

As rural Jola increasingly felt their covenant with *Emitaï* to be damaged or
broken, they began to rely less heavily on divine intervention for their agricultural efforts and started to invent new strategies to respond to their worsening plight, partly by relying more heavily on each other (as evidenced by
women's increasing collectivization of work and money). But discussions
about "what to do now," which were increasingly the focus of my interactions with Jola in Esana and neighboring villages, and were often the topic
of nightly conversations in Ampa Badji and Nho Keboral's house after we
had finished our collective bowl of rice, often included a mixture of Jola
approaches and orientations. Self-reliance, hard work, familial interdependence, and hopeful appeals to *Emitaï* all mingled together when Jola villagers contemplated their next steps for themselves and their children.

One of the most dramatic changes I have seen in the past decade concerning Jola orientations to their future has to do with the position of
school in the popular imaginary. In a relatively short period of time, the
overwhelming majority of Jola families in rural Guinea-Bissau have
moved from lukewarm and often resigned complacency regarding schools
to become enthusiastic supporters of their children's schooling, often
making great personal sacrifices and overcoming tremendous hurdles in
order to ensure their children attend school as much and for as long as
possible.[3] This has little to do with a shift in the actual school environment; the conditions of Guinean schools have, if anything, worsened.
Most schools in rural and urban areas alike have no books, are severely
short-staffed, and are regularly shut down due to teacher strikes. The
bankrupt Guinean state was unable to pay teachers' salaries for extended
periods of time between 2000 and 2005, and several of those years were
declared "*anos anulos*"—annulled years—given ongoing strikes. This situation was resolved somewhat with the payment of salary arrears, which
was largely funded by foreign aid organizations, and therefore does not
constitute a sustainable solution to funding state schools.

When I returned to Esana in 2010 I was surprised by the uniformly
strong support for schooling, especially among families who had—a decade

before—been satisfied when their children completed a few years of primary school in the village and then began to take their places alongside their parents in the rice paddies. Everywhere I went I heard an almost too consistent refrain: "School is the path now." "You can't do anything anymore if you don't have school." "We just have to suffer and get the children through school and then, if God wishes it, maybe one of them can succeed and help the rest." Such sentiments were felt in material terms by school administrators in the region. Reflecting on his tenure in the area, the director of the Esana school told me, "The main change I've noticed is increased attention to school and its importance. Now the population of each village contributes to building schools themselves."

In 2001 it was not uncommon to see eighteen-or nineteen-year-olds in first grade classrooms. Although the minimum age to begin schooling is seven years old, there is no maximum age for first entry, and children—especially from outlying villages—whose families had not allowed them to attend school would wait until they were legally autonomous and then enroll themselves. In 2010 these older students were few and far between, and the lower grades were packed with seven- and eight-year-olds, as their older

Second grade classroom, Cassolol 2003 *(photo by Joanna Davidson)*.

Nursery school classroom, Esana 2010 (*photo by Bobby Milstein*).

siblings went off to São Domingos and Bissau to continue their studies, and their parents struggled to pay their minimal fees and send them rice.

Ampa Badji and Nho Keboral are a case in point. As a member of one of the first cohorts of Jola boys who were brought into the PIME Mission in the mid-1960s—the only option for school in this region at the time— Ampa Badji stayed in school against his parents' will and completed fourth grade, after which he was eligible to become a teacher himself. He and his peers—all middle-aged heads of household now—comprise the corps of Mission-educated Jola teachers in Esana's current state-run and village-supported primary school. Ampa Badji was an early adopter of the "value of schooling" orientation, and he insisted that all six of his children stay in school for as long as possible. Nho Keboral, who never went to school herself, abided, but when I knew her in 2001–2003 she was not particularly enthusiastic about school, and she was more likely to complain about the cost—in actual expenses and decreased household labor—of supporting her children through school than to extol its virtues.

Once the older children finished the Esana primary school, Ampa Badji enrolled them in the São Domingos middle school, 50 km from Esana, where they roomed with various extended and fictive kin. The two oldest sons eventually finished middle school in São Domingos and went to Bissau to continue their schooling. Both boys lead precarious lives in Bissau; they often have only one meal a day, and they are frequently sick. Nho Keboral worries about them a great deal, but since 2003 and despite their travails she has changed her opinion regarding school and she now speaks enthusiastically about the value of formal education. Her hopes for the future rest almost entirely on her eldest son's job prospects, and on his future support and help for the remaining children. When I discussed this change of perspective with her, she told me,

> It's because we're tired. We're tired and fed up. This way of life is finished, there's nothing here for the children anymore. We have to rely on school now. It's the only way. . . . Before, children didn't go to school. Our mothers would say that school is bad, that we couldn't go to school. . . . People didn't know that things would change. We didn't know that school was a good thing. But now we have school and we understand that it's a good thing.

In 2003 most Jola villagers recognized their predicament—the declining rain and rice that made their lives so difficult—but the overall response to it was to work harder and, as Bulorim so aptly put it, "keep their feet in the fire." Now, many Jola families are pinning their hopes on their children's schooling, although it remains unclear what role rice cultivation will play in this still foggy vision.

It is also far too early to tell whether this strategy will come close to meeting Jola families' expectations. School is a friable thing to depend on for future security, especially in Guinea-Bissau. Not only are the schools themselves minimally equipped, but even those students who manage to get through have very few prospects once they graduate. It is a well-recognized risky scenario to build up cohorts of relatively more educated youth who have been taught to dream but have continually had their hopes dashed (Hoffman 2011; Mains 2012; Pureza 2012; Vigh 2006). They are far more likely to lead precarious (and perhaps violent) lives, especially now that drug trafficking has taken such a strong hold over life in the capital city.

As I reflected on these shifts, I recalled a particularly emotional discussion at Ampa Badji and Nho Keboral's house one night during the 2002 rainy season. All of Ampa Badji and Nho Keboral's children were home. Gregório, the eldest son, had returned from school in São Domingos and Sabina, the eldest daughter, was still in her parents' house along with her toddler daughter, Binta. The older children crowded around one bowl of rice and the adults around another. Binta ate from her own small bowl, and Tiago—Ampa Badji and Nho Keboral's youngest child—moved back and forth between the two larger bowls. After we had finished eating the children all went outside to the front veranda and the adults stayed inside with the door closed. Ampa Badji and Nho Keboral talked quietly between themselves for a bit and then Ampa Badji told me that they were discussing what they were going to do given the grave situation with rice. Since it had not rained enough yet there was very little paddy wet enough to plant. Ampa Badji had been to their largest tract of paddy the day before and there was no water there. The paddy that I had visited with them a few days earlier to broadcast seeds was also completely dry. Even though the seeds we scattered there had sprouted, Ampa Badji said he was sure they would die. "Rice is like ducks," he said. "They need water or they will die."

Since the rice they had stored in the granary the previous year had been depleted because of insects, they were starting this year without any rice in storage. The problem, they said, would come in February through May (and perhaps beyond), when the paddy rice ran out. Since they could not plant any rice now because of the lack of rain, they would not have a big enough harvest to see them through to the cashew season.

Nho Keboral said she had told Gregório that they might not be able to send him to school the following year because of these problems. Their main concern was not so much the small enrollment fee but the rice supply needed to feed him in São Domingos. We continued discussing the problem and the conversation turned to consider, more generally, the future prospects for their children. Ampa Badji insisted that as hard as it was to make the effort and investment, they needed to find a way to send their children to school; he was convinced that it would pay off in the long run. Nho Keboral agreed in principle, although it was harder for her to accept in practice when faced with the immediate challenge of the following year.

The conversation then turned to Sabina, their eldest child. They had a sense that Sabina had already decided to do something but that she was afraid to tell them. Gregório had told them that Sabina wanted to go back to school, and that she would be asking them for some support. But Marina—their third eldest child—told them that after they finished transplanting rice seedlings, Sabina wanted to go to the Gambia or somewhere else to look for work as a domestic, and perhaps earn enough money to go back to school. Ampa Badji remained solidly opposed to giving her anything; each time this came up, he told her to go to her boyfriend for help. Nho Keboral was more lenient, but was not altogether keen to take responsibility for raising Sabina's daughter, Binta. "It's not that I don't want her. I do. It's just that my own health is so bad. I'm sick all the time. How can I care for a baby?" Regardless, both Ampa Badji and Nho Keboral were waiting anxiously for Sabina to discuss her plans with them. They were both quite sure that she had already made up her mind, but they would wait for her to come to them. Confronting even their daughter on such matters did not fit within Jola communicative norms.

As for Gregório, they knew his intentions: he wanted to continue school and then try to get a scholarship to keep studying. I had heard so many teenaged boys and young men state the same intention, both in rural areas like Esana and in Bissau, and every time I heard it my heart sank a little. There were so many young men sitting around Bissau and all over the country, waiting and hoping and praying for a *bolsa* (a scholarship to study abroad). And there were fewer and fewer *bolsas* available every year, with international support for Guinea-Bissau on the wane and increasing corruption in the government handing the scant scholarships available to those with the right connections. Gregório, a hard-working and bright teenager from rural Jola-land, had very little chance at securing a *bolsa*. And yet I had never heard young men Gregório's age contemplate any alternatives. Sitting in the dark room with worried parents, I could not help feeling that the future, whether in Esana or Bissau, looked rather grim.

Eight years later, when I was back in Esana, I recalled that late-night conversation when Nho Keboral said to me, quite out of the blue, "If someone tells you that they know what to do about raising their kids, they are telling you a lie. It doesn't rain, so there's no way someone can tell you they know what to do. If they say so, it's a lie." Since I had left in 2003 Ampa Badji and Nho Keboral had managed to scrape together enough money to keep most of their children in school, although there were a few years in between when they simply did not have enough cash or rice and everyone returned to Esana and waited until the following year to see if there would be enough of either to go back to school.

"Now," Nho Keboral told me in 2010, "my sons are in Bissau. They'll come here, I'll pound some rice for them, Gregório will take his rice. . . . Angala will take his rice. What will be left? There won't even be enough during the rainy season. That's why I'm saying, if someone tells you 'I know what I'm doing this year,' he's telling a lie."

Gregório and Angala were each staying at different households in Bissau, and each of those households had their own children to feed. Nho Keboral felt an intense pressure to provide them with enough to eat.

> I don't want my children to cry of hunger, I who gave birth to them. I don't want to punish my children. If one says, today I want to eat, but my mother doesn't have anything, won't he go steal? If my child doesn't eat today, and doesn't eat tomorrow, won't he go see what you have and take it? He'll eat it! . . . That's what makes me so worried. . . . It would be better if I hadn't given birth to them just so they would be punished in this life.

Concerns such as these prompted many people in Esana not only to do everything they could to keep their children in school and send them rice, even if it meant they would go without enough in their own homes, but increasingly Nho Keboral and Ampa Badji and others in their cohort expressed their wish that they did not want their children to come back to Esana to be rice farmers. In 2001–2003, when I talked to men of Ampa Badji's generation who had some schooling and were teachers or had other professional, salaried jobs, all of them continued to insist that they were first and foremost—and proudly—rice farmers. But many, perhaps most, Jola parents in 2010 insisted that they did not want such a future for their own children. As Ampa Badji reflected,

> When I think about what I want for my children, how I would like to imagine their future, if I could choose . . . well, this is a big deal! I don't want a single one of them to be a farmer like me. . . . I don't want them to be farmers because farming, now, it has no strength. Nothing is there in farming. You farm, you give all your strength, but it won't sustain you. Maybe it'll get two or four months [of rice], but now it won't even get there. Now that it refuses to rain, you get nothing, absolutely nothing. We don't gain anything in this work here because of lack of rain, and that's why now, even when you want to work, you feel dismayed.
>
> Now, we are looking for white people's work, and white people's work is what? Well, white people's work is school. So now, currently, for us, you have to do what you can for your children to go to school. Because today's world isn't anything like yesterday's world. We, yesterday, we refused school. But nowadays we put all of our children in school. Before, if you had children and you put them in school, your own friends would tell you, 'So, you don't like your children.' . . . But I want my children, each one of them, to study until the day they say, 'I'm full up with school.' . . . This is essentially what I want, because I don't want my children to be like I was. . . .
>
> You see how different it is now. You see now boys who have some schooling, or have a profession, you can choose a girl, whichever girl you want that's the one that you'll choose. It's different now because if you are a farmer you'll never even find a worthwhile girl for yourself. Because girls, and not just girls, just about everyone, they don't give value to farming because it's outdated, it's expired. But it's outdated because of lack of rain; if it still rained it wouldn't have become outmoded.

In just one generation the basis for being a worthwhile person, for being able to find a marriage partner, for demonstrating the difference between life and death—all of which were bound up with the performance of hard work in the rice paddies—had shifted, according to Ampa Badji and his peers, to something quite different, although it is not yet clear what that something is. What is clear is that, now, farming is "outdated," farmers will "never find a wife," and hard work in the paddies is equivalent to a form of death rather than being an indication and expression of life.[4]

In Chapter One I discussed how plant breeders working to improve rice strains strive for "transgressive segregation," a condition in which the offspring does better than the best of its parents. As we have seen throughout their narratives, most adult Jola viewed their own lives as much harder and more precarious than those of their parents and grandparents. Their own experiences of hardship and increasing ineffectuality as rice farmers has led them to hope for a wholly different future for their own children, one that would entail the erosion of Esana beyond soil conditions in the paddies to the very population itself.

So where does this leave the value of hard work? Will the ethic of hard work translate to endeavors beyond rice cultivation? And how, given the physicality and the links with social relations and religious ideals, will this be taught to a generation of children that is not only occupied with schooling, but is far from the very relations—to people and land—that make such notions of hard work meaningful?

This all remains to be seen. Even Ampa Badji knows that his role is limited in this regard. He can continue to support his children's schooling, believing that it may provide the best security for their (and perhaps his) future. But what his children actually do is, as with most Jola notions of the future, up to *Emitaï* and each child's own proclivities; what, as Jola say, is "in their heart." "That's why I am always thinking about my children," Ampa Badji told me as I prepared to leave Esana again in 2010.

> You would think that maybe if it's true that there is a God, he might help my children so that they are saved, so that they won't fall in this type of exhaustion that people are fed up with now. But the truth is, I can't choose what they are going to do. Each one has his or her conviction, and each will choose what they will become.... I'm not going to pressure anyone. Each one will do what he or she can do. You see? You can't force a person to do what you want. He will decide. Each one will make his own final decision.... So, how do I imagine their lives in the future? Since they are now building their lives in the world, I hope they continue like this. For each and every one of them to leave Guiné and go study abroad, in white people's countries or in other countries in Africa that have better living conditions. Because if not for that, they're going to become like us.

Nho Keboral echoed many of the same sentiments in a separate conversation. "I don't want them to be farmers," Nho Keboral told me.

> Instead of them staying here and being farmers and not getting any-
> thing out of it, I ask God to help my children to find a job, even if it's a
> job in Bissau, that's fine, or a job in some foreign land, that's fine. That's
> what I think for my children. We, in these times, we're being punished.
> Even if you work SO hard—you *pabi*, *fura*, *labra*—there's nothing.
> Sometimes you till the paddies and the rain doesn't come; sometimes
> you tap the palm trees and get no wine; sometimes you *pabi* and you
> don't get any rice. So it's better for children to go away and look for their
> own work; it's better than looking for work here. It's not worth it to stay
> here in Esana because it's no good.

As Nho Keboral spoke these words, her friend Marijai nodded in
agreement. "My children," Marijai insisted, "I don't want them to be farmers, because farmers here, we don't gain anything, there's nothing in it,
just killing your body. Just look at me! Just look at their father! What do
you see? Nothing is here. So I want my children, each one of them, to leave
here and look for something in the city. . . . I want God to help my children
to find a good job."

"So they don't get worn out like us," Nho Keboral continued.

> Because look at us . . . you get up at dawn and go *pabi*, and only at night
> do you begin to leave the forest, and then insects eat your rice and birds
> eat your rice. . . . So what I see for my children is for God to help them so
> they can leave and find good work and help each other. . . . We, who gave
> birth to them, we're worn out. That's why I tell my children to stay in
> school, and their father tells them the same. That's the only thing that we
> wish for the future of our children: that they don't stay here.

The definition of hard work as rice cultivation, and of Jola personhood
as tied inextricably to the performance of this work regardless of the outcome, had shifted dramatically in a relatively short period of time. "Lots of
people, not just me, lots of people don't want this kind of work anymore,"
Nho Keboral told me.

> Everyone asks for another solution but there is no other solution, this is
> the situation we're in. That's why I think about my children. That's all I
> think about. My sons are in Bissau, so I ask God for just one of them to
> graduate, and then he can find a good job and rest. If he rests, then I can
> rest too. Instead of coming back here and punishing himself with work
> that doesn't result in anything, it's better if God gives him a good job.

As of this writing only Tiago, the youngest son, was still in the Esana primary school. Gregório and Angala were in Bissau. Angala was completing his penultimate year of secondary school, and Gregório, with his parent's help, had scrimped together enough money to enroll in a post-secondary accounting course. The week before registering, all of the money was stolen from his room in Bissau.

I will pick up the story of the daughters in the next chapter.

CHAPTER 7

....

Jopai, and the Limits of Legibility

[T]he notion of cultural construction ... explains things
when they are working well; what we do not know enough
about is how people cope and pull through when things fall
apart.

—Paul Richards (1996b),
Key Debates in Anthropology

....

I first met Marina, Ampa Badji and Nho Keboral's third eldest child,
when she was fourteen years old, although she didn't know it at the
time. It was December 2001 and I had recently moved from Bissau to
rural Jola-land. Marina's family was, for the time being, my home base in
Esana. I sat with her on my second morning in the village trying to make
conversation, and asked her how old she was. "I don't know," she replied
matter-of-factly. "But wait, I'll go get my friend's card and you can tell me."
Later that day, she showed me a tattered, yellow WHO immunization
record that belonged to her friend. "We were born on the same day, so
whatever is written there is the same for me. I lost my card." Based on the
card's information Marina (and her friend) has just turned fourteen two
weeks before. I told her this and said, "Happy Birthday." She shrugged.

It was through this interaction that I learned that Jola do not keep track
of their age, although they are fully aware of birth order, something that gets
reinforced in various public performances and rituals, such as funerals,
during which each gender dances around the corpse in a line from eldest to
youngest. In 2001 most people in Esana, including Marina, could not tell you
their numerical age. But in 2010 I had the following exchange with Marina:

"Marina, how old are you now?"
"Me? I turned twenty-three on December 13."

Of course, as the preceding chapters demonstrate, a lot more had changed in the intervening eight years than the ability of rural Jola to recite their age and birthdate. One of the most visible and widespread changes was that Marina, her friend with whom she shared a birthday, and every single member of her age group whom I had known as young schoolgirls had all become mothers, although unlike their own mothers, none was married. These young women not only told me their numerical ages, they also told me how many children they had (again, something their mothers would have been loathe to do), although they could not always tell me who the fathers were. Time and children now had numbers, but beyond even that, the calculus around having and raising them had shifted dramatically.

When I came back to Esana in 2010 Marina was living in her parent's house with her three-year old daughter, Deluza. Deluza's father, Armando, is a Balanta soldier who would come visit periodically from where he was stationed, bring Marina some money, and the two of them would hide away for hours in a little room on the exterior wall of the house—originally tacked on for Marina's brothers—as her parents went about their usual routines of backbreaking agricultural and domestic work and little Deluza played around the house and waited for her mother to emerge. One day, during one of these visits, Deluza was playing with something she found in the dirt and, as little kids tend to do, sucking on her found object. Although it was the middle of the day, Marina, bleary-eyed, came out from the room, spotted Deluza, and yanked what turned out to be a used condom from her daughter's mouth. By that point I had become aware of how widespread this new schoolgirls-as-mothers phenomenon was, how unhappy most of these girls were, and how much of a strain it was putting on their already stretched thin parents' households. So I found myself cynically wondering not so much about what Deluza might have ingested, but why Marina hadn't used a condom before (as she herself put it) she "went off track."

In Marina's family there was some precedent for out-of-wedlock pregnancy. It was Marina's older sister, Sabina, who was a pioneer in this regard. Sabina had finished primary school in Esana, and her parents had scraped together enough money and rice for her to continue her schooling in São Domingos. But during her first year there Sabina became pregnant by her Jola boyfriend—also in middle school—and came back to Esana, and her parent's home, with her baby girl. Ampa Badji once reflected on his own reactions when he found out his eldest daughter was pregnant:

> When Sabina got pregnant, the truth is, I felt bad. I felt bad, because I
> sent Sabina to São Domingos to continue her studies, to do her next level

of school. I sent her and she studied until, after some time, she came back home, she came here. One day I saw her, but I couldn't bring myself to ask her. But I said to her mother, 'Huh, your daughter is pregnant.' She said, 'Noo, my daughter's not pregnant.' I said, 'Yes she is.' So afterwards I asked her [Sabina], 'So, aren't you feeling well?' She said, 'No, it's only because of tiredness.' I said, 'Tiredness, huh?' And she said, 'Yes.' And I asked her, 'But what kind of tiredness are you feeling? You're eating. All the time you're eating your rice. I send you money for school and other needs, so you're taken care of. So what kind of tiredness do you have?' She said, 'Just tiredness, that's all.' I said, 'Fine. Any time you come, you'll find me here. I'm not going to die, I'm not going anywhere.' And that's how it was . . . she returned. She went back to school and continued there, April, May, June. She came back here, and her, her, her boyfriend came here. Her boyfriend came here and said, 'Well, Sabina is pregnant, but her pregnancy is mine.' Well, we didn't really react, because if we had reacted at that time, we wouldn't have, well, we couldn't have reacted. Since her, her boyfriend came to tell us. But we did react just a little bit by asking him, 'Why is it that we sent Sabina to São Domingos?' So, in this way, we reacted a little bit. We reacted a little bit.

When I started living with the family in 2001 Sabina and her baby were there, although they did not stay long (as I will soon explain). But at this time Sabina was the exception. A decade later such a situation—returned schoolgirls and their babies living back in their parents' homes—was the norm. So much so that the resident Colombian Catholic nuns had created a new group of them for specially targeted Mission activities and dubbed them *"Jopai,"* an abbreviation for *"jovens ku padi dja"*—unmarried youth who have already given birth. Such a trend had immediate consequences for the families involved and for the character of the educational dream. Schooling was becoming sharply gendered as young girls dropped out due to pregnancies and mothering. And the girls' families—already stretched thin in their ability to provide for their children—were struggling with the additional needs of their grandchildren.

In an effort to account for the emergence of *Jopai* several narratives were circulating around Esana. Padre Luigi, the reigning Italian Catholic priest who had been in the region for over thirty years, blamed the independence movement's "Africanization" tactics. After the liberation war in 1974 the PAIGC—in an effort to decolonize the population's consciousness—announced that "culture" was to be celebrated. This, according to the priest, involved "modern discoteca dancing;" that is, couples dancing close to one another. For Jola this kind of dancing had never been practiced, but the PAIGC declared it to be Guinean culture. They erected youth club discotecas in many of the villages—even the far outlying ones—and often supplied them with generators for music and lights, or if these were unavailable, stocked with them candles. As the priest recalled, "at certain points in the night, they would shut off all the lights or blow out all the candles, and this would be a signal for the boys to do anything they wished with the girls." This, according to the priest, was the start of moral decline and unwed pregnancy among Jola youth.

Others in the area were less concerned with post-independence dancing and more often than not pointed their fingers at the Catholic Mission itself for playing a part in the moral decline that has led to an increase in unwed pregnancy. I often heard villagers in Ampa Badji and Nho Keboral's generation—the first to be brought into the Mission—explain that conversion entailed leaving behind the highly effective punitive system based on spirit shrines. Prior to missionization, discipline and socialization revolved around both closer supervision by one's elders and spirit shrine sanctioning; a spirit could catch you if you committed a moral or social breach. There is no comparable disciplinary system among the newly converted, and it is quite true that the rates of unwed pregnancy in the village are higher among the missionized families.

Still others pointed to a more general breakdown in traditional socialization and supervision as the root of the current *Jopai* problem. Previously, young men of the same neighborhood would all sleep in common quarters in someone's house (not a separate dwelling, like a Melanesian long house, but a room in an adult's house. If everyone did not fit into one house then they would be divided among several houses). If a boy needed to get up in the middle of the night to urinate he would tap the boy sleeping next to him and tell him so, and the two of them would go out. If he did not do this he would be suspected of sneaking off to find girls. Multiple bodies in a room supervising each other and being supervised by the adult man of the house enabled a kind of social control over young men. Even more, if someone did manage to have a child out of wedlock (which I was often assured was an extremely rare occurrence) they would be severely punished, and sometimes excommunicated from the village. I often heard—especially from current head-of-household men in the village—that the breakdown of this supervisory and disciplinary system had led to the increase in *Jopai*.

Yet another explanation focused on the irresponsibility of young people, especially young men. Previously, a man could only have access to women once he had built his own house and had received enough paddy-land from his agnatic kin to provide for a family. Jola men and women were supposedly ignorant of even the mechanics of sex until their wedding night, when the eldest male and female members in their neighborhood would instruct them (cf. Chapter Four). With the recent widespread knowledge of sex, my neighbors would tell me, boys were all-too-ready to have girlfriends, but not willing to take on the responsibility that went along with them. Very few young men in Esana were building houses of their own, and most viewed the effort to till one's paddies in order to grow enough rice for a new family a futile and undesirable endeavor.

Finally, local and international development organizations took a different tack and, rather than highlighting newly gained sexual knowledge, they insisted that *lack* of sexual knowledge had led to increased out-of-wedlock pregnancy among Guinean youth nationwide, and even more alarmingly, increased HIV infection even in the previously low seroposi-tive rural areas. Sex education, UNAIDS and others insisted, was the key to curbing this trend.[1]

All of these explanations focused on the structural changes or gaps that have led to the emergence of *Jopai*. Whether because of post-independence "authenticity" efforts, the loss of spirit shrine-based punitive practices, a breakdown in previous socialization and supervision techniques, in-creased irresponsibility among youth, exposure to knowledge about sex, or, conversely, lack of appropriate sexual knowledge, each of these expla-nations attempted to make this new social group legible, even giving them a catchy name. But a major pitfall of legibility is simplification, which not only asserts synoptic authority at the expense of particularity and poten-tially relevant distinctions, but also, like a cadastral map, freezes "a scene of great turbulence" (Scott 1998:46). The proliferation and opposing per-spectives of these explanations suggests that this is a phenomenon that defies simplification. But, by imposing such manufactured views on the highly varied experiences of so-called *Jopai*, these efforts at legibility could very well lead to the implementation of facile and ineffective solutions. Even more, they may ultimately shape the reality that they try to render legible, becoming "an authoritative tune to which most of the population must dance" (Scott 1998:83).

This chapter considers the emergence of *Jopai* not in the moralistic terms typically tossed about by Catholic authorities and non-missionized "traditional" Jola alike, nor even in the development frame that primarily considers these youth as evidence of both socioeconomic and sociocul-tural decline and as prime targets for HIV (and general sex) education, or occasionally girls' empowerment programs. Rather, by focusing on one so-called *Jopai* and providing a more thorough and intimate portrayal of her life, I hope to bring out some of the elements often missed by these various discourses on the moral decline of youth, and counter the simplification of these young women's experiences with a more complicated and humanized rendering of what might still be their foreclosed lives.

Marina grew up just at the time when rural Jola were beginning to feel the pressures of climate change that shortened the rainy season and made their livelihoods increasingly precarious. Her mother, Nho Keboral, had worked her entire life in the forests and paddies that surround Esana, and she taught her three daughters—Marina in the middle—how to do typical Jola women's agricultural work. As discussed previously, the Jola agricultural economy depends on a labor scheme in which households work autonomously in their forest and paddy plots and are complemented in especially intense moments during the cultivation cycle by neighborhood-based gender-specific work groups. While children are still in their parents' household, boys accompany their fathers in the paddies and girls contribute their labor to help their mothers both in domestic and agricultural tasks. Marina began working alongside her mother as a child, perhaps eight or nine years old. As is the case for most rural primary school children in Guinea-Bissau, she would go to the village school for a few hours in the morning and then walk to the forest or paddies (depending on the season), often bringing a tin bowl of rice for her mother, and join her for lunch and work. (In her final year at the village school her schedule switched and she would go to the paddies in the morning, come back to the village around midday to get washed and dressed, and then attend school in the afternoon session.) Marina recalled her own pride in learning how to perform quintessential Jola women's work. Chief among the highly specialized gendered division of expertise and labor is *borokabu*—the process of transplanting rice seedlings from their forest nurseries to the inundated paddies, and manually pressing each plant into the moist mounds tilled by the men.

> My mother would tell me, "You hold the rice like this." There was a small plot that she set aside where my father had tilled; it was a very little plot. She told me, "You're the one who will transplant there." I would transplant them and they would be just right. Every year it would be like that; I would grow and my plot would get bigger. . . . When I started working I was thrilled, because before I had just gone to see those who worked, but I couldn't do it yet. But once I could do it, I was happy.

Jola are known throughout Guinea-Bissau as hard workers, but the discipline of hard work is one that is literally beaten into Jola children. As I discussed in the previous chapter, the only time I saw Jola adults hit children—their own and others—was as a punishment for laziness or theft, two things that are connected in Jola minds and are prevented through an emphasis on hard work. Marina's father, Ampa Badji, repeated this lesson often to his six children in words and by modeling his own efforts in the paddies, but I also saw him enforce this ethic in more physically forceful ways. One day, several months into my long-term fieldwork in Esana, Marina and her older sister did not join their mother in her agricultural work. Believing their father to be away in a neighboring village that day, they took advantage of his absence and hung out at the local military barracks, playing checkers with the few bored soldiers stationed there. But Ampa Badji came back to Esana earlier than they expected and spotted them at the barracks. He did not say a word to anyone about the matter, but at the end of the evening, after the family had finished eating from our collective rice bowl, he stood up and calmly barricaded the front door. When he handed me the baby sitting on his eldest daughter's lap and instructed me to "hold on to her tight," the children knew something was about to happen, but it was too late to escape. Ampa Badji took his machete and, clenching his eldest daughter's upper arm, brought the flat side of the machete down hard along her back and thighs. She shrieked out with pain and humiliation as the machete made a high-pitched whizzing sound again and again before it struck her. Next it was Marina's turn. The other children stuck to the back walls of the mud house, looking on with fear, and the youngest girl—although she remained untouched—cried along with her older sisters. I was paralyzed with surprise and confusion, and though I turned it over in my mind many times after the event, I could not find a way to intervene between Ampa Badji's machete and the girls. I sat and looked on dumbly with the rest of the family, doing my best to soothe the baby in my lap. After Ampa Badji sat down on a low stool and rested the machete across his knees, the beaten girls huddled in the farthest corner from him and whimpered, eventually moving to the small room in which all six children slept. Ampa Badji spoke calmly: "I will not have lazy children in my house. Either you work with your mother or you leave." Marina heeded the lesson, and for the duration of my fieldwork she was her mother's constant companion in the household chores, as well as in the forest grove and paddies. But Sabina took the latter option. Shortly after this incident she left the village with her baby, arranging to work in the cashew groves of her boyfriend's mother in another town.

In Ampa Badji's mind it was a dangerous prospect having children who did not work. Not only did it make Nho Keboral's daily burden heavier, but perhaps they would get used to their laziness and soon turn to theft, the most anti-social and strictly punished of all crimes among Jola. Ampa Badji emphasized to me the next day that no one would respect grown women or men who would not work, and that even though Jola work was admittedly hard, his daughters' lives would be even harder if they refused to work.

But all of this was shifting terrain, even as Ampa Badji spoke these words. Expectations around work were changing both because of an increased awareness of its futility in the declining environmental conditions of the rice paddies, and—partly as a consequence of this—because of a new emphasis on the importance of schooling beyond the village primary level as the only way out of what was beginning to feel for Jola like a rural trap: no rain, no rice, no way. As we have seen, Ampa Badji himself was an advocate of the "school is our best hope now" refrain, and even after his eldest daughter's debacle in São Domingos he still pushed his children to continue their education beyond Esana's limited offerings.

When it came time for Marina to leave the village and attend middle school in São Domingos, her father sat her down and told her that her mother did not want her to go to São Domingos for school because of what happened to Sabina, but he insisted that she go because "school is the only way now." He told her that she had to work hard—to *"pega tesu"*—in school, and that if she did what Sabina did and got pregnant and left school it would be a waste of their money. But as Ampa Badji put it, "She was barely even there. Wouldn't you know it? She was with that, that boy, that Balanta boy. . . ."

The contrast between Ampa Badji beating the lesson to "work hard" in the fields into his daughters' backs and his largely weak and ineffectual sermon to "work hard" at school highlights what might be the most frustrating shift for Marina's parent's generation. Given changing environmental and economic conditions in rural Jola-land, they cannot socialize their children into a life of hard agricultural work because they know there are no prospects in the paddies. And sending them to school, even when they buy into it as a path to future security, robs them of the power and authority to steer the course of their children's behavior.

From Marina's perspective, although she did not intend to get pregnant and she insists that she was fully focused on her schooling when "Deluza's father found me," her pregnancy was "God's destiny" and her intention is to stay loyal to her boyfriend in the hopes of his eventual decision to marry her. Marina distinguishes herself from the rest of her peers by saying, "Now that he made me pregnant, I don't want to be with anyone else, I don't want another guy. Other girls . . ."—indicating with juts of her chin in several directions toward households she knows I am aware of—"don't think like that."

> Like that one over there . . . [another chin thrust]. She has three kids, each with a different father. And that baby in her belly now? It's from a soldier. That girl, she's not going back to school, she's not going to do anything; she went to third grade and then she stopped. She's at her father's house now. All those kids, it's her own father and mother who take care of them now. I just don't get it. I'll sit and wait for Deluza's father. Whatever he tells me, I'll accept it, I'll do it.

Although Marina's monologue was intended to differentiate her situation and behavior from those "other girls," aside from the multiple children and boyfriends the conditions that she described with such disdain were not dissimilar to her own. This, I think, is less a matter of blindness to her own situation or cattiness toward her peers than it is a reflection of how each young woman does not quite see herself within the *Jopai* group to which others have assigned them membership. What defines them for onlookers—myself (dipping back into life in Esana after eight years away and being so struck by the seemingly obvious pattern of changing sexual and marital mores), the Catholic church, development organizations eager to educate them about sex, and perhaps even their own mothers who are now burdened with caring for their unclaimed grandchildren—is only a very partial piece of how they see themselves, each young woman a unique social drama unto herself.

In Marina's case, the plot does thicken rather quickly after Deluza's birth. Marina left São Domingos with her boyfriend and they stayed in his older brother's wife's house in Mansoa, a largely Balanta town further south. They lived together there, and eventually Armando, her boyfriend, came to Esana to tell Ampa Badji and Nho Keboral that he did, indeed, intend to marry her. Marina planned to continue her schooling in Mansoa, but about a year after Deluza was born Marina became sick with what was eventually diagnosed as epilepsy. Her seizures began in Mansoa, and her boyfriend sold the plot of land he had been saving to build a house on for their nascent family so he could pay for her treatment. But her condition worsened and he ran out of money, so he appealed to her parents for help. He brought Marina back to Esana, where Nho Keboral took over Deluza's care and took charge of Marina's treatment, covering her bases with traditional healing practices through a spirit shrine across the Senegalese border and by purchasing phenobarbital from the Catholic Mission's dispensary. To pay for Marina's treatment and medicine Ampa Badji and Nho Keboral spent all the money they had been saving—much of which they had collected from me over several years—to replace their thatch roof with corrugated zinc sheets, one of the most coveted quality-of-life improvements in rural Guinea-Bissau. Marina has now been living in her parent's home for several years, "getting stable again," and waiting for Armando to come whisk her away back to Mansoa. Hopeful as she is that this will happen, she also readily acknowledged that things might continue to go awry. "If he comes and tells me, 'Marina, what we talked about before, I can't do it anymore because I've gotten another girl pregnant,' I'll accept it. I'll just keep on with my life. Maybe I can continue going to school, or if I can't go back to school, I'll just stay in my parent's house."

Toward the end of my stay in 2010 Marina asked me to accompany her to the local clinic to discuss options for birth control with the midwife who made tours around the region. She wanted to get an intrauterine device (IUD) but wasn't quite sure how they worked and whether they were safe, so she asked me to come read the packaging for her. She also asked if I could provide the 2000 CFA (about US$4) for the IUD and procedure. We went together and sat with the midwife as I read the materials that came with the IUD and talked through the process and potential complications. The midwife strongly encouraged her to make an appointment, and Marina, who had been listening attentively, said she would think about it. Later, I asked if she was going to tell Armando about the IUD and she said, "No. If I do, he might think that I don't want to have more kids with him, and then he'll look elsewhere for someone to have kids with. I *do* want more children. But not until I'm healthy. I'm doing this because I'm sick." I gave her the 2000 CFA and told her that even if she decided not to use it for the IUD she could keep it to buy more condoms or get something Deluza needed. The following month she told me she had decided against the IUD and opted for Norplant, a form of birth control discontinued in the United States but still quite popular in much of rural Africa. Marina showed me where the Norplant rods had been implanted in her upper arm and said she hoped the small incision would become less noticeable before Armando's next visit.

Even amidst the rapid change in young women's lives, prospects, and experiences, this incident had a *déjà vu* quality for me, since I played a similar role many times with Marina's mother's generation the decade before. In 2001–2003 one of my more frequent functions for members in

my women's work group was as a resource—informational and financial—
for birth control. Many of them had given birth eight or ten or twelve
times, and they wanted to stop, or at least take a break. After her youngest
son was born Nho Keboral continued to get pregnant, but her pregnancies
always ended in miscarriage. Her body was getting weaker and she was
severely anemic. Nho Keboral miscarried at least twice, as far as I know,
early in my residence in Esana, and this was a major factor that contributed to her eventually confiding in me that she wanted my help in seeking
out birth control options. In 2003, after many conversations about various
birth control options with Nho Keboral, she asked me to take her across
the border to Senegal so she could get the Pill. Once she was no longer
having miscarriages her health improved considerably and she regained
much of her strength, which she immediately harnessed into unremitting
labor in the forests and paddies. Several of her peers—many of them my
closest companions in Esana—followed suit, and I often made trips across
the border with them so they could obtain birth control that they assumed
their elders—and often their husbands—would not approve of.

Birth control was another arena in which Nho Keboral drew clear distinctions between "then" and "now," but unlike most of her other assessments along these lines, enhanced knowledge about and access to birth
control was one of the few things that Nho Keboral counted as an improvement in Jola life. "In those days," Nho Keboral insisted,

> Women didn't know anything about birth control. Some older women
> had secrets about how to prevent pregnancy or even abort, but they
> would never tell you because that was taboo. So we didn't have family
> planning. I wanted to know these things but I didn't have anyone to teach
> me. But now, everyone goes to school and they know all of these things.
> In those days, we didn't know anything. Nothing! Your mother didn't tell
> you anything because she didn't know anything herself. So if she taught
> you something it would be a lie because she didn't know anything.

Nho Keboral and her peers now utilize a range of birth control options that none of them did when I first came to Esana. Their children are
instructed on basic sex education, AIDS awareness, and birth control options in school—much as their parents and grandparents feared they
would be when schools started in the 1960s and they hid their children in
the forest to protect their ears from being poisoned by such knowledge.
Nho Keboral and other women of her generation receive such instruction
when they bring their children to be vaccinated or treated for illnesses at
the village clinic. But now Nho Keboral and many members of her cohort

consider it an advantage to have such information, although the implications have quite a significant impact on ideas and practices around sexuality, family size, and gender relations.

To be sure, the pro-natalist ethos among Jola that often obligated women of Nho Keboral's generation (and those that preceded it) to, as one of my neighbors put it, "keep giving birth until your body dries up," had dissipated somewhat given changes in the environment that impinged upon agricultural work, as well as intensifying concerns over an increasingly cash-based economy and all the costs associated with buying—instead of growing—rice, not to mention the expenses of keeping children in school. Young women in Marina's generation did not feel the same pressures their mothers had to bear children in the double digits. As Marina put it:

> You have a lot of kids and they won't get work, they'll just sit around. Then, you as the mother, you have to go round and round to search for something for them to eat, give them clothing, until they grow up. To have a lot of kids, I'm not saying it's not good, it's good, because if you have a lot of kids you could get lucky even with just one, but if you have just two that could be good for you, too. Now if I come to have a lot of them, since I don't have work, Deluza's father just waits for his salary, sometimes they don't even pay them for three or four or more months. What will we give our children to eat? There won't be anything. That's why I don't want a lot of children.

Although the potential dangers, stakes, and calculus around using birth control have shifted considerably since I shuttled Nho Keboral and her friends across the border, Marina and her peers still have to navigate the murky waters of gendered double standards and perceived social stigma when they strategize about their reproductive roles.

Not only are they caught betwixt and between two economic models that promote radically different ideals around family size, they are caught up in a chronic African tension—the pushes and pulls of individual interest versus social/familial obligation—that is manifesting itself in new and perhaps not quite legible ways. Marina, for instance, often expressed contradictory statements about where she saw her life leading. Sometimes she would insist that she wanted to join Armando in Mansoa and establish an autonomous household with him far from Esana and Jola-land. But once, when I asked Marina whether she would go with Armando if he invited her back, she said, "I won't refuse. Only if my parents say that I can't go. If they tell me I can't go, I won't refuse, I'll obey only my parents. If it happens that they'll come and give me another husband, I'll stay. Or if it happens

they tell me, 'You can't go. You should go to school,' I'll go to school. Whatever God destines, that's what will be." Marina is caught between her own
desires for an autonomous life with Armando and her own sense of obedience and obligation to her parents—a confusing state best left in God's
hands. Whenever she contemplates a life with Armando in Mansoa she is
quick to qualify this by insisting that she'll come back to Esana to help her
mother transplant and harvest rice. Sometimes she even extends this obligation to Deluza and finesses her predicament by granting herself the free-
dom to move away by leaving her daughter behind. "I don't want Deluza to
leave this place, here in my father's hands, because my father, none of his
grandchildren are in his hands. Now I want to leave Deluza in this place so
she can help my mother, even when I'm not here, she will stay here and help
my mother. My mother will take her to teach her to transplant, she'll teach
her all the ways, so that she [Deluza] can help her."

This concern about leaving one's parents without the extra hands
needed for agricultural labor is a major one across Jola villages. Since Jola
families have begun sending their children to schools around the country
(and sometimes across the border), they can no longer split their day
between school in the morning and agricultural labor in the afternoon.
An aging head-of-household generation is, for the first time in Guinean
Jola-land, feeling the effect of scattered offspring increasingly reluctant, or
legitimately hard-pressed, to return home, even for the agriculturally intensive months during the shortened rainy season. This exacerbates the
already-intense pressures on rural Jola households to produce enough rice.
One might think that the return of unmarried young mothers to their natal
households would provide an unwitting resolution to this problem, particularly as their own young children are raised within the agricultural
knowledge system and demanding work regime of their grandparents. But
things have not quite panned out this way. Marina's expression of concern
and obligation toward her parents has not manifested itself in time spent
with her mother bending over rice seedlings in the paddies. It is a widely
acknowledged and often-commented-upon fact that Marina's generation is
not up to the kind of punishing manual labor that their mothers perform
each day. And unlike the previous decade, in my return visits I have not
seen any parents using the flat sides of their machetes to bodily correct this.

In Marina's family, the collective hopes are pinned on the eldest son's
academic success and the youngest daughter's chastity (or at least precau-
tion). If Gregório manages to finish his post-secondary accounting course
in Bissau the family believes he will find a job and be able to support them
all, or at least help out considerably. And as for the youngest daughter,

Noelza, her father decided to avoid the São Domingos middle school, given his other daughters' experiences there, and invest even more money in her schooling (and, perhaps more to the point, her supervision) by sending her to a private school run by nuns in Ingore, where she lives with her eldest sister, Sabina, and Sabina's four children.

When I asked Marina about Noelza's prospects, and whether she is preparing her younger sister to face the challenges of being away from the watchful eyes of her parents and extended kin, she told me, "Noelza should continue her schooling, now that we [Sabina and I] have cut off our own schooling because we gave birth; she shouldn't give birth yet. She should continue her schooling and if she finishes she will find work and help us; if our men don't have anything, she can help us, she can give my child something to wear. That would be the best thing." I asked Marina whether she discussed this with Noelza. "When she came here," she told me,

> We sat her down, me and Gregório, and we spoke with her and she agreed. But at night we didn't know where she went off to. She went off, wandering around. One day, my brother came and shut the door and told her he would beat her; she got scared and stopped. But in Ingore, where she is, in Sabina's hands, she doesn't go out anywhere. . . . They forbid her to go out. Sabina knows that, since she herself stopped her own schooling. Now my mother, all of her daughters, those of us— Sabina and I—have already given birth. Only Noelza is left. If Noelza also gets it in her head to give birth, that's even more. Who is going to come and give our children anything to eat? . . . No one.

When I last spoke to Ampa Badji and Nho Keboral, we caught each other up on our respective lives. I told them about my life and new job in Boston and they filled me in on their rainy season (or lack thereof) and the increasing cost of imported rice. They told me that Marina was feeling better and had not had seizures for several months. "And guess what?" they said. "Noelza is pregnant."

....

CHAPTER 8

Conclusions:
Structural Uncertainty

Souls are mixed with things and things with souls. . . .
Lives are mingled together, and this is how, among persons
and things so intermingled, each emerges from their own
sphere and mixes together.

—MARCEL MAUSS,
The Gift

Stories are redemptive, then, not because they preserve or
represent the truth of any individual life but because they
offer the perennial possibility that one see oneself as, and
discover oneself through, another, despite the barriers of
space, time, and difference.

—MICHAEL JACKSON,
The Politics of Storytelling

....

This is ostensibly a book about rice. By making rice one of the central characters in the story I have tried to convey its ubiquity and importance in Jola society. I have tried to capture, as much as any ethnographer can, what my interlocutors thought about, talked about, and organized their lives around. Although I did not go to Guinea-Bissau to study anything having to do with rice, the fact that it became so central to my research and ultimately found its way into the title of this book reminds us of a central tenet of ethnography captured by Peter Metcalf's quip that anthropologists end up studying whatever their informants want to talk about (Metcalf 2002).

But the focus on rice also evokes a longstanding anthropological approach to take seriously the seemingly mundane material stuff of life, not only because our interlocutors say so, but because it reveals a rather elusive concept: that people and things are inscribed in each other. For Jola and other rice cultivating people in this region rice is (or has been) the core material—the substance through which they have subsisted, but also so much more. Rice requires a certain kind of work, which in turn makes a certain kind of person. Rice elicits a certain constellation of appetites and desires, and its absence produces a certain kind of hunger and privation. The story of Jola villagers' preoccupation with rice reveals, in a larger sense, the entanglement of the material and the ideal. The concept of "sacred rice" does this by joining together in one phrase the supernatural and the natural, the spiritual and the material, the metaphysical and the physical, the intangible and the tangible, the religious and the secular, the extraordinary and the everyday.

All of this has implications for what broad concepts like "environment" and "development" mean. Although Jola and outside observers locate the primary culprit of their current hardships as the lack of rain, this does not mean that they are in the midst of an environmental crisis in the conventional sense. Rice and rain are not things outside of themselves, and the environment more generally is not merely "a space inhabited" (Croll and Parkin 1992:7). Rather, all of these are ontologically part of the Jola people; they comprise their cultural imagination of themselves. Rice and rain—whether abundant or depleted—are neither exterior to Jola society, nor located as separate entities to be managed or extracted or replaced. Their presence or absence ripples across all social and cosmological spheres and is entwined with Jola beliefs and practices around gender, knowledge, power, and work—in short, with Jola identity. So much so that, even from their refuge across the Senegalese border, Ampa Badji's grandfather's kin and friends risked Portuguese bullets to bury their dead in their own land, re-inscribing person and place as one indistinguishable entity. Eventually, they settled for an uneasy semblance of peace with Portuguese colonial officials in order to continue cultivating their central crop. Likewise, despite early orphanhood and childhood travails, Ampa Badji's parents became known as hard workers and successful rice cultivators, and they taught their only son to be the same. Even though he was schooled in the Mission and has spent most of his life teaching primary school, Ampa Badji repeatedly insisted "I am a rice farmer." For his generation, the hard work of rice farming was essential in defining a good Jola person, and a necessary prerequisite for marriageability. Throughout his

adult life, however, he and Nho Keboral have become increasingly cogni-
zant of the decreasing tenability of a rice-based livelihood. Nonetheless,
they continued to expend their time and energy in the paddies—to work
harder—and Nho Keboral began to spearhead collective efforts to address
their labor challenges. But their struggles to eke out a living in the forests and paddies have pushed them to reformulate their dreams for their
children, and they hope that their hard work to keep them in school—
combined with *Emitai*'s munificence—will lead their children far away
from farming life in Esana. These examples across several generations
suggest that it may be more productive to think of environmental change
as a social problem, not just a problem pertaining to science and nature.
Although I have detailed the particular Jola version of this, it serves as a
general reminder to re-inscribe the environment in a social world.

This ethnography also suggests several challenges to commonplace
development assumptions about power, practice, agency, and knowledge.
When Jola insist on "hard work," for instance, we have to understand that
work is not just tied to productivity and output, but also is crucially linked
to personhood, morality, and social structure. Development approaches
that see work solely as an economic activity geared toward such goals as
efficiency and growth not only betray their own moral prescriptions and
ideological underpinnings (in a word, their own culture), but they will
likely find themselves at odds with the very people they (supposedly) most
want to engage in a collective effort at betterment.

Likewise, Jola approaches to knowledge and the communicative strategies that surround them contrast in important ways with developmentalist—
and, more broadly, scientific and progressive political—epistemological
orientations: that it is good to ask, to learn as much as possible from as
many people as possible; that the way to address a given problem is to learn
about it rapidly and act even faster; and that, in a high-modernist version
of science, everything is ultimately knowable. As we have seen, Jola norms
regulate the circulation of knowledge—whether across generations, genders, or lineages—and concealment or avoidance are understood as protective strategies given the dangers inherent in certain kinds of knowledge.
Although this was most explicitly elaborated in Chapter Four, each chapter
touched on the problematic relationship between knowledge and practice.
The ethnographic data challenge what is often assumed—even by the most
progressive development practitioners—to be a direct link between knowing something and doing something directly about it. Jola know about
their changing environmental conditions. They know about the decrease
in rain—and the host of other changes—that challenge their work in the

rice paddies. They can articulate these problems clearly. But identifying these problems is not isomorphic with addressing them in ways that development experts or other outsiders might assume (or desire). Following Bourdieu, Jola practice—in the face of certain knowledge—may have a logic that is not that of logic, or at least the logic undergirding most development approaches.

Jola villagers are investing their energy and resources in various calculations, stakes, experiments, and gambles, each of which has serious individual and social costs and potentially profound transformative implications. At one level, the units of production and consumption are changing. Where the household was once the primary basis of the agricultural labor scheme, the work association has increased in importance in various ways. Given the increasingly dispersed household and the decreasingly favorable environmental conditions, this longstanding Jola institution is being deployed in new ways. Moreover, some producers have now become consumers: the children who once took their places alongside their parents in the paddies now rely on their parents' rural remittances of rice as they pursue further schooling far from Jola-land. Children and households are thus produced—and reproduced—in different ways, as are men and women. Men are no longer "made" through agricultural prowess, and so they seek both new and old ways of becoming and being men. One of the only ways women have been able to get their "feet out of the fire" is through the increased salience of collective work, and yet their daughters have not followed suit, so it remains unclear what being a Jola woman will mean (and entail) for Marina's generation. In the midst of these shifts in gender and socialization, parents continue to inculcate their children into a moral universe that values hard work and no theft. But although hard work retains its status in the Jola moral register, its currency has changed. one can no longer exhibit it in exchange for a spouse, but one may be able to trade on it for mutual help in times of extreme need. Likewise, Ampa Badji and Nho Keboral's continued insistence that their children not become thieves might seem to be a mere echo of expired parental expectations, a *non sequitur* in their current context. But their efforts to keep sending rice to their far-flung children in order to prevent them from stealing highlights their determination to instill a core tenet of Jola identity, and it is perhaps one of the only parenting strategies left to them: even in the capital city their children can still be Jola if they do not become thieves.

Throughout the narrative I have touched upon moments of misfortune in the lives of Ampa Badji and Nho Keboral's family. Nho Keboral's miscarriage while hauling heavy jerry-cans of palm oil across the Senegalese border resulted not only in the loss of her pregnancy, but—as she herself lamented—the loss of badly needed cash from her efforts to *kuji-kuji*. Later that same year insects invaded the family granary and depleted their meager stock of stored rice, making it impossible to support their older children's schooling through rural rice remittances. Several years later, after much scrimping and saving, Gregório's enrollment fees were stolen in Bissau. And Marina not only became pregnant against her parent's admonitions, but her efforts to establish an independent household with her boyfriend were thwarted when she developed epilepsy. We are witnesses to a great deal of bad luck, but we also begin to see the contours of the structural uncertainty that shapes these and other Jola lives. This kind of uncertainty extends beyond the season-to-season question about whether a particular harvest will suffice or even the perennial parental question about whether a particular son or daughter will succeed. Whole modes of being in the world are coming into question, and there is a general precariousness as to whether current techniques of material and social reproduction can fulfill their intended outcomes. Structurally, the system is in a moment of deep uncertainty as beliefs and practices around livelihood, personhood, gender, and religion are challenged to the core.

This is a problem that international development—as an ideology and an enterprise—thinks it knows how to fix. But the kinds of solutions that would come under the purview of development—many of which would require making Jola into a very different kind of people—do not map onto what or how Jola want to be in the world, nor would they be effective approaches among a people who have historically demonstrated their capacity to remain uncaptured (whether by Mandinka or other Muslims, French or Portuguese, missionaries or development practitioners).

There are, of course, both strengths and limitations in different approaches to work and knowledge (and even uncertainty), and one simply cannot ignore the fact that the norm of narrowly distributing information and the importance of self-reliance and household autonomy are part of the reason that it is so difficult for Jola to deal with their current predicament of declining rain and rice as a collective problem. A consequence of the ways in which Jola continue to define "hard work" as solely based on rice cultivation, combined with the ways in which they control knowledge, is that these dynamics maintain the status quo. This is not the same as saying such cultural processes *cause* Jola inaction and increasing poverty. Rather, these dynamics have the unintended consequence of buttressing continuity and being poorly suited to responsive changes in a changed set of circumstances. Ultimately, the ways in which Jola "work hard" and control the flow of information in both quotidian interaction and formal spheres are more than challenges to external agents of agricultural change. Collective and proactive responses from Jola themselves are inhibited by these norms, a predicament that is currently exacerbating the pressures on Jola households to make ends meet.

The impasse here is not one that pits progress against culture, nor modernity against tradition, nor innovation against conservatism. Jola are not passive in the face of their dilemma. Rather, there is a range of responses that Jola pursue as ways to "get their feet out of the fire." Their reactions and coping strategies do not isolate the material (rice), but often stress the link between the material and the ideal, with what it means to be Jola. Sometimes this means that individuals work harder but also find new ways to collectivize their work. Sometimes it means emphasizing certain aspects of religious and ritual life (like male initiation), or switching religions altogether. Sometimes it means sending one's children away to school, while reinforcing particularly powerful values (like no theft) even in the faraway context of the capital city. Some Jola romanticize the past while engaging in the backbreaking (and often heartbreaking) efforts to *kuji-kuji* in the present. In all of these efforts we see Jola conservatism, but also Jola creativity. Some things get accentuated, some things challenged, and some things find new expression.

When thinking about the future—or, as Charles Stafford put it, the "very common type of human question . . . what is going to happen next?" (Stafford 2007:57)—Jola have neither the "detached aspirations" (Bourdieu 2000) nor the indifferent "short-termism" (Day, Papataxiarchēs, and Stewart 1999) described by other anthropologists exploring responses among peoples grappling with precariousness and uncertainty. The people in this book make choices, make mistakes, and experience setbacks. But their capacity to choose or to overcome obstacles is severely constrained by the changing social structures over which they have little or no control. They actively shape their material worlds and make decisions about their own life trajectories, but they are also often unwittingly shaped by processes beyond the ken of their agency.

The story of Jola rice farmers in Guinea-Bissau thus captures a key aspect of globalization: the effort to make sense of dramatic changes wrought by forces beyond local control, and to respond based on local imaginings of what the good life is. But this book also challenges two key frameworks that organize most versions of globalization: the gloom-and-doom tale of local collapse or the celebratory story of cultural creativity and resistance. To be sure, there are both tragic and heroic moments, but neither of these tropes is singularly sufficient as an account of Jola lives. Ultimately, relying on such reductive assessments does a disservice to our attempts to render the full humanity of these lives, and smuggles in a version of the "single story" that has so often flattened representations of Africans—and especially rural Africans—at great cost (Adichie 2009).

In all of these ways, rice has served as a suitable focal point that ties together the personal narratives of the human characters and the contexts relevant to understanding and explaining the situations in which they find themselves. But, as it has for Jola themselves, rice has receded as the narrative moved forward, and by Chapter Seven it barely made it on the page. "I was so hungry I cried," Nho Keboral lamented to me as she related her brief experience in Portugal, away from her rice-oriented home. But she later confessed that the only thing she wished for her children was that "they don't stay here." Ampa Badji insisted, despite his salaried employment as a teacher, that he was first and foremost a rice farmer. But when reflecting on his children's prospects, he admitted that rice farming had become "outdated." Marina's concerns centered on distancing herself both from the exhausting work of her mother's generation and the foreclosed lives of her *jopai* peers. She set her sights on returning to school and to her boyfriend and, although she was a competent cultivator and hard worker, her sense of self was not tied to rice farming.

So, although this is a book about rice, it is also a book about several kinds of relationships: between a changing mode of livelihood and changes in every other part of a particular society; between knowledge and practice; between structure and agency; and, perhaps most importantly, among the people that populate this narrative themselves. Even through the particularity of their individual life histories and singular social dramas, these Jola villagers exemplify dilemmas rural people throughout West Africa (and probably elsewhere) face as they try to keep their families together and as they continue to farm and live in ways that give them a sense of accomplishment in their own eyes and in the eyes of their kin and neighbors, but in a world of circumstances that make those efforts increasingly precarious. By showing how Jola are thinking and feeling about, and responding to, those circumstances we gain insight into aspects of the human condition that are at times counterintuitive, but always revelatory, and hopefully resonant.

GLOSSARY
....

The languages I used throughout fieldwork included Crioulo (also known as Guinean Creole, Kiryol, Kriulo, Portuguese Creole, and Guineense) and Edjamat Jola. Crioulo is the *lingua franca* of Guinea-Bissau and its widespread use across the country makes it one of the strongest bases of Guinean national identity. Jola is spoken by members of the Jola ethnic group across Guinea-Bissau, Senegal, and the Gambia, although there are several different dialects and there is a high degree of linguistic variation even within the same dialect. The majority of Jola villagers in Guinea-Bissau speak both Edjamat Jola and Crioulo. The quotations from Edjamat Jola and Crioulo speakers included in this book have been translated by me into English. This glossary provides a list of words and phrases in both Edjamat Jola and Crioulo that can be found throughout the book.

JOLA

Adjadjau (sing.); *edjodjowai* (plural) Third male age grade; involves wrestling and dancing.

Adjamurau (sing.); *edjamurai* (plural) A married adult man with an autonomous household.

Ai (sing.); *ai-i* (plural) Highest level ritual authority at village level.

Amangen (sing.); *amangen-i* (plural) Ritual elder; usually referring to a shrine priest.

Apurau (sing.); *epurai* (plural) First age grade for boys; generally comprised of eleven- to twelve-year-olds; mostly involved in cow herding.

197

Aruntchikau (sing.); *eruntchikai* (plural)   Second age grade for boys; comprised of teenagers to early twenty-year olds; involved in wrestling, dancing, and the betrothal process.

Asubangilau (sing.); *esubangilai* (plural)   Final male age grade; involves building an autonomous house.

Badjolidjolabu   A headpiece worn by Jola boys; a mix of burnt jackfruit shell and palm oil is spread as black ash around head and white buttons are sewn into the hair.

Bakinabu (sing.); *ukinau* (plural)   Spirit shrine.

Bapendabu   Headpiece worn by *edjodjowai*.

Batolhabu   Burial specialists.

Borokabu   Transplanting rice seedlings from the forest nursery into the inundated paddy.

Botunabu   Widow inheritance (levirate) practice.

Bujandabu   Iron-tipped fulcrum shovel.

Bukut (bukutabu)   Male initiation.

Butat   Forest.

Butonda   Rice paddy.

Buyabu   A cohort of men and women who became engaged during the same year.

Ebandai   Marriage ceremony involving pig sacrifice.

Ebongai   Headpieces worn by boys to mark their age grade.

Edjalai   Harvesting.

Ehendjekurai   Final headpiece in male age grade system; the entire head is covered with white shells.

Embelengai (sing.); *bambelengabu* (plural)   A headpiece made of metal worn by *edjodjowai*.

Esaangai   Ceremony conducted every six years; related to male initiation proceedings.

Ewañai   Tilling a rice paddy.

Harimanahu   Part of funerary and grieving process during which relatives of the deceased remain in his or her house and courtyard for several days, composing and singing eulogistic songs about the deceased.

Hubohu   An educative process whereby older boys instruct younger ones on dances (especially *konkon*), work techniques, wrestling, and other gender-specific activities.

Hukulahu   Cleared circular space in each neighborhood, usually surrounded by large cottonwood trees, used for public gatherings such as funerals, celebrations, and meetings.

Hungómahu Metal headpiece worn by Jola boys.

Hurirahu A twisted white cloth with beads worn like tails by *esubangilai* at wrestling matches.

Huwokuñahu Girls' dance.

Kajanayaku Jola neologism for school; derived from Jola words for "ear" and "to hear"; encoded Jola concern that, at school, Jola children would hear things that were forbidden and perhaps even dangerous for them to know.

Kandaabaku Palm raffia belt used for climbing palm trees to tap them for wine.

Karenghaku Spirit shrine associated with male initiation.

Kasaabaku Corpse inquisition.

Kasaalaku Nickname.

Konkon Well-known male dance.

Kugabaku Headpiece worn by Jola boys; a row of white buttons is added to the star shape.

CRIOULO

Asosiason Collective work group.

Bagiche Sauce made from whipped hibiscus leaves and okra, sometimes used as a topping for rice.

Bolsa Scholarship (generally to study abroad).

Fura To tap oil palm trees for palm wine.

Kaneka Mug (mostly plastic; often used for drinking water or palm wine).

Kuji-kuji To hustle; to engage in small-scale activities in order to scrape enough cash together on a daily basis for basic needs.

Labra To cultivate; in particular, to till a rice paddy (similar to Jola *ewanai*).

Matu fitchadu Dense, uncut, largely impenetrable forest.

Pabi To clear-cut forest areas for cultivation.

Padi/ntera Literally: birth/burial; refers to high rates of infant mortality.

Pega tesu Strive; try hard.

Prasa Town (referring to any urban area).

Sipaios Portuguese colonial soldiers.

NOTES

....

Introduction

1. All names have been changed, except those of widely recognized political and historical figures.
2. Jola do not keep precise track of their age, but I estimate that Nho Keboral was approximately forty-seven years old at the time of this anecdote.
3. See Ohnuki-Tierney for similar observations among Japanese tourists: "Japanese, especially older Japanese who travel abroad, often complain that they do not feel satisfied after eating meals without rice; *manpukukan* (the full-stomach feeling) is not achieved without rice, no matter what else is eaten" (Ohnuki-Tierney 1993:41–42). Also, Nho Keboral's comment on Chinese rice "not tasting right" could be linked to evidence of West Africans' highly differentiated and fine-grained assessments of various characteristics (including taste) of rice varieties, especially new hybrids (see Temudo 2011).
4. See, for example, D'Almada (1594); Baum (1999); Lauer (1969); Linares (1970, 1981, 1985, 1992, 2005); Mark (1985); P. Pélissier (1958, 1966); Sapir (1970); Snyder (1973, 1981); Thomas (1959a, 1959b, 1963); Thomson (2006).
5. See Shipton (1994) for a review of similar symbolic and humanized approaches to land and its products in tropical Africa.
6. When my Jola interlocutors spoke about rice being sacred they often used the Crioulo word "sagradu." But they also discussed rice with Jola words and expressions that, although they might not literally translate to the English word "sacred," conveyed the many senses of sacred that I try to draw out here.

7. Although the Maussian framework is, I believe, the most pertinent here, there is another sense in which the Jola notion of "sacred rice" resonates with a Marxist understanding of the sacred being that which is outside the realm of use values.

8. See McCann (2005) for more on maize in Africa.

9. See also Andrieu (2008) for additional meteorological and geographical data on changes in rainfall and vegetation in the Gambia, southern Senegal, and Guinea-Bissau regions.

10. In this way, although Mauss advanced his concept of a total social phenomenon as a departure from Durkheimian sociology, his views on the dynamism of such phenomena echoes, in part, Durkehim's understanding of sacredness: that it was an ascribed rather than inherent aspect of things, and thus subject to change or even demise.

11. See Berry (1984, 1989); Bigman (1993); Carney and Watts (1991); Guyer (1978, 1983); Hart (1982); Linares (1981, 1985); Weil (1973).

12. See Carney and Watts (1991); Chazan and Shaw (1988); Cohen (1988); Commins, Lofchie, and Payne (1986); Franke and Chasin (1980); Glantz (1987); Linares (1985); Mortimore (1989); Watts (1983).

13. See also: McCann (1999); Leach and Mearns (1996); Broch-Due and Schroeder (2000).

14. See, for example, Becker and Yoboué (2009); Bigman (1993); Galli (1987b); Vogel (2005); Lofchie (1975); Moseley, Carney, and Becker (2010). Lofchie's assertion that "In Africa, political and economic arrangements have converted a problem of climactic unpredictability into an immense human catastrophe" (1975:554) clearly resonates with this case.

15. See Roitman for a creative critique of the orthodoxy of crisis as "an enabling blind spot for the production of knowledge" (2014:14).

16. Jola refer to imported rice as "sack rice" or "store rice." Most imported rice in Guinea-Bissau currently comes from China, Vietnam, and Thailand.

17. The dynamics around shifting levirate (*botunabu*) practices and the status of widows are quite complex. For now, what is important is to acknowledge that decreasing rice supplies play a significant part in the changes in social organization concerning widows.

18. See Dove (2014) for an expertly curated collection of the anthropology of climate change.

Chapter 1

1. This centrist approach to the history of agriculture, even when modified to account for multiple centers, has since fallen out of favor and an understanding of agricultural innovation—especially in Africa—has taken on a

more diffused and mosaic character. As Harlan et al. explain, "African agriculture appears to be basically non-centric in character. Not only do we fail to detect a particular center for the origin of indigenous African agriculture, but some African crops do not seem to have 'centers' either. . . . Our own analyses of the situation would call for a more diffused view. . . . The basic pattern is diffuse and noncentric rather than centric" (Harlan, De Wet, and Stemler 1976:5).

2. As Latham explains, "Water is more important than the type of soil, and given adequate water, rice will grow satisfactorily on many different soils, and in many different climatic conditions. Successful cultivation requires keeping the crop flooded for most of its growth period. . . . Yet paradoxically, the actual water needs of rice are no greater than that of any other dry crop, and it is the extra nutrients which rice can absorb under swamp conditions which make the difference" (Latham 1998:10–11).

3. See Sharma and Steele (1978) for an explanation of various hypotheses regarding the introduction of Asian rice to West Africa. There is currently significant varietal diversity of *Oryza sativa* in West Africa, particularly among upland varieties.

4. Interestingly, the introduction of *O. sativa* in Africa seems to bring out the lyrical in otherwise technical agronomist prose. *O. sativa's* history in Africa is "written on the wind" (Carpenter 1978:3) and "lost in the sands of time" (Sharma and Steele 1978:62).

5. Exemplary statements of this kind can be found in Buddenhagen (1978) who emphasizes the "primitivity" of both the cultigen and the cultivation practices: "To the observer familiar with Asian rice culture, the most notable characteristics of rice growing in Africa are its apparent newness and its primitive state. This generally primitive culture extends to most food crops in tropical Africa, and thus it is not due to the newness of rice in Africa, but rather to the character of peasant agriculture itself" (Buddenhagen 1978:11).

6. See Lansing (1991) for an excellent study of the repercussions of such Green Revolution approaches to rice cultivation in Bali.

7. According to McCann (2005), there was an earlier time in which colonial ecologists did, indeed, reflect "a deep understanding of African practice of agriculture, husbandry, and environmental management. . . . This tradition declined in the late 1930s and 1940s, superseded by the emergence of 'experts' trained more formally in the sciences of agriculture and medicine. . . . The new paradigm ignored the local in favor of the overarching structures of professionalizing science" (McCann 2005:138).

8. Eltis et al. argue against Judith Carney's "black rice" thesis (as well as Peter Wood and Daniel Littlefield's work, on which Carney's builds) by insisting

that "there is no compelling evidence that African slaves transferred whole agricultural systems to the New World; nor were they the primary players in creating and maintaining rice regimes in the Americas. . . . Furthermore, a close look at the slave trade from an Atlantic perspective suggests no evidence that the rice culture of South Carolina, Georgia, and Amazonia was any more dependent on skills imported from Africa than were its tobacco and sugar counterparts in the Chesapeake, the Caribbean, and Brazil. The evolving transatlantic connections, the age and sex composition of the slave trade, the broad shifts over time in transatlantic slaving patterns, and the structure of slave prices are all largely explained without reference to a supposed desire on the part of rice planters for slaves with rice-growing expertise developed in Africa" (Eltis, Morgan, and Richardson 2007:1335, 1357). See Hawthorne (2010) for a cogent response to Eltis et al.'s critique.

9. For the Asian "rice economies," Francesca Bray (1986, 1998) has argued for the limited value of a purely economistic interpretation of rice-based societies. Emiko Ohnuki-Tierney (1993) added to this contention with particular evidence from Japan: "Rice is a dominant metaphor of collective self for Japanese, especially in terms of how they have come to define and re-define themselves as a people in various cultural encounters. As each 'historical other' has emerged, rice (as food) and rice paddies (as land) have been the 'vehicles for deliberation' on the Japanese notion of self" (Ohnuki-Tierney 1993:5). This is best exemplified by post-agrarian Japan's protests over increasing importation of rice grown in the United States. Both Bray and Ohnuki-Tierney take a typical anthropological stance in arguing for the importance of cultural factors in addition to—or, in Ohnuki-Tierney's example, even more than— economic valuations of rice cultivation. The broad aim of my argument for Jola—that we must try to grapple with the complexity and multidimensionality of their relationship to rice—is the same. The context, however, is different. Ohnuki-Tierney's case (at least at the time she wrote it in the early 1990s) is based on an increasingly affluent population, where urbanized Japanese are holding on to a largely nostalgic image of rural wet rice paddies. Even as their own rice consumption is decreasing in favor of more flavorful and expensive side dishes (*fukushoku*), they insist on "pure" Japanese rice, and shift their valuation from quantity to quality of the crop. But what about in a context in which the standard of living is decreasing, and people still have to renegotiate their relationship to rice?

10. In terms of its value as an international trade commodity, the rice market is generally considered to be a structurally "thin" one. That is, most of the rice that is produced across the world is consumed by the producers and exporters themselves, and what enters the market is "residual," leftover rice

(Latham 1998; Sayamwala and Haykin 1983). Rice does not have a central market (such as the Chicago wheat market) and is mostly traded by governments rather than private entities. "Rice is often considered one of the most protected commodities in the world and only about 7% of global rice production is traded on the international market" (Seck et al. 2013:24).

11. Even prior to official independence, then-Portuguese Guinea's revolutionary leader, Amílcar Cabral, prioritized rice self-sufficiency as part of the independence struggle, aiming to "raise rice production in the zones controlled by the PAIGC by 20 percent, to create food storage facilities and to set up an infrastructure for domestic trade which would allow farmers to exchange rice for" other goods (Bigman 1993:63). Shortly after independence, however, the "anti-colonial revolutionaries became party-state bureaucrats whose policies more and more resembled those of the colonialists they had fought to replace" (Bigman 1993:124).

12. Other relevant institutions for rice research in West Africa—and international agricultural research and development more broadly—include: the International Rice Research Institute (IRRI) in Los Baños, Philippines (founded in 1960), the International Institute of Tropical Agriculture (IITA) in Ibadan, Nigeria (founded in 1967), the French Agricultural Research Centre for International Development (CIRAD), founded in 1984 (which incorporated nine French tropical agricultural research institutes, including IRAT—the Institut de Recherches Agronomiques Tropicales), and, finally, the French Institut de Recherche pour le Développement (IRD), formerly OSTROM, which was founded in the 1940s and currently works on rice cropping (among many other initiatives) in West Africa.

13. See Brooks (2010). See also Scoones, Devereux, and Haddad (2005) for a concise discussion of the problems of various technical, market-based, and policy fixes with regard to African agricultural development and Cernea (2005) for an important analysis of the persistent "uphill battle" to include social research in the CGIAR system.

14. See Richards (2006) for an excellent discussion of the pitfalls of such technocratic approaches to plant improvement strategies. See Offei et al. (2010) and Crane, Roncoli, and Hoogenboom (2011) for thoughtful extensions of Richards's work and useful suggestions for alternative approaches to seed science and agricultural development. But see, also, Tollens et al. (2013:13) for a more optimistic account of the successful adoption and increasing spread of NERICA varieties across West Africa. In 2011, AfricaRice began promoting a next generation of promising rice breeds, dubbed ARICA

(Advanced Rices for Africa), which, "unlike the NERICA varieties . . . are not restricted to interspecific crosses" (Kumashiro et al. 2013:75).

15. We cannot be sure, however, that the people farming rice in this region one thousand years ago considered themselves to be Jola. The origins of Jola ethnicity are debated.

16. Usually tilling the paddies with the *bujandabu* is considered quintessentially male labor, but there are some circumstances (such as widowhood) that lead women to use the heavy instrument to cultivate borrowed land.

17. Jola are most often referred to as "Felupe" in Guinea-Bissau, but I have opted to call them Jola as this is currently preferred among Jola themselves, who consider "Felupe" to be a Portuguese misnomer. The ethnonym "Jola" (other spellings include Diola and Djola) only became accepted in the nineteenth century, and there is some debate as to its provenance (see Thomas 1959b; Mark 1985; Nugent 2008).

18. Esana's total population was approximately 2,000. With the exception of a few shopkeepers, teachers, and other long-term residents from neighboring ethnic groups, all residents were Jola.

19. In addition to these three main dialects, there are several other dialects, some restricted to a single village. These include Buluf, Kombo, Narang, Gusilay, Karon, Kuwatay, and Mlomp (see Lewis, Simons, and Fennig 2014).

20. "Awasena" literally means "one who performs rituals" and refers specifically to the complex systems of spirit shrines that comprise Jola religious practice. But "awasena" has also become a kind of catch-all code to refer to any Jola practice deemed "traditional."

21. David Izadafir (UNODC Research Officer), personal communication.

22. Antonio Mazzitelli (former West Africa director of the UNODC), personal communication and quoted in Associated Press (2007).

23. Antonio Mazzitelli, quoted in Quist Arcton (2007).

24. Anonymous UN source, personal communication, May 2012. Likewise, a former UNODC representative in Dakar who was responsible for monitoring the drug trafficking situation in Guinea-Bissau was often asked by journalists to "verify that Guinea-Bissau is a narco-state," to which he regularly responded, "Well, to have a narco-state, you need to have a state. So perhaps it's a narco-economy" (Anonymous UNODC source, personal communication, May 2012).

25. Likewise, during the 1998 war, even though the majority of Bissau residents evacuated the capital, there were never any Internally Displaced Persons (IDP) or refugee camps, as the urban population was absorbed by rural households for the duration of the conflict.

Chapter 2

1. For example, see Barry (1981, 1998); Bigman (1993); Birmingham (1995, 1999); Bordonaro (2009); Brooks (1980a, 1980b, 1985, 1993); Chabal (1981); Cabral (1969, 1970); Chilcote (1977); Davidson (1969, 1981); Dhada (1993); Fage (1959); Forrest (1987, 1992, 1998, 2003); Galli (1987a, 1987b); International Crisis Group (2008); Lobban (1974); Lobban and Forrest (1988); Lobban and Mendy (1996, 2013); Lopes (1987); MacQueen (1997); Mark (1985, 1992, 1999); R. Pélissier (1989); Sangreman et al. (2008); Suret-Canale and Barry (1976); and Vigh (2006).

2. Fosterage in Jola families is quite common for a wide range of reasons, from the death of one's parents, as in Akabau's case, to extreme poverty or sickness in a family, or for less tragic reasons as a way to distribute children at different stages among those who do not have enough, whether because of their own reproductive problems or simply their stage in the life cycle. Most people I know in Esana have had some experience with either being fostered during some periods of their childhood, or taking in other children to foster, or often both. Such dynamics are quite widespread across African societies. See, for example, Alber, Martin, and Notermans (2013); Bledsoe (2002); Goody (1982); Johnson-Hanks (2006); and Shipton (2007).

3. There was an active trade in rice between the villagers who lived in the forested areas of Esana and the villagers from the reverine islands like Ellalab, Djifunku, Eosor, and Bullol, where palm trees did not grow. Jola in these villages were famous for growing the most rice in the region, as they had collectively engineered large dikes that enabled them to produce abundant paddy rice. This trade along the Jola axis of forest villagers (now referred to as *ginti di matu*) and water villagers (now referred to as *ginti di yagu*) persists to this day, with women from each side meeting each market day (*hiyeyehu*) in the Jola six-day week to trade small fish for products from the oil palm forests.

4. Like Ampa Badji's family, many Jola lineages were scattered in small hamlets around the forest for several hundred years, or as far back as any contemporary Jola can account for. But in the mid-1800s, a time of widespread internecine violence among Jola, they were brought together in an effort to consolidate the disparate populations into a militarily strong, confederated village. Although they settled in the various neighborhoods that eventually became the village of Esana, they maintained their land in the surrounding forests, and any Jola adult walking around these areas today can tell you the precise boundary lines between specific lineage holdings from this time. Often, when Ampa Badji tills this ground early in the rainy season to prepare it for growing seedlings that his wife will then transplant in the paddies, his

fulcrum shovel will uncover an old clay pipe or an earthenware pot left behind by his predecessors who inhabited the area before Esana was established as a confederated village.

5. *Kenyalen* has long been an active force in Jola society given the high incidence, especially prior to widespread WHO-sponsored immunizations, of infant mortality. Death of a child can be interpreted in many ways, but it generally has a social-spiritual dimension, which is in part what *kenyalen* members address through specific ceremonies and sometimes seclusion from would-be maleficent forces, be they human or supernatural. Women who enter *kenyalen* are worked extremely hard and are obliged to obey the *kenyalen* authorities in whose hands they are put. Ampa Badji's mother was made to pound rice for the whole household, to fetch water, and to complete all kinds of domestic tasks. Despite the hardship and required obedience, she was well cared for and given plenty to eat. Women taken into *kenyalen* are cared for entirely by the host's household, which covers their expenses and conducts ceremonies on their behalf. Even after she gives birth, a woman is kept in the *kenyalen* household until the baby has grown quite a bit. For more on *kenyalen*, see Journet (2007).

6. Payment for *kenyalen* is an ongoing struggle for most women who have gone through the rites, and many spend the rest of their lives paying back the *kenyalen* households that cared for them during their pregnancies and early motherhood. After Ampa Badji's mother gave birth to another child—a daughter this time—his parents raised a pig to pay at the spirit shrine. But payment does not release one from *kenyalen's* hold; whenever any concern regarding the child's health occurred, she was obliged to go back to them so they could attend to her and conduct the appropriate ceremonies.

7. The same process was repeated the following decade when Catholic missionaries first came to the area and wanted to set up their base of operations in Esana. Esana's elders again refused, and the Mission was sent off to outlying villages before coming back and insisting—with Portuguese backing—on establishing themselves in Esana.

8. For more on the Casamance separatist movement, see Faye (2006); Foucher (2002); Geschiere and van der Klei (1988); de Jong (2008); and Sonko (2004). The ongoing, low-grade Casamance conflict has been—and continues to be—a significant factor in local, regional, and national politics on both sides of the Senegal/Guinea-Bissau border, and it has had a substantial impact on the lives and experiences of Jola and other villagers in this area. An analysis of the relevance of the Casamance separatist movement for Guinean Jola does not, however, fall within the purview of this book.

9. There is evidence of active Jola resistance to Portuguese colonial presence in this region through a series of uprisings from the 1920s to the 1950s (see Chilcote 1972).

10. PIME, the *Pontificio Instituto Missioni Estere* (Pontifical Institute for Foreign Missions), is an Italian-based missionary group founded independently in Milan in 1850 and in Rome in 1874 as a society of diocesan priests whose explicit purpose is to dedicate their lives to missionary work across the globe. Pope Pius XI merged the two seminaries in 1926 when he officially recognized PIME as a Catholic missionary institution headquartered in Rome. PIME priests first came to what was then Portuguese Guinea in 1947 (Gheddo 1999). The Portuguese missionaries already active in the colony insisted on retaining their turf in Bissau, the new colonial capital. PIME priests had come through the imposition of the Vatican, and the Portuguese were not pleased about their presence in the colony (Gheddo 1999 and interviews with PIME priests). The policy of the Apostolic Prefect (there was no bishop in the region yet) was to reserve Bissau, Bula, Canchungo, and Mansoa for Portuguese Franciscan priests, and to send PIME priests, should they choose to stay, to "the bush." So, in 1947, six PIME priests and one monk began a series of expeditions into the interior, ultimately splitting into two groups: one settling in Bafatá and the other in Geba, both locations in the heart of Guinean Muslim country (Gheddo 1999:23). As of this writing, there are seventeen PIME priests and one PIME bishop in Guinea-Bissau.

11. The Italian PIME priests had two Portuguese Franciscan predecessors (a priest and a monk) who came to Esana in 1943. They set up their small mission in the center of town, across from the Portuguese army barracks, and attended only to the scant non-Jola population. They baptized six non-Jola African residents and set up a small school in which to teach them to read in Portuguese and pray in Latin. But they left in 1944 because, according to the current priest in Esana, they felt "it wasn't time yet" to be among the Jola since "they were too closed."

12. To compound matters, the site on which the Mission was developing its facilities was also home to an important women's spirit shrine—*karahayaku*. Women would regularly congregate there for ceremonies and weekly barter markets, and Padre Marmugi's attempts to hold mass or classes were often disrupted by these large gatherings, which sometimes included drinking, drumming, singing, and dancing. Marmugi decided that the two ceremonial sites—an expanding Catholic Mission and a longstanding women's spirit shrine—could not co-exist on the same turf, so he negotiated with village elders to move the women to a place behind the Mission walls. He gave the

elders a pig, some sugarcane liquor, and several bunches of tobacco and asked them for their help in moving the market and shrine. According to current accounts of this process, the negotiations were amicable (some more cynical residents say elders will do anything if you give them a little liquor), and a ceremony was held to remove the shrine and re-establish it where it currently sits, near the clearing that serves as Esana's traditional barter market.

13. Even though Padre Marmugi began his school with both boys and girls, after a few years he concentrated solely on boys. Girls had far more domestic duties than boys, and they were often sent to Senegal and the Gambia as domestics in order to earn enough money to acquire the basics for setting up a household once they were married, so their mobility disrupted Marmugi's plans for a stable Mission education.

14. He is also an invaluable resource on Jola linguistic matters. As soon as he arrived in Esana he began to study Jola language with Padre Marmugi, and he has since deepened and expanded his study so that, as many Jola villagers claim, Padre Luigi speaks better Jola than most Jola. He is clearly gifted with languages, and one of the only times I witnessed him becoming animated was when discussing linguistic matters. He compiled his linguistic studies into a small volume on Jola grammar (which I used in my own effort to learn the language) as well as in several editions of Jola dictionaries. Padre Luigi also translated much of the church liturgy and catechism lessons into Jola, and, unlike most priests around the country who have long since adopted Crioulo as the church *lingua franca*, he continues to conduct mass and give sermons in Jola.

15. When the Independence War broke out in 1963 and the Portuguese army occupied the Esana Mission, Padre Marmugi returned to Italy to get support and raise money for building a permanent Mission to advance PIME's work. Part of his plan included building a house for nuns, because, according to Padre Luigi, "he had come to the conclusion that, in order to enter among the Felupes, they would not accept us talking to the women. We needed other women to talk to Felupe women. If we didn't have nuns, we weren't going to get anywhere." He secured funds from various private donations in Italy and returned to construct many of the buildings that currently comprise the Mission facilities. The physical structures of the Mission buildings presently include the priests' dormitories and offices, with an attached kitchen and dining room; the nun's dormitory; a small health clinic run by the nuns; a women's center for sewing and canning activities; a carpentry and mechanic shop for Mission vehicles; a guest house (largely unused); the church; and the abandoned school house.

16. The impetus was two-fold: the Mission's own vehicles (the only ones in the area) needed regular repair from the inevitable damage wrought by rough or non-existent roads in the region; and Marmugi wanted to provide his Jola students with the opportunity to develop a set of practical and marketable skills beyond subsistence agriculture. Padre Luigi also cited another motive for developing the Mission workshop: by providing a local source of wage-earning jobs, he hoped to stem the flow of rural-urban migration of Jola youth looking to enter the cash economy, often with deleterious and destabilizing consequences for the migrants themselves and their home communities. Padre Luigi often repeated that it was one of his highest priorities to curb the flow of youth to urban areas, such as Bissau and Ziguinchor, as he saw the city as the site of much moral decay.

17. Not everyone treated the boys so well. Some soldiers would try to catch the boys when they hung around the barracks, and if they managed to catch one they beat him ruthlessly. Others would chase them away with a huge belt, whipping it at their legs. So Ampa Badji was always on the lookout for the "bad ones," and was generally able to avoid them. When he was being chased, he would quickly scamper under the barbed wire fence that surrounded the barracks, leaving the much larger soldiers on the other side. But most of the soldiers treated them well. "In truth," Ampa Badji recalled, "The Portuguese troops respected us."

18. Amílcar Cabral, an agronomist by training, was the revolutionary leader of Guinea-Bissau and Cape Verde's joint liberation struggle against Portuguese colonialism. He was assassinated in January 1973, just several months before Guinea-Bissau's official declaration of independence.

19. Padre Marmugi facilitated the establishment of this new neighborhood on land skirting the Mission walls for the first Jola Christian converts, although, at first, he did not want them to leave their natal neighborhoods, as he believed they were a vital link to reach out to the as-yet unbelievers in the village. He feared that by moving away from their neighborhoods they would lose contact with others in the village and the work of the Mission would not progress. These early adopters, however, were the targets of much abuse from their families and neighbors. Although they had not been baptized yet, they had begun to attend catechism and frequent Mission activities, and elders threatened them, saying that their children would die and they would not be able to have more children. Many of them were physically beaten. Once Padre Marmugi saw the physical dangers involved in their staying put, he arranged with the Portuguese authorities to use the land along the Mission walls to establish Santa Maria as the Jola Christian neighborhood. Six families built their houses there in 1964. Santa Maria has since grown to a

neighborhood of over sixty houses. Residents there maintain their claims to inherited rice paddies and forest groves, and thus continue to cultivate in their agnatic environment.

20. The bridge across João Landim, just outside Bissau, was completed in 2003 but officially inaugurated in 2005. The bridge across São Vicente was completed in 2009. Both projects were financed by Spain and effectively created a road link connecting Guinea-Bissau, Senegal, and the Gambia.

21. In transcribing Nho Keboral's self-recordings, I had ten single-spaced pages describing her various children's sicknesses. Angala, her fourth child was, as Nho Keboral put it, "the king of sickness." She was always rushing Angala to São Domingos to get treatment at the clinic there, as health resources were barely existent in Esana. Once he had cerebral malaria, a constant source of fear and dread in Jola-land that rapidly kills many children. During my first two years in the village I attended many funerals of small children who had succumbed to cerebral malaria. Another time a pain in his foot made it impossible for him to walk, so Nho Keboral and Ampa Badji would carry him everywhere until they eventually made it to the clinic in São Domingos. Although he was never clearly diagnosed, the doctor sent them on to Ziguinchor for treatment, and Ampa Badji and Nho Keboral spent the remainder of their scant savings on treatment for Angala. "I myself thought that Angala wouldn't live," Nho Keboral recalled.

Chapter 3

1. There are other reasons to resist the wholesale adoption of cashew farming, given massive fluctuations in the value of cashews in the international markets, as well as unpredictable shifts in national policies that regulate the cashew market. Guinea-Bissau's transformation from a net exporter of rice to a country now heavily dependent on rice imports is linked to the dramatic and widespread adoption, since the 1980s, of cashews as the dominant cash crop; currently, 98 percent of the country's export earnings comes from cashews (Abreu 2010) and despite its small size Guinea-Bissau is the world's second largest exporter of raw cashews (Temudo and Abrantes 2014). This all-too-familiar shift from food to cash crops has, as elsewhere on the continent, contributed to a decrease in overall food security (see Lofchie 1975). Some Jola villagers factored these risks into their decision-making, but most expressed more concern over the "laziness" that growing cashews would cultivate among Jola farmers.

2. See, for example, Atkins (1993); Coetzee (1988); Sodikoff (2004); Adas (1986); Jean Comaroff (1985); Ong (1987); Scott (1985); Taussig (1980); Cooper (1992); Pickering (2004); and Povinelli (1993).

3. See, for example, D'Almada (1594); Baum (1999); Brooks (1993); Coelho (1953); Crowley (1990); Dinis (1946); Gable (1997); Hawthorne (2003); Linares (1970, 1981, 1985, 1992); Lopes de Lima (1836); Mark (1985); Palmeri (2009); P. Pélissier (1966); Snyder (1973, 1981); Taborda (1950a, 1950b); Thomas (1959a, 1959b, 1963).

4. Even when Jola pool or exchange their labor with extended kin or work groups, the rice crop is always stored in the household granary of the conjugal family whose fields were cultivated. There are no communal granaries beyond the household level.

5. See also Berry (1993) and Fairhead and Leach (2005) for more on the importance of social relations in African agrarian systems. As Fairhead and Leach concisely explain, "Investment in social relations is investment in agriculture" (2005:87).

6. This is also where I depart from Netting's (1993) account of smallholders. Although Netting rightly refused both evolutionary and economically maximizing models to evaluate smallholders as a social form, he insisted that intensive cultivation was an adaptive—even ideal—type, glossing over the fact that some intensive cultivators can no longer maintain their practices in a sustainable way. Most of the characteristics that define smallholders, according to Netting, certainly apply to Jola. However, the aspects of high crop yield and sustainability so central to Netting's argument for a "smallholder alternative" (1993:9), at this juncture in Jola history, do not apply to them.

7. Ritual performances that evoke work, particularly during lifecycle transformations such as marriage and death, have symbolic dimensions that relate to productive and reproductive activities more generally. I provide more details on the symbolic aspects of funerary and other ritual activity in Davidson (2007).

8. Senegalese Jola have been migrating to urban areas—especially Dakar— for many decades (Lambert 2002; Linares 1992, 1987; Mark 1978; de Jong 1998, 2008).

Chapter 4

1. The intersection between these two types of production—agricultural and informational—reminds us of the etymology of the central anthropological concept of culture, which comes from the Latin *"colere,"*—to cultivate (see Williams 1985:87–93).

2. For studies that challenge the dichotomy between secrecy—especially around magicality—and modernity, see Lurhmann (1989) and West and Sanders (2003).

3. That said, given what was overall a prevailing ethos of secrecy around most things and my own reluctance to pry too much, I am acutely aware of the limits of my own knowledge of Jola lives.

4. "*Ukai beh*" is an abbreviated form of the complete question: "*Kama mukai ubeh.*"

5. See Goody (1978) for more on these dynamics. Linguistic anthropologists have also extensively studied such speech acts and communicative practices. My focus here is on the social organization of knowledge, rather than the sociolinguistics of knowledge, per se.

6. That religious knowledge resides within a priest class and is largely inaccessible to and unquestioned by lay people made for an initial comfortable (or at least familiar) fit between Jola religion and Catholicism (see Baum 1990:338).

7. Baum (1999) also discusses Jola techniques for acquiring knowledge in his study of Jola religious history. The two methods Jola employ to learn history, according to Baum (1999:16), are from stories told by elders and through use of special powers, such as dreams and visions. Moreover, van Tilburg (1998) explains that girls and women are not instructed in matters of reproduction—such as menarche and childbirth—until they are actually experiencing them. And it would be considered entirely inappropriate for anyone to ask about such matters.

8. See Linares (1970, 1992) for similar observations among Senegalese Jola.

9. One of the more prevalent themes that emerges from recent ethnographic literature on secrecy is the way in which various practices of secrecy disrupt our conventional understanding of egalitarianism and challenge typical models of the relationship between egalitarian and hierarchical forms of social and political organization (Gable 1997; Kratz 1990; Lurhmann 1989; Piot 1993).

10. In some Jola villages, 30 percent of households are headed by widows (Davidson 2007). In other Jola villages, the number of widows is not so high, primarily because the levirate system is still practiced, although it is starting to decline in these villages too.

11. There is no Jola word for widow. Women whose husbands have died, and men whose wives have died, are referred to in the same way as other women and men of their age, relative to who is addressing them. Sometimes widows and widowers are described as *apagnorol akem*, meaning "his/her husband died," but this is not used as a title or designation so much as a description.

12. There is a rich classic ethnographic literature on gendered domains of knowledge and secrecy—especially in reference to the body and bodily

processes—that I draw on here, especially Sally Falk Moore's (1976) analysis of why Chagga preserve the fiction that men's anuses are stitched closed during initiation, and Janis Irvine's (1976) study of Buu women's jural authority in matters of reproduction.

13. Women are prohibited from giving birth at home, and if they do the house becomes polluted and must either be ritually cleansed or torn down.

14. All of the Jola women in attendance had given birth to multiple children of both genders, and the information discussed, with the exception of the attempted conversation about birth control methods that I describe subsequently, remained within the purview of appropriate knowledge transmission among women of a certain reproductive status.

15. This analysis resonates with Fabian's (1990) key questions regarding power and performance: how Africans in diverse contexts use concealment as a strategic resource for the management of sociopolitical reality and, perhaps most importantly, how these strategies yield unintended consequences.

16. To be clear, there are no current development projects in northwestern Guinea-Bissau that seek, explicitly, to transform agricultural efforts, and this is not, therefore, an analysis of an actual development effort underway in this region. Rather, I bring to bear the ethnographic insights from this chapter to highlight the discursive contradictions between Jola cultivators and their would-be developers. And I ask broader questions about the assumptions that are entangled with efforts to access knowledge in its widest sense.

17. In this sense, I build on scholarship that explores the relationship between various kinds of indigenous knowledge and the goals and ambitions of participatory development projects, particularly those committed to interaction among agents of development and their would-be beneficiaries (e.g., Agrawal 1995; Ansell 2009; Arce and Long 1992; Bicker, Sillitoe, and Pottier 2004; Bornstein 2005; Cook and Kothari 2001; Elyachar 2005; Gupta 1998; Hendry and Watson 2001; Li 2007; Long and Long 1992; Pandian 2009; Pigg 1995a, 1995b, 1997; Rademacher 2011).

18. A counterpoint to this theme is developed by those who study the use of secrecy—particularly in the form of ambiguity and deception—as a "weapon of the weak" (Scott 1985; see also Jackson 1982).

19. See West and Sanders's (2003) edited volume that exposes such "retrograde" practices as magic in so-called modern contexts, thereby subverting the Enlightenment idea that transparency, as a mode of knowledge, replaces previous "irrational" forms.

Chapter 5

1. See Peter Mark (1992) for a detailed description and analysis of Jola male initiation in the northern Casamance region of Senegal. See also Ferdinand de Jong (1998, 2002, 2008) for thoughtful discussions on the transformations in these ceremonies in Senegal brought about by increased migration, shifts in Senegalese national politics, and the expanding influence of Islam in this region, among other factors.

2. Padre Luigi's general orientation to Jola male initiation is in stark contrast to other Catholic priests in Jola communities to the north (in Senegal's Casamance region), as well as Catholic priests with active missionary presence among other ethnic groups in Guinea-Bissau. The general trend has been to accept—and in some cases encourage—a convert's participation in male initiation and circumcision. Some priests in the Casamance have even begun to accompany Jola Christian boys and young men into the initiation forest. Esana's Jola population is aware of this difference, and the Jola Christians who participated in the 1998 *bukutabu* regularly brought this up to indicate Padre Luigi's outlier (and, by implication, unfair) approach to male initiation.

3. "Theology," in the way I intend its use here, refers to the study and discussion of the nature of religious truths, especially in reference to God. Even though the more generic term "religion" might seem to avoid some of the problematic associations that come with "theology," it actually confuses matters in a context where religion is not a separate domain of belief and practice but infuses all realms of Jola life (including agriculture and gendered personhood). Therefore, I use the term "theology" to signal discussions specifically focused on doctrine and debates about "religious truths."

4. I was unable to date the initial use of buttons. Jola have had trading relationships with other Africans and Europeans for many hundreds of years, and I can only surmise that buttons became a trading object early on in these encounters. Until very recently, buttons were used only for decoration rather than as a functional item on clothing.

5. For a provocative analysis of Jola beliefs about consanguinity and conception, see Sapir (1977).

6. A more direct link between these two—fire and blood—is revealed in a longstanding practice in Jola maternity houses. During childbirth, if a woman is bleeding excessively her attendants will put fire close under her back in order to curb the flow of blood.

7. A now defunct dance—*huwokuñahu*—demonstrates the opposite move on the women's side. (In Esana, the last *huwokuñahu* dance was in the early 1980s.) Young women who have been declared as brides—that is, formally engaged to men who have already built their new home but who have yet to move in—wear a red cloth skirt at this dance. This announces their proximity to becoming wives, and literally clothes them in fertility.

Chapter 6

1. Copyright © 1941 Richard Wright. Reprinted by permission of John Hawkins & Associates, Inc., and the Estate of Richard Wright.
2. Although Jola often remark upon their anti-theft values and practices as particularly *Jola* traits, they are by no means *exclusively* Jola. Other ethnic groups in the region have similar practices with regard to theft. When Jola assert their ethnic distinctiveness in this respect they are most likely alluding to a contrast with their Balanta neighbors.
3. See Lambert (2002:140–141) for a discussion of similar—although differently inflected—dynamics concerning the impact of schooling among the Jola of Mandégane in Senegal.
4. Lambert (2002) also observes shifts in the "logic of marriage" among Mandégane Jola in Senegal due to increasing urban migration and the decreasing salience of rural agricultural labor as a mark of masculinity (see especially pp. 154–158).

Chapter 7

1. See UN News Centre (UN News Centre 2011).

BIBLIOGRAPHY

Abreu, Alexandre. 2010. Threats to Food Sovereignty in Guinea-Bissau. *IPRIS Lusophone Countries Bulletin* 5. http://www.ipris.org/php/download.php?fid=104.academia.edu/225896/Threats_to_Food_Sovereignty_in_Guinea-Bissau.

Adams, Vincanne, and Stacy Leigh Pigg, eds. 2005. *Sex in Development: Science, Sexuality, and Morality in Global Perspective.* Durham, N.C.: Duke University Press.

Adas, Michael. 1986. From Footdragging to Flight: The Evasive History of Peasant Avoidance Protest in South and Southeast Asia. *Journal of Peasant Studies* 13 (2): 64–86.

Adichie, Chimamanda Ngozi. 2009. *The Danger of a Single Story.* Video file. http://www.ted.com/talks/chimamanda_adichie_the_danger_of_a_single_story.html.

Africa Rice Center (WARDA). 2009. Policy Changes. http://www.africarice.org/warda/story-policy.asp (accessed June 15, 2014).

Agboh-Noameshie, Afiavi, Abdoulaye Kabore, and Michael Misiko. 2013. Integrating Gender Considerations in Rice Research for Development in Africa. In *Realizing Africa's Rice Promise,* eds. Marco C. S. Wopereis, Benin David E. Johnson, Nourallah Ahmadi, Eric Tollens, and Abdulai Jalloh, 343–354. Oxfordshire: CABI.

Agrawal, Arun. 1995. Dismantling the Divide Between Indigenous and Scientific Knowledge. *Development and Change* 26 (3): 413–439.

Alber, Erdmute, Jeannett Martin, and Catrien Notermans, eds. 2013. *Child Fostering in West Africa: New Perspectives on Theory and Practices.* Boston: Brill.

Alliance for a Green Revolution in Africa (AGRA). 2009. Learning from Farmers. http://www.agra-alliance.org/ (accessed June 3, 2009).

Alpern, Stanley B. 2008. Exotic Plants of Western Africa: Where They Came From and When. *History in Africa* 35: 63–102.

Andrieu, Julien. 2008. *Dynamique des Paysages dans les Régions Septentrionales des Rivières-du-Sud (Sénégal, Gambie, Guinée-Bissau)*. PhD dissertation, Department of Geography, Université Paris Diderot – Paris 7.

Ansell, Aaron. 2009. "But the Winds Will Turn Against You": An Analysis of Wealth Forms and the Discursive Space of Development in Northeast Brazil. *American Ethnologist* 36 (1): 96–109.

Appiah, Kwame Anthony. 1985. *Assertion and Conditionals*. Cambridge: Cambridge University Press.

Arce, Alberto, and Norman Long. 1992. The Dynamics of Knowledge: Interfaces Between Bureaucrats and Peasants. In *Battlefields of Knowledge: The Interlocking of Theory and Practice in Social Research and Development*, eds. Norman Long and Ann Long, 211–247. New York: Routledge.

Arendt, Hannah. 1958. *The Human Condition*. Chicago: University of Chicago Press.

Arens, W., and Ivan Karp, eds. 1989. *Creativity of Power: Cosmology and Action in African Societies*. Washington, D.C.: Smithsonian Institution Press.

Associated Press. 2007. Torrent of Cocaine Threatens to Destabilize Country— Officials Worry That an Influx of Drug Traffic Would Swamp the Economy of Tiny Guinea-Bissau. *Tampa Bay Times*, November 4. http://www.sptimes.com/2007/11/04/Worldandnation/Torrent_of_ cocaine_th.shtml (accessed September 5, 2012).

Atkins, Keletso. 1993. *The Moon Is Dead! Give Us Our Money! The Cultural Origins of an African Work Ethic, Natal, South Africa, 1843–1900*. Portsmouth, N.H.: Heinemann.

Aw, Djibril. 1978. Rice Development Strategies in Africa. In *Rice in Africa: Proceedings of a Conference Held at the International Institute of Tropical Agriculture Ibadan, Nigeria, 7–11 March 1977*, eds. I. W. Buddenhagen and G. J. Persley, 69–74. London: Academic Press.

Badawi, Abd El-Azeem T., Milad A. Maximos, Ibrahim R. Aidy, R. A. Olaoye, and S. D. Sharma. 2010. History of Rice in Africa. In *Rice: Origin, Antiquity and History*, ed. S. D. Sharma, 373–410. Enfield, N.H.: Science Publishers; Distributed by CRC Press, Boca Raton, Fla.

Barry, Boubacar. 1981. Economic Anthropology of Precolonial Senegambia from the Fifteenth through the Nineteenth Centuries. In *The Uprooted of the Western Sahel: Migrants' Quest for Cash in the Senegambia*, ed. Lucie Gallistel Colvin, 27–57. New York: Praeger.

———. 1998. *Senegambia and the Atlantic Slave Trade*. Cambridge: Cambridge University Press.

Barth, Fredrik. 1975. *Ritual and Knowledge Among the Baktaman of New Guinea*. New Haven, Conn.: Yale University Press.

Baum, Robert M. 1990. The Emergence of a Diola Christianity. *Africa* 60 (3): 370–398.

———. 1999. *Shrines of the Slave Trade: Diola Religion and Society in Precolonial Senegambia.* Oxford: Oxford University Press.

Becker, Laurence, and N'guessan Yoboué. 2009. Rice Producer-Processor Networks in Côte D'Ivoire. *Geographical Review* 99 (2): 164–185.

Beidelman, T. O. 1982. *Colonial Evangelism: A Socio-Historical Study of an East African Mission at the Grassroots.* Bloomington: Indiana University Press.

Bellman, Beryl L. 1984. *The Language of Secrecy: Symbols and Metaphors in Poro Ritual.* New Brunswick, N.J.: Rutgers University Press.

Berry, Sara. 1984. The Food Crisis and Agrarian Change in Africa: A Review Essay. *African Studies Review* 27 (2): 59–112.

———. 1989. Social Institutions and Access to Resources. *Africa* 59 (1): 41–55.

———. 1993. *No Condition Is Permanent: The Social Dynamics of Agrarian Change in Sub-Saharan Africa.* Madison: University of Wisconsin Press.

Bicker, Alan, Paul Sillitoe, and Johan Pottier, eds. 2004. *Development and Local Knowledge: New Approaches to Issues in Natural Resources Management, Conservation and Agriculture.* London: Routledge.

Bigman, Laura. 1993. *History and Hunger in West Africa: Food Production and Entitlement in Guinea-Bissau and Cape Verde.* Westport, Conn.: Greenwood Press.

Birmingham, David. 1995. *The Decolonization of Africa.* Athens: Ohio University Press.

———. 1999. *Portugal and Africa.* New York: St. Martin's Press.

———. 2006. *Empire in Africa: Angola and Its Neighbors.* Athens: Ohio University Press.

Bledsoe, Caroline H. 2002. *Contingent Lives: Fertility, Time, and Aging in West Africa.* Chicago: University of Chicago Press.

Bohannan, Laura. 1964. *Return to Laughter.* Garden City, N.Y.: Natural History Library.

Bohannan, Paul. 1963. *Social Anthropology.* New York: Reinhart and Winston.

Bok, Sissela. 1979. *Lying.* New York: Vintage.

———. 1982. *Secrets.* New York: Pantheon Books.

Bordonaro, Lorenzo I. 2009. Introduction: Guinea-Bissau Today: The Irrelevance of the State and the Permanence of Change. *African Studies Review* 52 (2): 35–45.

Bornstein, Erica. 2005. *The Spirit of Development: Protestant NGOs, Morality, and Economics in Zimbabwe.* New York: Routledge.

Bourdieu, Pierre. 2000. Social Being, Time and the Sense of Existence. In *Pascalian Meditations,* 206–245. Cambridge: Polity Press.

Bravman, Bill. 1998. *Making Ethnic Ways: Communities and Their Transformations in Taita, Kenya, 1800–1950.* Portsmouth, N.H.: Heinemann.

Bray, Francesca. 1986. *The Rice Economies: Technology and Development in Asian Societies.* Oxford: Blackwell.

————. 1998. A Stable Landscape? Social and Cultural Sustainability in Asian
    Rice Systems. In *Sustainability of Rice in the Global Food System*, eds.
    N. G. Dowling, S. M. Greenfield, and K. S. Fischer, 45–60. Manila:
    Pacific Basin Study Center and International Rice Research Institute.
Broch-Due, Vigdis, and Richard A. Schroeder, eds. 2000. *Producing Nature and
    Poverty in Africa*. Uppsala: Nordiska Afrikainstitutet.
Brooks, George E. 1980a. *Kola Trade and State Building: Upper Guinea Coast and
    Senegambia, 15th–17th Centuries*. Working Paper 38, African Studies
    Center, Boston University.
————. 1980b. *Luso-African Trade and Settlement in the Gambia and Guinea-Bissau
    Regions*. Working Paper 24, African Studies Center, Boston University.
————. 1985. *Western Africa to C1860 A.D.: A Provisional Historical Schema
    Based on Climate Periods*. Bloomington: Indiana University Press.
————. 1993. *Landlords and Strangers: Ecology, Society, and Trade in Western
    Africa, 1000–1630*. Boulder, Colo.: Westview Press.
Brooks, Sally. 2010. *Rice Biofortification: Lessons for Global Science and
    Development*. London: Earthscan.
Buddenhagen, I. W. 1978. Rice Ecosystems in Africa. In *Rice in Africa:
    Proceedings of a Conference Held at the International Institute of Tropical
    Agriculture Ibadan, Nigeria, 7–11 March 1977*, eds. I. W. Buddenhagen and
    G. J. Persley, 11–27. London: Academic Press.
Buddenhagen, I. W., and G. J. Persley, eds. 1978. *Rice in Africa: Proceedings of a
    Conference Held at the International Institute of Tropical Agriculture
    Ibadan, Nigeria, 7–11 March 1977*. London: Academic Press.
Cabral, Amílcar. 1969. *The Struggle in Guinea*. Cambridge, Mass.: Africa
    Research Group.
————. 1970. *Revolution in Guinea: Selected Texts by Amílcar Cabral*, ed.
    Richard Handyside. New York: Monthly Review Press.
————. 1973. *Return to the Source: Selected Speeches by Amílcar Cabral*.
    New York: Monthly Review Press.
————. 1980. *Unity and Struggle: Speeches and Writings*, trans. Michael Wolfers.
    Partido Africano de Independência da Guiné e Cabo Verde, London:
    Heinemann.
Carney, Judith. 2001. *Black Rice: The African Origins of Rice Cultivation in the
    Americas*. Cambridge, Mass.: Harvard University Press.
————. 2004. "With Grains in Her Hair": Rice in Colonial Brazil. *Slavery and
    Abolition* 25 (1): 1–27.
Carney, Judith, and Michael Watts. 1991. Disciplining Women? Rice,
    Mechanization, and the Evolution of Mandinka Gender Relations in
    Senegambia. *Signs* 16 (4): 651–681.
Carpenter, A. J. 1978. The History of Rice in Africa. In *Rice in Africa: Proceedings
    of a Conference Held at the International Institute of Tropical Agriculture
    Ibadan, Nigeria, 7–11 March 1977*, eds. I. W. Buddenhagen and
    G. J. Persley, 3–10. London: Academic Press.

Cernea, Michael M. 2005. Studying the Culture of Agri-Culture: The Uphill Battle for Social Research in CGIAR. *Culture and Agriculture* 27 (2): 73–87.

Chabal, Patrick. 1981. National Liberation in Portuguese Guinea, 1956–1974. *African Affairs* 80 (319): 75–99.

———.1983. *Amílcar Cabral: Revolutionary Leadership and People's War.* Cambridge: Cambridge University Press.

Chakrabarty, Dipesh. 1988. Conditions for Knowledge of Working-Class Conditions: Employers, Government and the Jute Workers of Calcutta, 1890–1940. In *Selected Subaltern Studies,* eds. Ranajit Guha and Gayatri Chakravorty Spivak, 259–310. New York: Oxford University Press.

Chandler, Robert F. 1979. *Rice in the Tropics: A Guide to the Development of National Programs.* Boulder, Colo.: Westview Press.

Chang, Te-Tzu. 1976a. The Origin, Evolution, Cultivation, Dissemination, and Diversification of Asian and African Rices. *Euphytica Euphytica* 25 (1): 425–441.

———. 1976b. Rice: *Oryza sativa* and *Oryza glaberrima* (Gramineae-Oryzeae). In *Evolution of Crop Plants,* eds. N. W. Simmonds, 98–104. London: Longman.

Chazan, Naomi, and Timothy M. Shaw, eds. 1988. *Coping with Africa's Food Crisis.* Boulder, Colo.: Lynn Rienner.

Chilcote, Ronald H. 1967. *Portuguese Africa.* Englewood Cliffs, N.J.: Prentice-Hall.

———. 1972. *Emerging Nationalism in Portuguese Africa: Documents.* Stanford: Hoover Institution Press, Stanford University.

———. 1977. Guinea-Bissau's Struggle: Past and Present. *Africa Today* 24 (1): 31–39.

———. 1991. *Amílcar Cabral's Revolutionary Theory and Practice: A Critical Guide.* Boulder, Colo.: Lynn Rienner.

CIA. 2015. The World Factbook. https://www.cia.gov/library/publications/the-world-factbook/geos/pu.html (accessed March 22, 2015).

Clark, John Desmond. 1970. The Spread of Food Production in Sub-Saharan Africa. In *Papers in African Prehistory,* eds. J. D. Fage and Roland Anthony Oliver, 25–42. Cambridge: Cambridge University Press.

Clifford, James. 1988. *The Predicament of Culture: Twentieth-Century Ethnography, Literature and Art.* Cambridge, Mass.: Harvard University Press.

Coelho, Francisco de Lemos. 1953. Duas Descrições Seiscentistas da Guiné. In *Manuscritos Inéditos Publicados,* ed. Damião Peres, Lisboa.

Coetzee, J. M. 1988. *White Writing: On the Culture of Letters in South Africa.* New Haven, Conn.: Yale University Press.

Cohen, Ronald. 1988. *Satisfying Africa's Food Needs: Food Production and Commercialization in African Agriculture.* Boulder, Colo.: Lynn Rienner.

Comaroff, Jean. 1985. *Body of Power, Spirit of Resistance: The Culture and History of a South African People.* Chicago: University Chicago Press.

Comaroff, John L., and Jean Comaroff. 1991. *Of Revelation and Revolution, Vol. 1: Christianity, Colonialism, and Consciousness in South Africa.* Chicago: University Chicago Press.

———. 1997. *Of Revelation and Revolution, Vol. 2: The Dialectics of Modernity on a South African Frontier.* Chicago: University of Chicago Press.

Commins, Stephen K., Michael F. Lofchie, and Rhys Payne, eds. 1986. *Africa's Agrarian Crisis: The Roots of Famine*. Boulder, Colo.: Lynn Rienner.

Cooke, Bill, and Uma Kothari, eds. 2001. *Participation: The New Tyranny?* New York: Zed Press.

Cooper, Frederick. 1992. Colonizing Time: Work Rhythms and Labor Conflict in Colonial Mombasa. In *Colonialism and Culture*, ed. N. B. Dirks, 209–245. Ann Arbor: University of Michigan Press.

Cormier-Salem, Marie-Christine, ed. 1999. *Rivières du Sud: Sociétés et Mangroves Ouest-Africaines*, Vols. 1 and 2. Paris: IRD Editions.

Coser, Rose Laub. 1962. *Life in the Ward*. East Lansing: Michigan State University Press.

———. 1979. *Training in Ambiguity: Learning Through Doing in a Mental Hospital*. New York: Free Press.

Crane, T. A., C. Roncoli, and G. Hoogenboom. 2011. Adaptation to Climate Change and Climate Variability: The Importance of Understanding Agriculture as Performance. *Journal of Life Sciences* 57 (3–4): 179–185.

Croll, Elisabeth, and David J. Parkin, eds. 1992. *Bush Base: Forest Farm: Culture, Environment, and Development*. London: Routledge.

Crosby, Alfred W. 1972. *The Columbian Exchange: Biological and Cultural Consequences of 1492*. Westport, Conn.: Greenwood Press.

Crowley, Eve Lakshmi. 1990. *Contracts with the Spirits: Religion, Asylum, and Ethnic Identity in the Cacheu Region of Guinea-Bissau*. PhD dissertation, Department of Anthropology, Yale University.

D'Almada, A. Alvares. 1594. *Tratado Breve Dos Rios De Guiné Do Cabo Verde*. Lisboa: Editorial L.I.AM.

Da Silva, C. S. 1978. Guinea-Bissau. In *Rice in Africa: Proceedings of a Conference Held at the International Institute of Tropical Agriculture Ibadan, Nigeria, 7–11 March 1977*, eds. I. W. Buddenhagen and G. J. Persley, 324–325. London: Academic Press.

Davidson, Basil. 1969. *The Liberation of Guiné: Aspects of an African Revolution*. Harmondsworth: Penguin.

———. 1981. *No Fist Is Big Enough to Hide the Sky: The Liberation of Guinea-Bissau and Cape Verde*. London: Zed Press.

Davidson, Joanna. 2007. *Feet in the Fire: Social Change and Continuity Among the Diola of Guinea-Bissau*. PhD dissertation, Department of Anthropology, Emory University.

———. 2009. "We Work Hard": Customary Imperatives of the Diola Work Regime in the Context of Environmental and Economic Change. *African Studies Review* 52 (2): 119–141.

———. 2010. Cultivating Knowledge: Development, Dissemblance, and Discursive Contradictions among the Diola of Guinea-Bissau. *American Ethnologist* 37 (2): 212–226.

———. 2012a. Basket Cases and Breadbaskets: Sacred Rice and Agricultural Development in Postcolonial Africa. *Culture, Agriculture, Food and Environment* 34 (1): 15–32.

———. 2012b. Of Rice and Men: Climate Change, Religion, and Personhood among the Diola of Guinea-Bissau. *Journal for the Study of Religion, Nature and Culture* 6 (3): 363–381.

Day, Sophie, Evthymios Papataxiarchēs, and Michael Stewart, eds. 1999. *Lilies of the Field: Marginal People Who Live for the Moment.* Boulder, Colo.: Westview Press.

De Datta, S. K. 1975. Cultural Practices for Upland Rice. In *Major Research in Upland Rice*, ed. IRRI, 160–183. Los Baños, Philippines: International Rice Research Institute.

De Jong, Ferdinand. 1998. The Production of Translocality: Initiation in the Sacred Grove in Southern Senegal. *Focaal* 30–31: 61–83.

———. 2002. Politicians of the Sacred Grove: Citizenship and Ethnicity in Southern Senegal. *Africa* 72 (2): 203–220.

———. 2008. *Masquerades of Modernity: Power and Secrecy in Casamance, Senegal.* Bloomington: Indiana University Press.

Dhada, Mustaffa. 1993. *Warriors at Work: How Guinea Was Really Set Free.* Boulder, CO: University Press of Colorado.

Dinis, Antonio J. Dias. 1946. As Tribos da Guiné Portuguesa na História. *Portugal em Africa*, Second Series 2: 206–215.

Dove, Michael, ed. 2014. *The Anthropology of Climate Change: An Historical Reader.* Malden, MA: John Wiley & Sons.

Écoutin, Jean-Marc. 1999. Aménagement Technique du Milieu. In *Rivières du Sud: Societes et Mangroves Ouest-Africaines, Vol. 1*, ed. Marie-Christine Cormier-Salem, 209–268. Paris: IRD Editions.

Eltis, David, Philip Morgan, and David Richardson. 2007. Agency and Diaspora in Atlantic History: Reassessing the African Contribution to Rice Cultivation in the Americas. *The American Historical Review* 112 (5): 1329–1358.

Elyachar, Julia. 2005. *Markets of Dispossession: NGOs, Economic Development, and the State in Cairo.* Durham, N.C.: Duke University Press.

Embaló, Garcia Bacar. 2008. A Vulnerabilidade da População às Alterações Agro-Ecologicas: Estudo de Caso no Sector de Pirada, Região de Gabu, Guiné-Bissau, Masters thesis, Instituto Superior de Agronomia, Universidade Técnica de Lisboa. http://hdl.handle.net/10400.5/2061.

Engelke, Matthew. 2004. Discontinuity and the Discourse of Conversion. *Journal of Religion in Africa* 34: 82–109.

Etherington, Norman. 1983. Missionaries and the Intellectual History in Africa. *Itinerario* 7 (2): 116–143.

Fabian, Johannes. 1990. *Power and Performance: Ethnographic Explorations Through Proverbial Wisdom and Theater in Shaba, Zaire.* Madison: University of Wisconsin Press.

———. 1991. *Time and the Work of Anthropology: Critical Essays, 1971–1991.* Philadelphia: Harwood Academic Publishers.

Fage, J. D. 1959. *An Introduction to the History of West Africa.* Cambridge: Cambridge University Press.

Fairhead, James, and Melissa Leach. 1996. *Misreading the African Landscape: Society and Ecology in a Forest-Savanna Mosaic.* Cambridge: Cambridge University Press.

———. 2005. The Centrality of the Social in African Farming. *IDS Bulletin* 36 (2): 86–90.

Faye, Wagane. 2006. *The Casamance Separatism: From Independence Claim to Resource Logic.* Masters Thesis, Naval Postgraduate School, Monterey, CA. http://hdl.handle.net/10945/2750.

Ferguson, James. 1994. *The Anti-Politics Machine: "Development," Depoliticization, and Bureaucratic Power in Lesotho.* Minneapolis: University of Minnesota Press.

Fernandez, James W. 1978. African Religious Movements. *Annual Review of Anthropology* 7: 195–234.

———. 1986. The Argument of Images and the Experiences of Returning to the Whole. In *The Anthropology of Experience,* eds. Victor Turner and Edward Bruner, 159–187. Urbana: University of Illinois Press.

Fields-Black, Edda L. 2008. *Deep Roots: Rice Farmers in West Africa and the African Diaspora.* Bloomington: Indiana University Press.

Forrest, Joshua B. 1987. Guinea-Bissau Since Independence: A Decade of Domestic Power Struggles. *Journal of Modern African Studies* 25 (1): 95–116.

———. 1992. *Guinea-Bissau: Power, Conflict, and Renewal in a West African Nation.* Boulder, Colo.: Westview Press.

———. 1998. State Peasantry in Contemporary Africa: The Case of Guinea-Bissau. *Africana Journal* 17: 1–26.

———. 2003. *Lineages of State Fragility: Rural Civil Society in Guinea-Bissau.* Athens: Ohio University Press.

Fortes, Meyer. 1966. Religious Premises and Logical Technique in Divinatory Ritual. *Philosophical Transaction of the Royal Society of London,* Series B. 251: 409–422.

Foster, George. 1965. Peasant Society and the Image of the Limited Good. *American Anthropologist* 67 (2): 293–315.

Foucher, Vincent. 2002. *Cheated Pilgrims: Education, Migration, and the Birth of Casamançais Separatism.* PhD dissertation, University of London, School of Oriental and African Studies.

Franke, Richard W., and Barbara H. Chasin. 1980. *Seeds of Famine: Ecological Destruction and the Development Dilemma in the West African Sahel.* New York: Universe Books.

Gable, Eric. 1990. *Modern Manjaco: The Ethos of Power in a West African Society.* PhD dissertation, Department of Anthropology, University of Virginia.

———. 1997. A Secret Shared: Fieldwork and the Sinister in a West African Village. *Cultural Anthropology* 12 (2): 213–233.

———. 2000. The Culture Development Club: Youth, Neo-Tradition, and the Construction of Society in Guinea-Bissau. *Anthropological Quarterly* 73 (4): 195–203.

Galli, Rosemary E. 1987a. On Peasant Productivity: The Case of Guinea-Bissau. *Development and Change* 18 (1): 69–98.

———. 1987b. The Food Crisis and the Socialist State in Lusophone Africa. *African Studies Review* 30 (1): 19–44.

———. 1990. Liberalisation Is Not Enough: Structural Adjustment and Peasants in Guinea-Bissau. *Review of African Political Economy* 17 (49): 52–69.

Galli, Rosemary E., and Jocelyn Jones. 1987. *Guinea-Bissau: Politics, Economics, and Society*. London: F. Pinter.

Gell, Alfred. 1974. Understanding the Occult. *Radical Philosophy* 9: 17–26.

Geschiere, Peter, and Jos van der Klei. 1988. Popular Protest: The Diola of South Senegal. In *Religion & Development: Towards an Integrated Approach*, eds. Philip Quarles van Ufford and J. M. Schoffeleers, 209–229. Amsterdam: Free University Press.

Gheddo, Piero. 1999. *Missione Bissau: I 50 Anni del Pime in Guinea-Bissau (1947–1997)*. Bologna: SERMIS.

Glantz, Michael H., ed. 1987. *Drought and Hunger in Africa. Denying Famine a Future*. Cambridge: Cambridge University Press.

Gofman, Alexander. 1998. A Vague but Suggestive Concept: The 'Total Social Fact'. In *Marcel Mauss: A Centenary Tribute*, ed. Wendy James, 63–70. New York: Berghahn Books.

Goody, Esther N., ed. 1978. *Questions and Politeness: Strategies in Social Interaction*. Cambridge: Cambridge University Press.

———. 1982. *Parenthood and Social Reproduction: Fostering and Occupational Roles in West Africa*. Cambridge: Cambridge University Press.

Griffiths, Tom. 2007. The Humanities and an Environmentally Sustainable Australia. *Australian Humanities Review* 43: 1–11.

Grist, D. H. 1959. *Rice*. London: Longman.

Gupta, Akhil. 1998. *Postcolonial Developments: Agriculture in the Making of Modern India*. Durham, N.C.: Duke University Press.

Guyer, Jane I. 1978. *Women's Work in the Food Economy of the Cocoa Belt: A Comparison*. Working Paper 7, African Studies Center, Boston University.

———. 1983. *Anthropological Models of African Production: The Naturalization Problem*. Working Paper 152, African Studies Center, Boston University.

Habermas, Jürgen. 1972. *Knowledge and Human Interests*, trans. Jeremy J. Shapiro. Boston: Beacon Press.

———. 1979. *Communication and the Evolution of Society*, trans. Thomas McCarthy. Boston: Beacon Press.

———. 1989. *The Structural Transformation of the Public Sphere: An Inquiry into a Category of Bourgeois Society*, trans. Thomas Burger. Cambridge: MIT Press.

Handem, Diana Lima. 1987. A Guine-Bissau Adaptar-se a Crise. *Soronda* 39: 52–76.

Harlan, Jack R., Jan M. J. De Wet, and Ann B. L. Stemler, eds. 1976. *Origins of African Plant Domestication*. The Hague: Mouton.

Hart, Keith. 1982. *The Political Economy of West African Agriculture.* Cambridge: Cambridge University Press.

Hawthorne, Walter. 2003. *Planting Rice and Harvesting Slaves: Transformations Along the Guinea-Bissau Coast, 1400–1900.* Portsmouth, N.H.: Heinemann.

———. 2010. From "Black Rice" to "Brown": Rethinking the History of Risiculture in the Seventeenth- and Eighteenth-Century Atlantic. *The American Historical Review* 115 (1): 151–163.

Hendry, Joy, and C. W. Watson, eds. 2001. *An Anthropology of Indirect Communication.* London: Routledge.

Hocart, A. M. 2004 [1952]. *The Life-giving Myth and Other Essays,* ed. Lord Raglan. London: Methuen.

Hoffman, Danny. 2011. *The War Machines: Young Men and Violence in Sierra Leone and Liberia.* Durham, N.C.: Duke University Press.

Horton, Robin. 1975a. On the Rationality of Conversion: Part I. *Africa* 45 (3): 219–235.

———. 1975b. On the Rationality of Conversion: Part II. *Africa* 45 (4): 373–399.

Huang, Xuehui, Nori Kurata, Xinghua Wei, et al. 2012. A Map of Rice Genome Variation Reveals the Origin of Cultivated Rice. *Nature* 490 (7421): 497–501.

International Crisis Group. 2008. *Guinea-Bissau: In Need of a State.* Africa Report No. 142. Brussels.

———. 2014. *Guinée-Bissau: Les Élections, et Après?* Briefing Afrique No. 98. Dakar/Bruxelles.

IRIN. 2006. *Famine Warning Issued in South.* http://www.irinnews.org (accessed May 20, 2006).

Irvine, Frederick Robert. 1974. *West African Crops.* London: Oxford University Press.

Irvine, Janis. 1976. Changing Patterns of Social Control in Buu Society. In *A Century of Change in Eastern Africa,* ed. W. Arens, 215–228. The Hague: Mouton.

Jackson, Michael. 1982. *Allegories of the Wilderness: Ethics and Ambiguity in Kuranko Narratives.* Bloomington: Indiana University Press.

———. 2013. *The Politics of Storytelling: Variations on a Theme by Hannah Arendt.* 2nd ed. Denmark: University of Copenhagen, Museum Tusculanum Press.

James, Wendy. 1988. *The Listening Ebony: Moral Knowledge, Religion, and Power Among the Uduk of Sudan.* Oxford: Oxford University Press.

———. 1996. For the Motion (1) [1990 Debate: Human Worlds Are Culturally Constructed]. In *Key Debates in Anthropology,* ed. Tim Ingold, 105–111. New York: Routledge.

Johnson-Hanks, Jennifer. 2006. *Uncertain Honor: Modern Motherhood in an African Crisis.* Chicago: University of Chicago Press.

Journet, Odile. 1987. Le Sang des Femmes et le Sacrifice: l'Example Joola. In *Sous le Masque de l'Animal: Essais sur le Sacrifice en Afrique Noire,* ed. M. Cartry, 241–266. Paris: University Press of France (PUF).

———. 2007. *Les créances de la terre: chroniques du pays Jamaat (Jóola de Guinée-Bissau),* Turnhout, Belgium: Brepols.

Journet, Odile, and Jean Girard. 1976. *Rôles et Statuts des Femmes Dans la Société Diola (Basse Casamance).* Thèse de 3e cycle, Sociologie. Université de Lyon-II.

Keen, Ian. 1994. *Knowledge and Secrecy in an Aboriginal Religion: Yolngu of North-east Arnhem Land.* Oxford: Oxford University Press.

Kratz, Corinne. 1990. Sexual Solidarity and the Secrets of Sight and Sound: Shifting Gender Relations and their Ceremonial Constitution. *American Ethnologist* 17 (3): 449–469.

Kumashiro, Takashi, Koichi Futakuchi, Moussa Sié, Marie-Noëlle Ndjiondjop, and Marco C.S. Wopereis. 2013. A Continent-Wide, Product-Oriented Approach to Rice Breeding in Africa. In *Realizing Africa's Rice Promise.* eds. Marco C. S. Wopereis, Benin David E. Johnson, Nourallah Ahmadi, Eric Tollens, and Abdulai Jalloh, 69–78. Oxfordshire: CABI.

La Fontaine, Jean S. 1985. *Initiation.* Wolfeboro, N.H.: Manchester University Press.

Lambert, Michael C. 2002. *Longing for Exile: Migration and the Making of a Translocal Community in Senegal, West Africa.* Portsmouth, N.H.: Heinemann.

———. 2007. Politics, Patriarchy, and New Traditions: Understanding Female Migration Among the Jola. In *Cultures of Migration: African Perspectives,* eds. Hans Peter Hahn and Georg Klute, 129–148. Münster: LIT Verlag.

Lansing, J. Stephen. 1991. *Priests and Programmers: Technologies of Power in the Engineered Landscape of Bali.* Princeton, N.J.: Princeton University Press.

Latham, A. J. H. 1998. *Rice: The Primary Commodity.* London: Routledge.

Latour, Bruno. 1993. *We Have Never Been Modern.* Cambridge, Mass.: Harvard University Press.

Lauer, Joseph J. 1969. *Rice in the History of the Lower Gambia-Geba Area.* Masters thesis, Department of History, University of Wisconsin.

Leach, Melissa, and Robin Mearns, eds. 1996. *The Lie of the Land: Challenging Received Wisdom on the African Environment.* Oxford: International African Institute, James Currey.

Lehmann de Almeida, Carlos. 1955. Inquérito Etnográfico sobre a Alimentação dos Felupes. *Boletim Cultural da Guiné Portuguesa* 10 (40): 617–634.

Lewis, M. Paul, Gary F. Simons, and Charles D. Fennig, eds. 2014. Jola-Fonyi. *Ethnologue: Languages of the World.* Dallas, Tex.: SIL International. http://www.ethnologue.com/language/dyo (accessed September 28, 2014).

Li, Tania Murray. 2007. *The Will to Improve: Governmentality, Development, and the Practice of Politics.* Durham, N.C.: Duke University Press.

Linares, Olga F. 1970. Agriculture and Diola Society. In *African Food Production Systems: Cases and Theory,* ed. Peter F. M. McLoughlin, 195–227. Baltimore, Md.: Johns Hopkins University Press.

———. 1981. From Tidal Swamp to Inland Valley: On the Social Organization of Wet Rice Cultivation Among the Diola of Senegal. *Africa* 51 (2): 557–595.

———. 1985. Cash Crops and Gender Constructs: The Jola of Senegal. *Ethnology* 24 (2): 83–93.

———. 1987. Deferring to Trade in Slaves: The Jola of Casamance, Senegal in Historical Perspective. *History in Africa* 14:113–139.

———. 1992. *Power, Prayer, and Production: The Jola of Casamance, Senegal.* Cambridge: Cambridge University Press.

———. 2002. African Rice (*Oryza glaberrima*): History and Future Potential. *Proceedings of the National Academy of Sciences* (PNAS) 99 (25): 16360–16365.

———. 2005. Jola Agriculture at a Crossroads. *Canadian Journal of African Studies/La Revue canadienne des études africaines* 39 (2): 230–252.

Littlefield, Daniel C. 1981. *Rice and Slaves: Ethnicity and the Slave Trade in Colonial South Carolina.* Baton Rouge: Louisiana State University Press.

Lobban, Richard. 1974. Guinea-Bissau: 24 September 1973 and Beyond. *Africa Today* 21 (1): 15–24.

Lobban, Richard, and Joshua B. Forrest. 1988. *Historical Dictionary of the Republic of Guinea-Bissau.* Metuchen, N.J.: Scarecrow Press.

Lobban, Richard, and Peter Karibe Mendy. 1996. *Historical Dictionary of the Republic of Guinea-Bissau.* 3rd ed. Lanham, Md.: Scarecrow Press.

———. 2013. *Historical Dictionary of the Republic of Guinea-Bissau.* 4th ed. Plymouth, U.K.: Scarecrow Press.

Lofchie, Michael F. 1975. Political and Economic Origins of African Hunger. *Journal of Modern African Studies* 13 (4): 551–567.

Long, Norman. 1968. *Social Change and the Individual: A Study of the Social and Religious Responses to Innovation in a Zambian Rural Community.* Manchester: Manchester University Press.

Long, Norman, and Ann Long, eds. 1992. *Battlefields of Knowledge: The Interlocking of Theory and Practice in Social Research and Development.* London: Routledge.

Lopes, Carlos. 1987. *Guinea-Bissau: From Liberation Struggle to Independent Statehood.* London: Zed Books.

Lopes de Lima, J. J. 1836. Memória dos Felupes. *Jornal de Sociedade dos Amigos das Letras* 3:68–69.

Luh, Bor Shiun. 1991. *Rice.* New York: Van Nostrand Reinhold.

Lurhmann, T. M. 1989. *Persuasions of the Witch's Craft: Ritual Magic in Contemporary England.* Cambridge, Mass.: Harvard University Press.

MacQueen, Norrie. 1997. *The Decolonization of Portuguese Africa: Metropolitan Revolution and the Dissolution of Empire*. London: Longman.

Mains, Daniel. 2012. *Hope Is Cut: Youth, Unemployment, and the Future in Urban Ethiopia*. Philadelphia: Temple University Press.

Mark, Peter. 1978. Urban Migration, Cash Cropping, and Calamity: The Spread of Islam Among the Diola of Boulouf (Senegal), 1900–1940. *African Studies Review* 21 (2): 1–14.

———. 1985. *A Cultural, Economic, and Religious History of the Basse Casamance Since 1500*. Stuttgart: F. Steiner.

———. 1992. *The Wild Bull and the Sacred Forest: Form, Meaning, and Change in Senegambian Initiation Masks*. Cambridge: Cambridge University Press.

———. 1999. The Evolution of "Portuguese" Identity: Luso-Africans on the Upper Guinea Coast from the Sixteenth to the Early Nineteenth Century. *Journal of African History* 40 (2): 173–191.

Masco, Joseph. 2006. *The Nuclear Boderlands: The Manhattan Project in Post–Cold War New Mexico*. Princeton, N.J.: Princeton University Press.

Mauss, Marcel. 1967. *The Gift: Forms and Functions of Exchange in Archaic Societies*. Trans. W. D. Halls. New York: Norton.

McCann, James. 1999. *Green Land, Brown Land, Black Land: An Environmental History of Africa, 1800–1990*. Portsmouth, N.H.: Heinemann.

———. 2005. *Maize and Grace: Africa's Encounter with a New World Crop, 1500–2000*. Cambridge, Mass.: Harvard University Press.

Mendy, Peter Karibe. 2006. Amílcar Cabral and the Liberation of Guinea-Bissau: Context, Challenges and Lessons for Effective African Leadership. *African Identities* 4 (1): 7–21.

Metcalf, Peter. 2002. *They Lie, We Lie: Getting on with Anthropology*. London: Routledge.

Mintz, Sidney W. 1985. *Sweetness and Power: The Place of Sugar in Modern History*. London: Penguin.

Molina, Jeanmaire, Martin Sikora, Nandita Garud, et al. 2011. Molecular Evidence for a Single Evolutionary Origin of Domesticated Rice. *Proceedings of the National Academy of Sciences* (PNAS) 108 (20). 8351–8356.

Moore, Sally Falk. 1976. The Secret of Men: A Fiction of Chagga Initiation and its Relation to the Logic of Chagga Symbolism. *Africa* 46 (4): 357–370.

———. 1978. *Law as Process: An Anthropological Approach*. London: Routledge and Kegan Paul.

Moormann, F. R., and W. J. Veldkamp. 1978. Land and Rice in Africa: Constraints and Potentials. In *Rice in Africa: Proceedings of a Conference Held at the International Institute of Tropical Agriculture Ibadan, Nigeria, 7–11 March 1977*, eds. I. W. Buddenhagen and G. J. Persley, 29–43. London: Academic Press.

Mortimore, Michael. 1989. *Adapting to Drought: Farmers, Famines, and Desertification in West Africa*. Cambridge: Cambridge University Press.

Moseley, William G., Judith Carney, and Laurence Becker. 2010. Neoliberal Policy, Rural Livelihoods, and Urban Food Security in West Africa: A Comparative Study of The Gambia, Côte d'Ivoire, and Mali. *Proceedings of the National Academy of Sciences* (PNAS) 107 (13): 5774–5779.

Murphy, William P. 1980. Secret Knowledge as Property and Power in Kpelle Society: Elders Versus Youth. *Africa* 50 (2): 193–207.

———. 1981. The Rhetorical Management of Dangerous Knowledge in Kpelle Brokerage. *American Ethnologist* 8 (4): 667–685.

———. 1990. Creating the Appearance of Consensus in Mende Political Discourse. *American Anthropologist* 92 (1): 24–41.

———. 1998. The Sublime Dance of Mende Politics: An African Aesthetic of Charismatic Power. *American Ethnologist* 25 (4): 563–582.

Netting, Robert McC. 1993. *Smallholders, Householders: Farm Families and the Ecology of Intensive, Sustainable Agriculture.* Stanford: Stanford University Press.

Nugent, Paul. 2008. Putting the History Back into Ethnicity: Enslavement, Religion, and Cultural Brokerage in the Construction of Mandinka/Jola and Ewe/Agotime Identities in West Africa, C. 1650–1930. *Comparative Studies in Society and History* 50 (4): 920–948.

Offei, S. K., C. Almekinders, T. A. Crane, et al. 2010. Making Better Seeds for African Food Security—A New Approach to Scientist-Farmer Partnerships. *Aspects of Applied Biology* 96: 141–148.

Ohnuki-Tierney, Emiko. 1993. *Rice as Self: Japanese Identities Through Time.* Princeton, N.J.: Princeton University Press.

Ong, Aihwa. 1987. *Spirits of Resistance and Capitalist Discipline: Factory Women in Malaysia.* Albany: State University of New York Press.

Osseo-Asare, Fran. 2005. *Food Culture in Sub-Saharan Africa.* Westport, Conn.: Greenwood Press.

Ottenberg, Simon. 1989. *Boyhood Rituals in an African Society: An Interpretation.* Seattle: University of Washington Press.

Palmeri, Paolo. 2009. *Living with the Diola of the Mof Evvì: The Account of an Anthropological Research in Sénégal.* Padova: CLEUP.

Pandian, Anand. 2009. *Crooked Stalks: Cultivating Virtue in South India.* Durham, N.C.: Duke University Press.

Parkin, David J. 1994. *Palms, Wine, and Witnesses: Public Spirit and Private Gain in an African Farming Community.* Prospect Heights, Ill.: Waveland Press.

Pearson, Scott R., Josiah Dirck Stryker, and Charles P. Humphreys. 1981. *Rice in West Africa: Policy and Economics.* Stanford: Stanford University Press.

Peel, J. D. Y., and Paul Richards. 1981. Introduction. *Africa* 51 (2): 553–556.

Pélissier, Paul. 1958. *Les Diola: étude sur l'habitat des riziculteurs de Basse-Casamance,* Dakar-Fann: Département de géographie, Faculté des lettres, Université de Dakar.

———. 1966. *Les Paysans Du Sénégal: Les Civilisations Agraires du Cayor à la Casamance.* Saint-Yrieix, France: Imprimerie Fabrègue.

Pélissier, René. 1989. *Naissance de la Guiné: Portugais et Africains en Sénégambie, 1841–1936*. Orgeval, France.

Pickering, Kathleen Ann. 2004. Decolonizing Time Regimes: Lakota Conceptions of Work, Economy and Society. *American Anthropologist* 106 (1): 85–97.

Pigg, Stacy Leigh. 1995a. Acronyms and Effacement: Traditional Medical Practitioners (TMP) in International Health Development. *Social Science and Medicine* 41 (1): 47–68.

———. 1995b. The Social Symbolism of Healing in Nepal. *Ethnology* 34 (1): 17–36.

———. 1997. 'Found in Most Traditional Societies': Traditional Medical Practitioners between Culture and Development. In *International Development and the Social Sciences*, eds. Frederick Cooper and Randall Packard, 259–290. Berkeley: University of California Press.

Piot, Charles D. 1993. Secrecy, Ambiguity, and the Everyday in Kabre Culture. *American Anthropologist* 95 (2): 353–370.

Pitt-Rivers, Julian Alfred. 1971. *The People of the Sierra*. Chicago: University of Chicago Press.

Portères, Roland. 1970. Primary Cradles of Agriculture in the African Continent. In *Papers in African Prehistory*, eds. J. D. Fage and Roland Anthony Oliver, 43–58. Cambridge: Cambridge University Press.

———. 1976. African Cereals: Eleusine, Fonio, Black Fonio, Teff, *Brachiaria, Paspalum, Pennisetum* and African Rice. In *Origins of African Plant Domestication*, eds. Jack R. Harlan, Jan M. J. De Wet, and Ann B. L. Stemler, 409–452. The Hague: Mouton.

Povinelli, Elizabeth A. 1993. *Labor's Lot: The Power, History, and Culture of Aboriginal Action*. Chicago: University of Chicago Press.

Pureza, José Manuel, Sílvia Roque, and Katia Cardoso. 2012. *Jovens e Trajetórias de Violências: Os Casos de Bissau e da Praia*. Coimbra: Almedina.

Purseglove, J. W. 1976. The Origins and Migrations of Crops in Tropical Africa. In *Origins of African Plant Domestication*, eds. Jack R. Harlan, Jan M. J. De Wet, and Ann B. L. Stemler. The Hague: Mouton.

Quist-Arcton, Ofeibea. 2007. A Small Nation Tries to Tackle Big Drug Traffickers. *NPR.org*. http://www.npr.org/templates/story/story .php?storyId=15152837 (accessed September 30, 2014).

Rademacher, Anne. 2011. *Reigning the River: Urban Ecologies and Political Transformation in Kathmandu*. Durham, N.C.: Duke University Press.

Ranger, Terence. 1987. Religion, Development and African Christian Identity. In *Religion, Development and African Identity*, ed. Kirsten Holst Petersen, 29–57. Uppsala: Scandinavian Institute of African Studies.

Ribeiro, Rui. 1989. Causas da Queda de Produção de Arroz na Guiné-Bissau: A Situação no Sector de Tite, Região de Quinara. *Revista Internacional de Estudos Africanos* 10 (11): 227–265.

Richards, Paul. 1985. *Indigenous Agricultural Revolution: Ecology and Food Production in West Africa*. Boulder, Colo.: Westview Press.

————. 1986. *Coping with Hunger: Hazard and Experiment in an African Rice-Farming System*. London: Allen & Unwin.

————. 1996a. *Fighting for the Rain Forest: War, Youth & Resources in Sierra Leone*. Portsmouth, N.H.: Heinemann.

————. 1996b. Against the Motion (2) [1990 Debate: Human Worlds Are Culturally Constructed]. In *Key Debates in Anthropology*, ed. Tim Ingold, 123–146. New York: Routledge.

————. 2006. The History and Future of African Rice: Food Security and Survival in a West African War Zone. *Africa Spectrum* 41 (1): 77–93.

Roitman, Janet L. 2014. *Anti-Crisis*. Durham, N.C.: Duke University Press.

Sangreman, Carlos, Fernando Sousa Júnior, Guilherme Rodrigues Zeverino, and Miguel José de Barros. 2008. Guiné-Bissau (1994–2005). Um Estudo Social das Motivações Eleitorais num Estado Frágil. *Lusotopie* 15 (1): 3–25.

Sanni, Kayode Abiola, Daniel D. Tia, David K. Ojo, et al. 2013. Diversity of Rice and Related Wild Species in Africa. In *Realizing Africa's Rice Promise*, eds. Marco C. S. Wopereis, Benin David E. Johnson, Nourallah Ahmadi, Eric Tollens, and Abdulai Jalloh, 87–94. Oxfordshire: CABI.

Sapir, J. David. 1970. Kujaama: Symbolic Separation Among the Diola-Fogny. *American Anthropologist* 72 (6): 1330–1348.

————. 1977. The Fabricated Child. In *The Social Use of Metaphor*, eds. J. David Sapir and J. Christopher Crocker, 193–223. Philadelphia: University of Pennsylvania Press.

Sarró, Ramon. 2009. *The Politics of Religious Change on the Upper Guinea Coast: Iconoclasm Done and Undone*. Edinburgh: Edinburgh University Press.

Sauer, Jonathan D. 1993. *Historical Geography of Crop Plants: A Select Roster*. Boca Raton, Fla.: CRC Press.

Sayamwala, Amma, and Stephen Haykin. 1983. *The World Rice Market: Structure, Conduct, and Performance*. Washington, D.C.: International Food Policy Research Institute.

Schloss, Marc R. 1988. *The Hatchet's Blood: Separation, Power, and Gender in Ehing Social Life*. Tucson: University of Arizona Press.

Scoones, Ian, Stephen Devereux, and Lawrence Haddad. 2005. Introduction: New Directions for African Agriculture. *IDS Bulletin* 36 (2): 1–12.

Scott, James C. 1985. *Weapons of the Weak: Everyday Forms of Peasant Resistance*. New Haven, Conn.: Yale University Press.

————. 1998. *Seeing Like a State: How Certain Schemes to Improve the Human Condition Have Failed*. New Haven, Conn.: Yale University Press.

Seck, Papa Abdoulaye, Ali A. Touré, Jeanne Y. Coulibaly, Aliou Diagne, and Marco C. S. Wopereis. 2013. Africa's Rice Economy Before and After the 2008 Rice Crisis. In *Realizing Africa's Rice Promise*, eds. Marco C. S. Wopereis, Benin David E. Johnson, Nourallah Ahmadi, Eric Tollens, and Abdulai Jalloh, 24–34. Oxfordshire: CABI.

Sembène, Ousmane, dir. 1971. *Emitaï*. Sénégal: Filmi Domirev.

Sharma, S. D., ed. 2010. *Rice: Origin, Antiquity and History*. Enfield, N.H.; Science Publishers; Distributed by CRC Press, Boca Raton, Fla.

Sharma, S. D., and W. M. Steele. 1978. Collection and Conservation of Existing Rice Species and Varieties of Africa. In *Rice in Africa: Proceedings of a Conference Held at the International Institute of Tropical Agriculture Ibadan, Nigeria, 7–11 March 1977*, eds. I. W. Buddenhagen and G. J. Persley, 61–67. London: Academic Press.

Sheridan, Michael J., and Celia Nyamweru. 2008. *African Sacred Groves: Ecological Dynamics & Social Change*. Oxford: James Currey.

Shils, Edward A. 1956. *The Torment of Secrecy: The Background and Consequences of American Security Policies*. Glencoe, Ill.: Free Press.

Shipton, Parker MacDonald. 1994. Land and Culture in Tropical Africa: Soils, Symbols and the Metaphysics of the Mundane. *Annual Review of Anthropology* 23: 347–377.

———. 2007. *The Nature of Entrustment: Intimacy, Exchange, and the Sacred in Africa*. New Haven, Conn.: Yale University Press.

Simmel, Georg. 1950. *The Sociology of Georg Simmel*, ed. and trans. Kurt H. Wolff. Glencoe, Ill: Free Press.

Smoltczyk, Alexander. 2013. Africa's Cocaine Hub: Guinea-Bissau a "Drug Trafficker's Dream." *Spiegel Online*, August 3. http://www.spiegel.de/international/world/violence-plagues-african-hub-of-cocaine-trafficking-a-887306.html (accessed September 28, 2014).

Snyder, Frances G. 1973. L'Evolution du Droit Foncier Diola de Basse Casamance (Republique du Sénégal), PhD dissertation, Université de Paris I, Pantheon, Sorbonne.

———. 1981. *Capitalism and Legal Change: An African Transformation*. New York: Academic Press.

Sodikoff, Genese. 2004. Land and Languor: Ethical Imaginations of Work and Forest in Northeast Madagascar. *History and Anthropology* 15 (4): 367–398.

Sonko, Bruno. 2004. The Casamance Conflict: A Forgotten Civil War? *CODESRIA Bulletin* (3/4): 30–33.

Stafford, Charles. 2007. What is Going to Happen Next? In *Questions of Anthropology*, eds. Jonathan Parry, Rita Astuti, and Charles Stafford, 55–75. Oxford: Berg.

Suret Canale, J., and Boubacar Barry. 1976. The Western Atlantic Coast to 1800. In *History of West Africa, Vol. 1*, eds. J. F. A. Ajayi and Michael Crowder, 456–511. New York: Columbia University Press.

Taborda, António da Cunha. 1950a. Apontamentos Etnográficos sobre os Felupes de Susana: Generalidades. *Boletim Cultural da Guiné Portuguesa* 5 (18): 187–223.

———. 1950b. Apontamentos Etnográficos sobre os Feulpes de Susana, Capítulo 2: Vida Psíquica. *Boletim Cultural da Guiné Portuguesa* 5 (20): 511–561.

Taussig, Michael T. 1980. *The Devil and Commodity Fetishism in South America.* Chapel Hill: University of North Carolina Press.
———. 1999. *De-face-ment: Public Secrecy and the Labor of the Negative.* Stanford: Stanford University Press.
Tefft, Stanton K., ed. 1980. *Secrecy: A Cross-Cultural Perspective.* New York: Human Sciences Press.
Temudo, Marina Padrão. 2011. Planting Knowledge, Harvesting Agro-Biodiversity: A Case Study of Southern Guinea-Bissau Rice Farming. *Human Ecology* 39 (3): 309–321.
Temudo, Marina Padrão, and Manuel Bivar Abrantes. 2014. The Cashew Frontier in Guinea-Bissau, West Africa: Changing Landscapes and Livelihoods. *Human Ecology* 42 (2): 217–230.
———. 2015. The Pen and the Plough: Balanta Young Men in Guinea-Bissau. *Development and Change* 46 (3): 464–485.
Temudo, Marina Padrão, and Ulrich Schiefer. 2003. Disintegration and Resilience of Agrarian Societies in Africa - The Importance of Social and Genetic Resources: A Case Study on the Reception of Urban War Refugees in the South of Guinea-Bissau. *Current Sociology* 51 (3/4): 393–416.
Thomas, Louis Vincent. 1959a. Les Diola (Part II). *Mémoires de l'Institut Français d'Afrique Noire,* No. 55. Dakar: IFAN.
———. 1959b. Les Diola: Essai d'Analyse Fonctionelle sur une population de Basse Casamance. *Mémoires de l'Institut francais d'Afrique noire,* Nos. 58–59. Dakar: IFAN.
———. 1963. Essai Sur Quelques Problèmes Relatifs au Régimes Foncier des Diola de Basse-Casamance (Sénégal). In *African Agrarian Systems,* ed. D. Biebuyck, 314–330. Oxford: Oxford University Press.
Thompson, E. P. 1963. *The Making of the English Working Class.* New York: Vintage Books.
———. 1993. *Customs in Common.* New York: The New Press.
Thomson, Steven K. 2006. *Children of the Village: Peace and Local Citizenship in a Multiethnic Gambian Community.* PhD dissertation, Department of Anthropology, Boston University.
Tollens, Eric, Matty Demont, Moussa Sié, et al. 2013. From WARDA to AfricaRice: An Overview of Rice Research for Development Activities Conducted in Partnership in Africa. In *Realizing Africa's Rice Promise,* eds. Marco C. S. Wopereis, Benin David E. Johnson, Nourallah Ahmadi, Eric Tollens, and Abdulai Jalloh, 1–23. Oxfordshire: CABI.
UN News Centre. 2011. *Guinea-Bissau Receives Boost from UN to Promote Sex Education in Schools.* UN News Centre, September 16. http://www.un.org/apps/news/story.asp?NewsID=39574#.VQx_NWbfjOo (accessed September 17, 2011).
United States Department of Agriculture. 2014. Guinea-Bissau Milled Rice Imports by Year (1000 MT). *Index Mundi.* http://www.indexmundi.com/

agriculture/?country=gw&commodity=milled-rice&graph=imports (accessed October 1, 2014).

Van Binsbergen, Wim. 1988. *The Land As Body: An Essay on the Interpretation of Ritual Among the Manjaks of Guinea-Bissau. Medical Anthropology Quarterly* 2 (4): 386–401.

Van Tilburg, Mariette. 1998. Interviews of the Unspoken: Incompatible Initiations in Senegal Fieldwork. *Anthropology and Humanism* 23 (2): 177–189.

Vigh, Henrik. 2006. *Navigating Terrains of War: Youth and Soldiering in Guinea-Bissau.* New York: Berghahn Books.

Vogel, Coleen. 2005. "Seven Fat Years and Seven Lean Years"? Climate Change and Agriculture in Africa. *IDS Bulletin* 36 (2): 30–35.

Walsh, John R. 2001. *Wide Crossing: The West Africa Rice Development Association in Transition, 1985–2000.* Aldershot: Ashgate.

WARDA. 2008. *2007 Africa Rice Trends.* Cotonou, Benin.

Watts, Michael. 1983. *Silent Violence: Food, Famine, & Peasantry in Northern Nigeria.* Berkeley: University of California Press.

Weil, Peter M. 1973. Wet Rice, Women, and Adaptation in The Gambia. *Rural Africana* 19 (Winter): 20–29.

Werbner, Richard P. 1989. *Ritual Passage, Sacred Journey: The Process and Organization of Religious Movement.* Manchester: Manchester University Press.

West, Harry, and Todd Sanders, eds. 2003. *Transparency and Conspiracy: Ethnographies of Suspicion in the New World Order.* Durham, N.C.: Duke University Press.

Will, H. 1978. The Research Programme of the West African Rice Development Association (WARDA). In *Rice in Africa: Proceedings of a Conference Held at the International Institute of Tropical Agriculture Ibadan, Nigeria, 7–11 March 1977,* eds. I. W. Buddenhagen and G. J. Persley, 215–222. London: Academic Press.

Williams, Raymond. 1977. *Marxism and Literature.* Oxford: Oxford University Press.

———. 1985. *Keywords: A Vocabulary of Culture and Society.* New York: Oxford University Press.

Wood, Peter H. 1974. *Black Majority: Negroes in colonial South Carolina from 1670 through the Stono Rebellion.* New York: Knopf; Distributed by Random House.

Wright, Richard. 1941. *12 Million Black Voices.* New York: Viking Press.

Zahan, Dominique. 1979. *The Religion, Spirituality, and Thought of Traditional Africa,* trans. Kate E. Martin and Lawrence M. Martin. Chicago: University of Chicago Press.

INDEX

....

Note: Page numbers in *italics* indicate photographs and illustrations.

Africanization, 178
African Party for the Independence of
  Guinea and Cape Verde (PAIGC)
  and the Catholic Mission, 69
  and Christian influences, 149
  and the international political
    environment, 46
  and out-of-wedlock pregnancies,
    178–79
  and Portuguese colonial forces, 73
  and rice self-sufficiency, 204n11
Africa Rice Center (AfricaRice), 29–30
agoto, 156
agricultural practices
  Arendt on, 85
  author's experience with, 87–88
  and climate change, 181, 187–88
  and end-of-season parties, 93,
    162–63, 165
  and institutional history of rice
    science, 26–33
  Jola calendar wheel, *38*
  and Jola work ethic, 85–87, 88–90,
    94–98, 99, 100, 105, 106, 120,
    157–58, 161
  and paradoxes of custom, 98–100
  and social dynamics, 12, 90–94

agricultural reforms, 131
AIDS and HIV, 180–81, 186–87
ai-i (religio-political officials)
  and esoteric knowledge, 128–29
  and Jola boyhood, 138
  and Jola funeral practices, 101–6
  and the Jola rice complex, 39
  and Jola work ethic, 97
  and male maturation rites,
    143–44, *144*
  and secrecy in Jola culture, 110
Akabau
  and Ampa Badji's family, 56–58
  and fosterage, 206n2
  home, 74–75
  kinship ties, *61*
  and Portuguese colonialism,
    65–66
Alliance for a Green Revolution for
  Africa (AGRA), 32, 131–32
amangen-i (shrine priests/ritual elders)
  and Jola funeral practices, 101–2,
    104, 105
  and the Jola rice complex, 39
  and Jola work ethic, 97
  and responsibility for spirit
    shrines, 76

236

and ritual knowledge in Jola
culture, 128–29
and secrecy in Jola culture, 114
Ampa Badji
and age in Jola culture, 176–77
and author's field work, 50–51,
53–55
and changing Jola culture, 155,
157–58, 193
and economic struggles, 80–82
and education in Jola culture, 166,
168–73
and family background, 56–62,
206n4
and funeral practices, 102, 191
and historical milestones, 13–14
and Jola male initiation, 136–38,
138–40, 146–52
and Jola work ethic, 85–86, 94,
96–97
and kenyalen, 207n6
and Nho Keboral's background,
78–79
and out-of-wedlock pregnancies,
179, 182–85, 189
and perceptions of a better past,
83–84
and Portuguese colonialism, 64–66,
72–77, 210n17
and responsibility for spirit
shrines, 76
and rice farmer identity, 48–49, 196
and ritual knowledge, 129
and secrecy in Jola culture, 113,
116–17
self-recordings, 54
Ampa Bontai, 95, 99, 159
Ampa Kapeña, 101–5, 112, 123, 128
Amumau, 11
Aneki, 94
Angala
birth, 81
and education, 171, 175

illnesses, 211n21
kinship ties, 61
Angola, 63
animal herding, 141
animal sacrifice, 6, 92, 128
Apekua, 61, 78
Appiah, Kwame Anthony, 127
apurau, 141–42, 146
aquatic rice, 36. See also wet rice
cultivation
archaeological evidence, 34
Arendt, Hannah, 85
Armando, 61, 177, 184–85, 187–88
aruntchikau, 141, 142, 144–45, 146
Asia, 19, 23
asubangilau, 142, 146
Atlantic slave trade, 62–63, 202–3n8
authoritarianism, 133
autonomy, 113–14, 149
awasena, 39, 149, 205n20
awassau, 91

badjolidjolabu, 141, 146
Bafatá Mission, 68
bakinabu (ukinau pl.), 57–58, 128.
See also spirit shrines
Balanta ethnicity, 216n2
bapendabu, 141, 146
batolhabu, 101, 128
Baum, Robert, 4, 107, 149, 213n7
betrothal in Jola culture, 67–68, 141
Bijagós Islands, 63
Binta, 61, 169–70
biographical approach, 51
birth control, 82, 125–26, 185–87,
214n14
Bissau, 80, 164
"black rice" thesis, 202–3n8
bolsa, 171
Bontai, 61, 77–78
borokabu, 22, 38, 91, 181
botunabu, 11, 198, 201n17
Bourdieu, Pierre, 193

Bray, Francesca, 203n9
breeding programs for rice, 23–24,
    30–31, 32–33, 173
bridges, 80, 211n20
British colonialism, 63
Buddenhagen, I. W., 23–24, 202n5
bujandabu (fulcrum shovel), *37*
    and gender roles, 205n16
    and Jola households, 116
    and Jola male initiation, 140
    and the Jola rice complex, 37
    and Jola work ethic, 85–86, 90,
        94, 96
Bukekelil neighborhood, 77
bukutabu (male initiation), 107,
    135–38, 150, 153–54, 215n2
Bulorim, 156–57, 169
burial practices, 65, 191
butat, 57, *90, 112,* 198. *See also*
    forestland plots *(butat)*
butonda, 57, 90–91. *See also* rice
    paddies

Cabral, Amílcar, 74, 204n11, 210n18
Cape Verde, 62–63
Carney, Judith, 25, 202n8
Casamance region
    and Jola male initiation, 215n2
    and the Jola rice complex, 39
    and labor migration, 80
    and Portuguese colonialism, 64
    and rice taxes, 6
    and secrecy in Jola culture, 107
    and separatist movement, 207n8
cash cropping, 10, 187, 211n1
cashew farming
    and author's field work, 52
    and cash-cropping, 211n1
    and changing Jola culture, 159, 162
    and education in Jola culture, 170
    and Jola family structure, 182–83
    and Jola work ethic, 89, 100
Catholic Church

    and climate change, 11
    and cultural changes in Jola-land,
        48–49
    and early Jola converts, 74
    and Jola male initiation, 136–37,
        147–54, 215n2
    and Jola work associations, 163
    and out-of-wedlock pregnancies,
        178–80, 184–85
    and Portuguese colonialism, 207n7,
        208n10
    and resistance to missionization, 39
    and ritual knowledge in Jola
        culture, 123, 126
    and secrecy in Jola culture, 213n6
    See also *Pontifico Instituto Missioni
        Estere* (PIME)
cemeteries, 101
childbirth
    and Jola male initiation, 151
    and *kenyalen* birth society, 56, 58,
        62, 74, 207n5, 207n6
    and maternity houses, 124, 127, 215n6
    and secrecy in Jola culture,
        107, 114, 124
    and traditional medicine, 215n6
    See also reproductive knowledge
China, 19
Christianity, *71,* 135–37, 150–54.
    See also Catholic Church;
    missionaries; *Pontifico Instituto
    Missioni Estere* (PIME)
circumcision, 124, 126–27, 135–36,
    146, 151, 215n2
climate change
    and Christian missionization,
        153–54
    and development practices, 192–93
    and economic struggles, 81
    and education in Jola culture,
        169, 171
    and esoteric knowledge, 129–30
    and global economy, 16

impact on Jola rice culture, 9–12, 13,
    181, 187–88, 192
and Jola work ethic, 99
and rainfall declines, 7–8, 99
cocaine trade, 43–45
code names, 54 55
cohort groups, 110
collective funds, 163–66
collective labor, 36–37, 37–38, 98, 162,
    192. *See also* work associations
Colombian drug cartels, 45
colonialism
    and agricultural practices, 202n7
    and Cabral, 210n18
    and Catholic missionaries, 66–69,
        207n7, 208n10, 208n11
    and Christian converts, 210n19
    and cultural changes in
        Jola-land, 49
    and domestication of rice, 20–21
    and "Felupe" term, 205n17
    and food security, 10
    and the Independence War, 209n15
    and the international political
        environment, 46
    and Jola dialects, 39
    and Jola male initiation, 137, 147
    and Jola social organization, 42
    and Jola work ethic, 85–86, 91
    and Portuguese influence, 62–66
    and Portuguese soldiers, 72–74,
        210n17
    and rice cultivation, 24, 27–28, 33, 191
    and rice self-sufficiency, 204n11
    and ritual knowledge in Jola
        culture, 124
    and secrecy in Jola culture, 106, 116
color symbolism, 143–45
commercialization, 9
Consultative Group on International
    Agricultural Research (CGIAR),
    28–29, 204n13
consumption of rice, 38

corruption, 171
coups d'état, 46, 47
"cradles of agriculture" thesis, 20–21
Crioulo language, 91, 199
crue/décrue techniques, 21, 25
cultigens of rice, 19, 23, 25, 33, 202n5
cultivating rice
    and author's field work, 52
    and changing Jola culture, 156, 194
    and Christian influences, 152
    and climate change, 11, 47
    and development programs, 132
    and education in Jola culture, 170
    and gender, 152
    and Japanese culture, 203n9
    and Jola family structure, 188
    and Jola funeral practices, 105
    and the Jola rice complex, 7, 34,
        36 38
    and Jola work ethic, 87–88, 89–91,
        97–99
    and Nho Keboral, 1
    and secrecy in Jola culture, 114,
        120, 121
cultural knowledge, 130. *See also*
    esoteric knowledge
curses, 53, 159

dance, 103, 109–10, 216n7
death in Jola culture, 15, 53, 96–97.
    See also funeral practices
Deluza, 61, 177, 183 85, 187 88
democracy, 44
demographic trends, 26
desertification, 7
development organizations and
    policies
    and climate change, 12, 17
    and ethnographic practices, 192–94
    and Jola work associations, 162–63
    and out-of-wedlock pregnancies,
        180, 184
    and secrecy in Jola culture, 131–33

dialects of Jola, 39, 205n19
Dinesen, Isak, 1
Diola, 4, 205n17
discotecas, 178–79
domains of knowledge
    and the Catholic Mission, 67
    and Christian influences, 152–54
    and ritual knowledge, 122–28
    and secrecy in Jola culture, 107, 109
    See also gender roles
domestication of rice, 18–24, 25, 31
domestic labor, 79–80
drought, 9. See also climate change
drug trafficking, 12, 43–45, 169,
    205n24
dry rice cultivation, 87. See also
    cultivating rice
Durkheimian sociology, 201n10

East Africa, 21
ebandai, 141
ebongai, 141, 144, 146, 147, 151
edjalai, 91
Edjamat dialect, 39
edjodjowai, 141, 144–45, 146
education
    and birth control, 185–87
    changing attitudes toward, 166–75
    and changing Jola culture, 157–58,
        167, 193
    and climate change, 11–12
    and Jola agricultural labor, 86
    and Jola male initiation, 147–48
    and out-of-wedlock pregnancies,
        177–89
    and Portuguese colonial soldiers, 74
    and responsibility for spirit shrines,
        76–77
egalitarianism, 118–22, 213n9
ehendjekurai, 142, 145, 146
Ehing people, 107
elderly persons in Jola culture, 95–96
Elia (village), 73, 126

eluupai, 145
embelengai, 141, 142
Emitaï (Jola supreme deity)
    and changing Jola culture, 156, 192
    and education in Jola culture,
        166, 173
    and Jola agricultural practices, 66
    and Jola male initiation, 151
    and the Jola rice complex, 4
    and Jola work ethic, 86
    Ousmane Sembène film (1971), 6
    and secrecy in Jola culture, 115, 134
environmental changes, 10, 13, 93,
    129–30. See also climate change
environmental conditions, 9
epurai, 141, 146
esaangai proceedings, 76
Esana (village)
    and age in Jola culture, 176
    and Ampa Badji's family, 56–62
    and Ampa Badji's leadership, 84
    and author's field work, 50–52,
        54–55
    and the Catholic Mission, 66–72,
        68, 69, 70, 71, 208–9n12
    and changing Jola culture, 157,
        160–61, 192
    and cultural changes in
        Jola-land, 49
    and economic struggles, 81–82
    and education in Jola culture,
        166–68, 171–75
    and fosterage, 206n2
    healthcare resources, 211n21
    and huwokuñahu dance, 216n7
    and the Independence War, 209n15
    and Jola funeral practices, 101–5
    and Jola lineages, 206n4
    and Jola male initiation, 135–38,
        139, 147–51, 215n2
    and Jola work associations, 163–64
    and local trade, 206n3
    location, 41

and missionaries, 207n7, 208n11
and Nho Keboral's background, 78
and out-of-wedlock pregnancies,
   177–78, 180–88
population of, 205n18
and Portuguese colonialism, 64–65,
   72–77, 208n11
and rice cultivation, 37, 85–86, 87,
   93, 95, 97
and ritual knowledge in Jola
   culture, 124
and secrecy in Jola culture, 107, 111,
   113, 116–17
sketch of, 59
esoteric knowledge, 106–7, 108–9,
   111–12, 122, 127, 128–29
esubangilai, 142, 146
ethnicity of Jola people, 4, 205n15
ethnographic practices, 104–5, 106–7,
   107–12
eulogistic couplets, 153
ewañai, 37, 38, 91

Fabian, Johannes, 114
Fairhead, James, 9, 18
family structure, 14, 37–38, 137.
   See also gender roles
feasts, 92
Felupes, 149
Ferguson, James, 32
Fields-Black, Edda L., 25
Fonyi dialect, 39
food insecurity, 9, 12
foods of Jola culture, 73
forestland plots (butat), 57, 90, 112, 198
forest-savannah complex, 9
formal knowledge, 129
Fortes, Meyer, 154
fosterage, 79, 206n2
Foucauldian theory, 127
French Agricultural Research Centre
   for International Development
   (CIRAD), 204n12

French colonialism, 63
Fula merchants, 89
funeral practices
   and age in Jola culture, 176
   and death of an ai, 101–6
   and eulogistic couplets, 153
   and the Jola rice complex, 35
   and Jola work ethic, 96–97
   and kasaabaku, 57–58, 102, 114
   and Portuguese colonialism, 65
   and ritual performances, 212n7
   and secrecy in Jola culture,
      109–10, 128

Gable, Eric, 108, 118–20
Gambia, 39, 79–80, 162
Gambia River, 21
gender roles
   and collective labor, 37–38
   and domains of knowledge, 67, 107,
      109, 127–28, 152–54, 213n12
   and education, 157–58
   and Jola funeral practices, 176
   and Jola male initiation, 135–38,
      138–40, 140–46, 146–54
   and missionary efforts, 209n15
   and out-of-wedlock pregnancies, 178
   and rice cultivation, 52, 90–91
   and secrecy in Jola culture, 122–28,
      129, 130
genetics research, 20, 30–31, 132, 173
geopolitical environment, 42–47
Geschiere, Peter, 107
Ghana, 3
The Gift (Mauss), 5, 190
global economy, 16, 26, 31, 203–4n10
global food crisis, 10
globalization, 195–96. See also
   development organizations and
   policies
Gofman, Alexander, 5–6
Gondwanaland, 30–31
Green Revolution, 24, 26–27, 30, 32, 131

Gregório
  birth, 81
  education, 194
  and education in Jola culture,
    169–71, 175
  kinship ties, *61*
  and out-of-wedlock pregnancies,
    188–89
  and responsibility for spirit
    shrines, 76
Griffiths, Tom, 15–16
Guinea-Bissau, *40*
  and agricultural development, 214n16
  and Cabral, 210n18
  and Casamance separatist
    movement, 207n8
  and climate change, 12, 26
  and development projects, 12,
    16–17, 131–33, 162–63, 180, 184,
    192–93, 194, 214n16
  and drug trafficking, 14, 43–45, 47,
    205n24
  and economic centralization, 31–32
  and education, 166, 169, 171
  and globalization, 195
  and healthcare NGOs, 1
  institutional change in, 84
  and the international political
    environment, 42–47
  Jola villages of, *41*
  and labor migration, 79–80
  languages of, 197
  and rice culture, 4, 7, 33, 36,
    38–42, 190
  and rice imports, 28, *29,* 201n16
  roads and bridges, *40, 41,* 47, 80, 89,
    159, 211n20
  War of Independence, 46, 69, 86,
    209n15

Habermas, Jürgen, 133
harimanahu, 53
Hawthorne, Walter, 25

healers, 60
healers and health care, 194. *See also*
  medicine
hierarchical relations, 123, 127
high-yield rice varieties, 30
hippopotamuses, 77
HIV/AIDS, 180–81, 186–87
Hocart, A. M., 1
household organization, 116, 162
hubohu, 139–40, 146–47, 148, 151
hukulahu, 97, 102–3
hungómahu, 141, 143–44, *146*
hunting, 77–78
hurirahu, 142, 145
huwokuñahu, 216n7
hybrid rice varieties, 30

illness and disease, 60–62, 82, 211n21
imports of rice, *28, 29. See also* sack
  rice
indigenous knowledge, 131–32
Indus Valley, 19
infant mortality
  and Ampa Badji's family, 56, 60,
    62, 74
  and childhood diseases, 211n21
  and gendered domains of
    knowledge, 124
  and Jola work ethic, 86
  and *kenyalen,* 207n5
  and Nho Keboral, 77–78
  and perceptions of a better past, 83
  and Portuguese colonialism, 65
informal information, 129
infrastructure of Guinea-Bissau, *40,*
  41, 47, 80, 89, 159, 211n20
initiation practices
  and Ampa Badji background,
    57, 62
  and changing Jola culture, 195
  and Christian influences, 147,
    151–54
  and esoteric knowledge, 129, 130

and gendered domains of
knowledge, 122–24, 126–28
and the Jola rice complex, 34
and male maturation in Jola culture,
135–38, 145, *145*, 215n2
and responsibility for spirit shrines,
77, 84
and secrecy in Jola culture, 107,
111–12, 133–34
Inner Delta of the Niger River, 21, 25
Institut de Recherche pour le
Développement (IRD), 204n12
Institut de Recherches Agronomiques
Tropicales (IRAT), 204n12
institutional change in
Guinea-Bissau, 84
Instituto Nacional de Estudos e
Pesquisa (INEP), 42
interactional knowledge, 112–22
Internally Displaced Persons (IDP),
205n25
International Institute of Tropical
Agriculture (IITA), 204n12
International Monetary Fund
(IMF), 10
International Rice Research Institute
(IRRI), 204n12
intrauterine devices (IUDs), 185
Iraq War, 42
Islam, 19, 39, 137

Jackson, Michael, 48, 114, 190
James, Wendy, 135
Japan, 19, 203n9
Jola culture. *See specific facets of Jola
culture such as marriage practices,
initiation practices, funeral
practices, etc.*
Jones, Monty, 30
Jopai, 177–89

kajanayaku, 67, 148
karahayaku, 208n12

Karenghaku shrine, 57–58, 75–76.
See also spirit shrines
kasaabaku (corpse inquisition), 57–58,
102, 114
Kasa dialect, 39
Kassompa, 153
Katama neighborhood, 74
kenyalen birth society, 56, 58, 62, 74,
207n5, 207n6
kin-based reciprocal labor, 37–38
King Baudouin International
Agriculture Research Award, 30
konkon, 138, 139, 141, 142
kugabaku, 141, *146*
Kugelh neighborhood, 140
kuji-kuji practice, 80–83, 165,
194, 195
Kurijol, *61,* 64, 66
kutangu, 33

labra, 174
land tenure, 57–58, 121, 212n6
Leach, Melissa, 9, 18
legitimacy, 92–94
levirate system, 11, 151, 198, 201n17,
213n10
liberalization, economic, 32
liberation struggles, 49
Linares, Olga, 4, 92, 93–94
lineage in Jola culture, 55, 57,
74–77, 206n4

Madagascar, 19, 20
magic, 122, 133, 214n19
Mali, 3
Mandinka people, 25, 76, 80, 107, 194
mangroves
and distribution of Jola people, 39
and domestication of rice, 21, 25
foods gathered from, 56, 138
as refuge, 3
and rice cultivation, 10, 12, 34, 36
and salt production, 87

Manjaco ethnic group, 118–19
Marijai, 165, 174
Marina
    and age in Jola culture, 176–77
    birth, 81
    and changing Jola culture,
        193–94, 196
    children of, 14
    and education in Jola culture, 170
    kinship ties, *61*
    and out-of-wedlock pregnancy,
        181–89
Mark, Peter, 107
market economics, 32
Marmugi, Spartaco, *68*
    and Christian converts, 210n19
    and Christian influences, 147–50
    and education of Jola children,
        209n13
    and history of the Catholic Mission,
        66–71
    and the Independence War,
        209n15
    and Jola language, 209n14
    and Jola spirit shrines, 208n12
    and the Mission workshop, 210n16
marriage practices
    and Ampa Badji's family, 58
    and betrothal in Jola culture,
        67–68, 141
    and the Catholic Mission, 67–68
    and centrality of rice cultivation,
        191–92
    and Jola agricultural practices,
        94–95
    and Jola male initiation, 141, 151
    and Jola work ethic, 91
    and lineage issues, 74–76
    and out-of-wedlock pregnancies,
        176–89
    and ritual performances, 212n7
Marxist theory, 127, 201n7
masculinity, 137–38, 153

maternity huts, 124, 127, 215n6
maturation, 140–46
Mauss, Marcel, 5–6, 8–9, 16, 190,
    201n10
McCann, James, 202n7
medicine
    and childbirth, 215n6
    and secrecy in Jola culture, 114
    traditional practices, 125–26,
        184–85, 215n6
Mesopotamia, 20
Metcalf, Peter, 190
micro-financing, 164
migration patterns
    and colonialism, 56–57
    and distribution of Jola people, 57
    and domestication of rice, 19, 23
    and education, 98, 164, 168–70,
        177–78
    and Fula merchants, 89
    and Jola work ethic, 99
    and marriage practices, 216n4
    and the rice economy, 7
    and Senegal, 212n8
    as threat to Jola social
        organization, 93
    and wage labor, 210n16
military of Guinea-Bissau, 46, 64.
    See also colonialism
miscarriages, 56, 62, 82, 125, 186, 194
missionaries
    and changing Jola culture, 194
    and Christian influences, 147, 153
    establishment in Esana, 207n7
    and establishment of PIME,
        208n10
    and gendered domains of
        knowledge, 123
    and Jola male initiation, 137–38,
        215n2
    and Jola resistance, 39
    and the Jola rice complex, 42
    and Jola work ethic, 93

and Portuguese colonialism, 66
and secrecy in Jola culture, 115, 118
See also Catholic Church; Pontifico
    Instituto Missioni Estere (PIME)
modernization, 96–97, 192
monogamy, 137
Moore, Sally Falk, 93, 213–14n12
Mozambique, 63
mutual aid societies, 164–66

nahote, 82–83
narco-state status of Guinea-Bissau,
    43–45, 205n24
neoliberal economics, 32, 33
Neolithic Revolution, 20
Netting, Robert McC, 212n6
New Rice for Africa (NERICA)
    varieties, 30–31
Nha Buhel, 56, 58, 60–62, 61, 66
Nhakun neighborhood, 74–75
Nho Keboral
    and age in Jola culture, 176
    and Ampa Badji's family, 56–62
    and author's field work, 50–55
    background, 77–80
    and changing Jola culture, 155, 157–
        62, 192–93
    and economic struggles, 80–83
    and education in Jola culture, 166,
        168–72, 174
    estimated age, 200n2
    health problems, 82–83
    and historical milestones, 13
    and Jola funeral practices, 102,
        105–6
    and Jola work associations, 163–66
    and Jola work ethic, 86, 87
    marriage, 75–77
    and out-of-wedlock pregnancies,
        179, 181, 183–87, 189
    and perceptions of a better past,
        83–84
    on rice varieties, 2, 200n3

and ritual knowledge in Jola
    culture, 125–26
and secrecy in Jola culture, 113,
    116–17
self-recordings, 211n21
travels to Portugal, 1–4, 196
nicknames, 83, 152–53, 154
Niger River, 21, 25
nightmare egalitarianism, 118, 122
Noelza, 61, 81, 189
nongovernmental organizations
    (NGOs), 1–2, 124–25
Norplant, 185

oficina, 71–72
Ohnuki-Tierney, Emiko, 203n9
Oryza glaberrima, 21, 23, 25, 30–31, 33
Oryza sativa, 19–20, 20, 23–24, 30–31,
    202n3, 202n4
out-of-wedlock pregnancies, 14, 176–
    89

pabi, 174
padi/ntera, 62, 74. See also infant
    mortality
Padre Luigi
    and Ampa Badji, 76
    and the Catholic Mission, 68–72
    and Christian influences, 148, 150,
        152–53
    and the Independence War, 209n15
    and Jola language, 209n14
    and Jola male initiation, 135–36,
        215n2
    and the Mission workshop, 210n16
    and out-of-wedlock pregnancies,
        178
palmatorios, 64
palm oil, 81, 82
palm trees, 60
palm wine
    and Ampa Badji, 56
    and author's field work, 50

palm wine (*continued*)
and Jola funeral practices, 101, 103
and Jola identity, 48
and Jola male initiation, 138
and Jola work associations, 162–63
and Jola work ethic, 92, 97
and *kuji-kuji* practice, 81–82
and ritual knowledge in Jola
    culture, 126
and secrecy in Jola culture, 116
paradox of custom, 98–100, 156
Parkin, David J., 90, 98
patriclan structures, 55, 58
Peacebuilding Commission, 45
pearl millet, 6
physical discipline, 157–59, 182–83
polygyny, 151
Pontifico Instituto Missioni Estere
    (PIME), *37, 68, 69, 70, 71*
and Ampa Badji, 76
background of, 66–72
and Christian converts, 210n19
and Christian influences, 147,
    149–52, 153–54
and education, 168, 191, 209n13
establishment of, 207n7, 208n10
and the Independence War, 209n15
and Jola funeral practices, 103–4
and Jola male initiation, 136–38
and Jola spirit shrines, 208n12
and Jola work associations, 164
and Jola work ethic, 86
location, 59
mechanic's shop, 48, 71, *72*, 209n15,
    210n16
and out-of-wedlock pregnancies,
    178–79
and Portuguese colonial soldiers,
    73–74
predecessors of, 208n11
population growth, 26
Portères, Roland, 20–21
Portuguese Guinea, 63. *See also*
    colonialism

post-conflict countries, 45
poverty
and fosterage, 306n2
and *kuji-kuji* practice, 80–83
and secrecy in Jola culture, 105,
    117–18, 121–22, 129
power relationships, 108–9, 113–14
pregnancy
and childbirth, 107, 114, 124, 151,
    214n14, 215n6
and infant mortality, 56, 60, 62, 65,
    74, 77–78, 83, 86, 124, 207n5,
    211n21
and *kenyalen,* 207n6
and secrecy in Jola culture, 107,
    112–13
"prehending the occult," 154
privacy in Jola culture, 51, 111, 113–14,
    115–22. *See also* secrecy in Jola
    culture
Protestantism, 11, 39, 115
"public secrets," 104, 128

religious beliefs and practices
conversion, 39, 71–72, 74, 137, 148,
    151, 179, 210n19, 215n2
and education, 173–74
and *kenyalen,* 207n5
and secrecy in Jola culture, 114
traditional practices, 39–42
See also *awasena*; spirit shrines
remittances, 46–47, 194
reproductive knowledge, 123–28, 148,
    150, 151, 213n7
resistance movements, 64–65
rhetorical strategies, 15–16
Rice Coast, 3, 27
rice knowledge systems, 25
rice paddies, 21–23, *37,* 57, 90–91
Richards, Paul, 24, 176
ritual collusion, 106
ritual knowledge, 112, 122–28
ritual mimesis, 96–97
rural/urban divide, 13, 46–47

Sabina, *61*, 81, 169–70, 177–78,
    182–83, 189
sack rice, 10–11, *28*, 75, 81, 117, 201n16
sacred forests, 126–27
"sacred rice" concept, 5–8, 191, 200n6
Santa Maria neighborhood, 74, 210n19
São Domingos
    and cashew farming, 89
    and condition of roads, 159
    and education of Jola youth, 98, 164,
        168–70, 177–78
    and health care, 101–2, 211n21
    and out-of-wedlock pregnancies,
        183–84, 189
Scott, James C., 32, 135
secrecy in Jola culture
    and ethnographic research, 106–7,
        107–12, 213n9
    and gendered domains of
        knowledge, 67, 107, 109, 127–28,
        152–54, 213n12
    and hiding possessions, 115–22
    and personal privacy, 114
    and ritual knowledge, 122–28,
        128–29
self-sufficiency ethic, 28, 122, 164,
    166, 204n11
Sembène, Ousmane, 6
Senegal, 27–28, 39, *41*, 80–81, 162
separatist movements, 64, 67, 107, 207n8
sex education, 149–50, 180, 184, 186
silence, 130–34
Simmel, Georg, 101, 108, 110–11,
    122, 130–31
slave trade, 62–63, 202–3n8
smallholders, 212n6
Snyder, Francis, 4
social organization of Jola society
    and agricultural labor, 90–94, 100
    and collective work, 162–66
    and environmental change, 13
    and information flow, 131
    and Jola work ethic, 98–100
    and legitimation, 92–93, 92–94

and out-of-wedlock pregnancies,
    180
and rice cultivation, 18–24, 24–26
and secrecy in Jola culture, 130–34
social security systems, 11
songs, 53, 82–83
sorghum, 6
Southeast Asia, 19
spirit shrines
    and "Awasena" term, 205n20
    and changing Jola culture, 11
    and conflict resolution, 47
    and curses, 159
    and Jola male initiation, 137,
        149 51, 153
    and *kenyalen,* 207n6
    and out-of-wedlock pregnancies,
        179, 180
    and rice cultivation, 92–93
    sacrifices at, 4–5
    and secrecy in Jola culture, 107, 111,
        128–29
    spiritual significance of, 57–58
    and traditional healing, 185
    and women's society, 208n12
    work associations compared to, 98
Stafford, Charles, 195
state services, 47
stereotypes, 89–90, 106
Steudel, Ernst Gottlieb von, 21
storytelling, 15–16, 48, 50–51,
    53 54, 190
structural adjustment policies,
    10, 31, 32
structural uncertainty, 15–16, 194–95
supernatural beliefs, 106–7
sustainability, 212n6
symbolism, 143

Taussig, Michael T., 104
taxation, 47
Tegilosso, 60–62, *61*
Temudo, Marina, 10, 28, 31–32, 36
Ten Commandments, 151

terrorism, 44
theft
    and Jola work ethic, 5, 157–60, 193
    and other ethnicities, 216n2
    and physical discipline, 157–59,
        182–83
theology, 137–38, 150, 215n3
Tiago, *61*, 81, 169, 175
"total social phenomenon," 5–6, 8, 16,
    201n10
"transgressive segregation," 32–33, 173

Ukai beh, 112–15, 120, 213n4
ukinau. See *bakinabu*
United Nations Office of Drugs and
    Crime (UNODC), 43–44
universal salvation religions, 137
unmarried parents, 14. *See also*
    out-of-wedlock pregnancies
UN Security Council, 45
upland rice, 36, 38, 202n3
Upper Guinea Coast
    and cultural changes in
        Jola-land, 49
    and domestication of rice,
        20–21, 24
    and the Jola rice complex, 34
    and migration patterns, 57
    and Rice Coast, 3
    and rice cultivation, 23–24, 24–26
urbanization, 26, 96, 216n4

van Tilburg, Mariette, 107, 123, 133,
    213n7
Vavilov, Nikolai, 20–21
Vaz, José Mário, 46
virilocality, 58–59, 91

Walsh, John R., 30
water resources, 1–2, 202n2
Weber, Max, 92–93
weddings, *34. See also* marriage
    practices

West Africa, 21, 25, 26
West African Rice Development
    Association (WARDA), 28–29
wet rice cultivation
    and changing Jola culture, 156
    and Christian influences, 152
    and development programs, 132
    and Japanese culture, 203n9
    and Jola funeral practices, 105
    and the Jola rice complex, 7, 34
    and Jola work ethic, 87–88, 89–90,
        97–98, 98–99
    and secrecy in Jola culture, 120
widows
    and changes in agricultural
        production, 11
    households headed by, 213n10
    and Jola language, 213n11
    and Jola work associations, 165
    and levirate system, 201n17
    and secrecy in Jola culture,
        121–22, 131
    See also levirate system
Williams, Raymond, 87
witchcraft, 53, 58, 60, 76, 77, 133, 143
Women's Association of Esana, 164
work associations
    and division of rice crop, 212n4
    gender-exclusivity, 91, 162
    and the Jola rice complex, 4, 37–38
    neighborhood work associations,
        52, 56, 91, 96, 97, 140, 181
    women, 50, 52, 82, 87–88, 91–92,
        112, 116, 155–56, 157,
        162–65, 186
    youth, 86, 98, 140, 152, 160–61
work ethic
    and changing Jola culture, 161
    and history of rice cultivation,
        85–87
    and Jola family structure, 157–58
    and Jola funeral practices, 96–97,
        104–5

and Jola male initiation, 138–40, 152
and the Jola rice complex, 36–37
and Jola work ethic, 94–98,
    99, 100
and secrecy in Jola culture,
    106, 120, 134
and structural economic changes,
    190–96
and value of agricultural labor,
    88–90
wrestling
    and esoteric knowledge, 128

and Jola masculinity, 138–39,
    141–46, *145,* 152
and the Jola rice complex, 33, *35*
and Nho Khboral's nickname, 55
and spirit shrine ceremonies, 11,
    128–29
Wright, Richard, 155

yams, 6
Yangtze River, 19

Ziguinchor, 112–13, 125